Laptops
FOR
DUMMIES®
2ND EDITION

Laptops
FOR
DUMMIES®
2ND EDITION

by Dan Gookin

WILEY

Wiley Publishing, Inc.

Laptops For Dummies®, 2nd Edition

Published by
Wiley Publishing, Inc.
111 River Street
Hoboken, NJ 07030-5774
www.wiley.com

WILEY

About the Author

After physically destroying three typewriters, **Dan Gookin** bought his first computer in 1982 at the urging of the guy in the typewriter repair shop. Contrary to his prejudices, Dan quickly discovered that computers were about more than math and he quickly took to the quirky little devices.

Twenty-five years later Mr. Gookin has written over 100 books on computers and high tech, gone through more than 50 computers, including a dozen or so laptops and portables. He's achieved fame as one of the first computer radio talk show hosts, editor of a magazine, national technology spokesman, and occasional actor on the community theater stage.

Today, Dan still considers himself a writer and computer "guru" whose job it is to remind everyone computers are not to be taken too seriously. His approach to computers is light and humorous, yet very informative. He knows the complex beasts are important and can do a great deal to help people become productive and successful. Dan mixes his vast knowledge of computers with a unique, dry sense of humor that keeps everyone informed — and awake. His favorite quote is, "Computers are a notoriously dull subject, but that doesn't mean I have to write about them that way."

Dan Gookin's most recent books are *PCs For Dummies,* 10th Edition, *Troubleshooting Your PC For Dummies*, and some new titles he can't yet discuss under threat of death. He holds a degree in Communications / Visual Arts from UCSD. Dan currently dwells in North Idaho where he enjoys woodworking, music, theater, riding his bicycle, and spending time with his boys.

Publisher's Acknowledgments

We're proud of this book; please send us your comments through our online registration form located at www.dummies.com/register/.

Some of the people who helped bring this book to market include the following:

Acquisitions, Editorial, and Media Development

Sr. Project Editor: Mark Enochs

Executive Editor: Greg Croy

Copy Editor: Becky Whitney

Technical Editor: Mark L. Chambers

Editorial Manager: Leah Cameron

Media Development Manager: Laura VanWinkle

Editorial Assistant: Amanda Foxworth

Sr. Editorial Assistant: Cherie Case

Cartoons: Rich Tennant (www.the5thwave.com)

Composition Services

Project Coordinator: Jennifer Theriot

Layout and Graphics: Carl Byers, Lauren Goddard, Denny Hager, Stephanie D. Jumper, Alicia B. South

Proofreaders: John Greenough, Jessica Kramer, Christine Pingleton, Charles Spencer, Techbooks

Indexer: Techbooks

Publishing and Editorial for Technology Dummies

    Richard Swadley, Vice President and Executive Group Publisher

    Andy Cummings, Vice President and Publisher

    Mary Bednarek, Executive Acquisitions Director

    Mary C. Corder, Editorial Director

Publishing for Consumer Dummies

    Diane Graves Steele, Vice President and Publisher

    Joyce Pepple, Acquisitions Director

Composition Services

    Gerry Fahey, Vice President of Production Services

    Debbie Stailey, Director of Composition Services

Contents at a Glance

Table of Contents

Introduction

・・

*T*ips. Suggestions. Examples. Good advice. Information. Stir it all up with a dash of humor and you have *Laptops For Dummies*, now in its lustrous second edition.

You hold in your hands the next-best thing you could buy, other than a laptop computer itself. Whether you have used a laptop before, are thinking about buying one, or have a laptop and have decided to give yourself a boost, you've found the best book on the shelf.

Now what? Honestly, I could just fill the next few pages with random words or Chinese characters because studies show that few people read introductions. In fact, I could divulge the key to happiness here, the real answer to life after death, and the simple directions for creating a perpetual-motion machine, and no one other than my copy editor would ever notice. Hopefully, if you've made it this far, you're different!

This reference is just for the laptop user, with no desktop PC bias or attitude. Laptop users often feel like second-class citizens, struggling through desktop references that don't consider the special needs of laptop users and the special features that laptops offer. The laptop probably came with a thin pamphlet — no manual. The Internet doesn't help. And, desktop users may think that they understand laptops — nay, they are but fools! If you've felt frustrated at the lack of good laptop information, rest assured: Your days of second-class citizenship are over!

This book covers your portable computer from laptop to lap-bottom, inside and out, on the road or resting at home. The information here runs the gamut from those who are just out laptop shopping to the old hands, from introducing your laptop to making your first wireless connection at some swanky cybercafé. Soon, you and your laptop will do the merry dance of happiness and cooperation.

About This Book

This book covers all aspects of the laptop or notebook computer. Trivial history is noted, I give you tips for buying a laptop, and then information on setup and orientation is provided. This book covers all the laptop necessities, including managing the battery and doing the ever-so-trendy wireless thing.

This book is organized as a reference; it's not intended for you to read each chapter one after the other. Instead, merely find the tidbit of information, the knowledge nugget you need to know, and then be on your merry way. Everything is cross-referenced, so if you need to look elsewhere in the book for more information, you can easily find it.

In writing this book, I assume that you may know a bit about computers, as most folks do today. But you may be utterly fresh on the idea of *portable* computing. Despite what they tell you, a laptop computer is not merely a desktop computer with a handle attached. There's more to it, and this book is here to show you the ropes — and let you take full advantage of what the laptop has to offer.

I divide the laptop experience into six handy parts:

Part I contains an overview of laptop computing, plus a handy how-to guide for buying a laptop to fill your portable computing needs.

Part II discusses how to use your laptop and its basic features and how Windows works with a laptop, plus important information on power management (a subject you won't find in a desktop computer book or reference).

Part III is about networking and the Internet and getting your laptop to communicate with the rest of the world.

Part IV deals with taking your laptop on the road, and includes a special chapter on the hot topic of laptop security.

Part V covers laptop troubleshooting as well as various ways to upgrade your laptop's hardware and software.

Part VI is the traditional *For Dummies* Part of Tens — various lists for review or to help you get on your way.

And Just Who Are You?

Let me jump to the conclusion that you're a human being, not a robot or an alien living on Earth in disguise. Furthermore, you either own a laptop PC or want to buy one. You may already have a desktop computer, or perhaps you had a laptop a long, long time ago. Things have changed.

(You'll find that I use the word *laptop* here to describe the common portable computer. Others use the term *notebook*. You can read in Chapter 1 why I prefer the term *laptop*.)

This book assumes that you have a PC-compatible laptop, one that runs the Windows operating system — either Windows Vista or Windows XP. This book doesn't cover the Apple line of Macintosh laptop and notebook computers, nor does it address any PC laptops running the Linux operating system or any other operating systems known or unknown, from this or any parallel universe or dimension.

This book doesn't describe the basic operations of a computer, Windows, or your software. I've tried to keep the information specific to the portable aspects of the laptop computer. Beyond that, if you need more information about running your computer, any standard PC or Windows reference will work fine.

Icons Used in This Book

The Tip icon notifies you about something cool, handy, or nifty or something that I highly recommend. For example, "Check your teeth for spinach *before* you go in for that job interview."

Don't forget! When you see this icon, you can be sure that it points out something that you should remember, something I said earlier that I'm repeating because it's very important and you'll likely forget it anyway.

Danger! Ah-oogah! Ah-oogah! When you see the Warning icon, pay careful attention to the text. This icon flags something that's bad or that could cause trouble. For example, "Don't try to shift your car into Reverse when you're going 75 m.p.h. down the freeway just because you would like to see what happens."

This icon alerts you to something technical, an aside or some trivial tidbit that I just cannot suppress the urge to share. Feel free to skip over this book's technical information as you please.

Where to Go from Here

You can start reading this book anywhere, as a reference. Open up the Table of Contents and pick a spot that amuses you or concerns you or has piqued your curiosity. Everything is explained in the text, and stuff is carefully cross-referenced so that you don't waste your time reading repeated information.

I offer, as a supplement to this book, a Web site as well as support forums. You can visit the Web site at

```
www.wambooli.com
```

Specific information for this book can be found at

```
www.wambooli.com/help/laptops/
```

The support forums are found at

```
http://forums.wambooli.com/
```

Finally, I enjoy hearing feedback. If you want to send me e-mail, my personal address is dgookin@wambooli.com. I'm happy to answer questions specific to this book, or just to say "Hello." Please be aware that I am not listing my e-mail address here to provide free troubleshooting or support for your computer. If you need support, contact your laptop dealer or manufacturer. Thank you for understanding.

Enjoy your laptop computer. I'll see you on the road!

Part I
Getting Your Very Own Laptop

The 5th Wave   By Rich Tennant

"You know if we can all keep the tittering down, I, for one, would like to hear more about Ken's new pointing device."

In this part . . .

Contrary to the name *laptop,* very few people actually put laptop computers in their laps. Doing such a thing would be kind of dangerous — laptops generate heat (maybe not as much heat as a scalding cup of coffee, but heat nonetheless). Plus, the human lap is not the most stable platform for an expensive technological gizmo.

The laptop computer is the answer to the question "How can I take my computer with me?" Surprisingly, the desire for portable computing is an old one. If you've been stuck inside with your PC, your yearning for the freedom a laptop computer offers is a deep one. Or, maybe you're just curious about why so many people like their desktop PCs but *love* their laptops. Either way, this part of the book introduces the concept of the laptop computer, including many reasons that you should get yourself one as well as providing a handy shopping guide to help you find a laptop that's perfect for your lap.

Chapter 1

Sometimes You Can Take It with You

The notion of computing on the road is as old as the computer itself. I'm pretty certain that sometime after one of those huge, room-size computers was first turned on in the late 1940s, someone with thick glasses and a crewcut dreamed of putting the thing on wheels and using it outside on a sunny day.

The dream of computing elsewhere is an old one, deeply rooted in the computer community yet only recently realized. To help you better understand the concept of portable computing, and how the modern-day laptop came into being, I present this chapter: a brief and informative history of portable computing.

The Power Cord Can Stretch Only So Far

The concept of portability isn't anything new. Basically, it goes like this: Just attach a handle. *Presto!* It's portable! Such marketing gimmickry makes a 19 lb. television or a 25 lb. table saw instantly portable. Wow! I suppose that even a handle on an elephant would make it portable. (Oh, but the legs! Right.)

Real portability implies more than a handle, however. It means that the thing cannot only be lugged around, but that it's also designed to do so. Adding a handle may make something easier to tote, but when you still need to plug in the device, is it truly portable? Nope. You need batteries. The ability to be lightweight, run from battery power, *and* be useful is what's required to make something truly portable.

The desire to take a computer on the road has been around a long, long time. Back around 1970, long before the notion of the personal computer existed, Xerox PARC developed the Dynabook concept. Today, you'd recognize it as a Tablet PC: the Dynabook was to be about half an inch thick with the width and breadth of a sheet of paper. The top part would be a screen; the bottom would be a keyboard.

The Dynabook never left the lab, remaining only a dream. Yet the desire to take a computer on the road wouldn't go away. For the next three decades after the Dynabook, many attempts were made at creating truly portable computers.

The ancient portable computer

Long before people marveled over credit-card-size calculators (solar powered), there existed the world's first portable, human-powered calculator. Presenting the *abacus,* the device used for centuries by merchants and goat herders to rapidly perform calculations that would break human fingers.

Abacus comes from the Greek word meaning "to swindle you faster." Seriously, the abacus, or *counting board,* is simple to master. Many kids today learn the abacus in elementary school. In the deft hands of an expert, an abacus can perform all the operations on a calculator — including the square and cubic roots. In his short story *Into the Comet,* science fiction author Arthur C. Clarke wrote of stranded astronauts using multiple abacuses to plot their voyage home when the spaceship's computer broke down.

The Osborne 1

The first successful portable computer was the Osborne 1, created by Adam Osborne in 1980. A computer book author and publisher, Adam believed that for personal computers to be successful, they would have to be portable.

Adam's design for the Osborne 1 portable computer was ambitious for the time: The thing would have to fit under an airline seat — and this was *years* before anyone would dream of actually using a computer on an airplane.

The Osborne 1 portable computer (see Figure 1-1) was a whopping success. It featured a full-size keyboard, two 5¼-inch floppy drives, but a teensy, credit-card-size monitor. It wasn't battery powered, but it did have a handy carrying handle so that you could lug around the 24-pound beast like an overpacked suitcase. Despite its shortcomings, they were selling 10,000 units a month (at $1,795 each, which included software — a first for the time). The cash was rolling in.

Figure 1-1: A late-model Osborne.

By late 1983, sadly, Adam's company floundered, suffering from the onslaught of the new IBM PC and its legion of compatibles and clones. Yet the Osborne 1 proved that computers could be portable. In fact, it founded a new class of computer: the *luggable*.

The loveable luggables

The Osborne was portable, but not conveniently so. Face it: The thing was a *suitcase!* Imagine hauling the 24 lb. Osborne across Chicago's O'Hare airport. Worse: Imagine the joy of your fellow seatmates as you try to wedge the thing beneath the seat in front you.

Portable wasn't the proper word to describe the Osborne 1. People in the computer world yearned for portability. They wanted to believe the advertising images of carefree people toting the Osborne around — people with arms of equal length, no less. But no hip marketing term could mask the ungainly nature of the Osborne: Portable? Transportable? Wispy? Nope. Credit some wag in the computer press for dreaming up the term *luggable* to describe the new category of portable computers.

The luggable was an extremely popular class of computer. Never mind its weight. Never mind that most never ventured from the desktops they were first set up on — luggables were the best the computer industry could offer in the arena of portable computing.

In the end, it wasn't the Osborne computer's weight that doomed it. No, what killed the Osborne was that the world wanted IBM PC compatibility. The Osborne lacked that. Instead, an upstart Texas company called Compaq introduced luggability to the IBM world with the Compaq 1, shown in Figure 1-2.

Figure 1-2:
The
luggable
Compaq 1.

The Compaq 1, introduced in 1983 at $3,590, proved that you could have your IBM compatibility and haul it on the road with you — as long as a power socket was handy.

Yet the power cord can stretch only so far. It became painfully obvious that for a computer to be truly portable — as Adam Osborne intended — it would have to lose that power cord.

The Model 100

The first computer that even remotely looks like a modern laptop, and was fully battery powered, was the Radio Shack Model 100, shown in Figure 1-3. It was an instant, insane success.

Figure 1-3:
The Radio
Shack
Model 100.

The Model 100 wasn't designed to be IBM PC compatible, which is surprising considering that PC compatibility was all the rage at the time. Instead, it offered users a full-size, full-action keyboard, plus a tiny, 8-row, 40-column LCD display. It came with several built-in programs, including a text editor (word processor), communications program, and scheduler and appointment book, plus the BASIC programming language, which allowed users to create their own programs or buy and use BASIC programs written by others.

Portability and communications

Long before the Internet came around, one item that was deemed necessary on all portable computers was the ability to communicate. The laptop computer had to be able to not only talk with the desktop computer, to exchange and update files, but also use a *modem* to communicate electronically over phone lines.

Nearly every portable computer from the Radio Shack Model 100 onward had to have a modem, or at least an option for installing one. This was in an era when modems were considered optional luxuries for a desktop computer. On the road, portable computers required a modem to be able to keep in touch with their companion desktop systems. Special software was required, but after the connection was made, it was possible to keep files on the laptop updated even from the most remote locations.

The Radio Shack Model 100 was really all that was needed for portability at the time, which is why the device was such a resounding success.

- ✔ The Model 100 provided the *form factor* for laptops of the future. It was about the size of a hardback novel. It ran for hours off of standard AA batteries. And, it weighed just 6 pounds.

- ✔ So popular was the Model 100 among journalists that it was common to hear the clackity-clack of its keyboard during Presidential news conferences.

- ✔ Despite its popularity and versatility, people wanted a version of the Model 100 that would run the same software as the IBM PC. Technology wasn't ready to shrink the PC's hardware to Model 100 size, but the Model 100 set the goal for what users wanted in a laptop's dimensions.

The lunch buckets

Before the dawn of the first true laptop, some ugly mutations wandered in, along with a few rejects from various mad scientists around the globe. I call them the *lunch bucket* computers because they assumed the shape, size, and weight of a typical hardhat's lunch box. The Compaq III, shown in Figure 1-4, was typical of this type of portable computer.

Figure 1-4:
The
Compaq III.

- ✔ The lunch box beasts weighed anywhere from 12 to 20 or more pounds, and most weren't battery powered.

- ✔ The lunch bucket portables were the first PCs to use LCD monitors. (The Osborne and Compaq portables used glass CRTs.)

- ✔ Incidentally, around the same time as the lunch bucket computers became popular, color monitors were becoming standard for desktop PCs. All portables at the time, even those with LCD monitors, were monochrome.

- ✔ Honestly, the lunch buckets did offer something over the old trans-portable or luggables: less weight! A late-model lunch bucket PC weighed in at about 12 pounds, or half the weight and about ⅛ the size of the suitcase-size luggables.

Early PC laptops

The computer industry's dream was to have a portable computer that had all the power of a desktop computer, plus all the features, yet be about the same size and weight as the Model 100. One of the first computers to approach that mark was the Compaq SLT, back in 1988, shown in Figure 1-5.

Figure 1-5:
The Compaq
SLT.

The Compaq SLT was the first portable computer that actually looks like one of today's laptops: A hinged lid swings up and back from the base, which contains the keyboard. This is the *clamshell* design.

Feature-wise, the SLT had what most PC desktop users wanted in a portable system: It featured a full-size keyboard, full-size screen, floppy drive (no hard drive or CD-ROM), and 286 microprocessor, which meant that the computer could run the then-popular DOS operating system.

Weight? Alas, the SLT was a bowling ball, at 14 pounds!

What the Compaq SLT did was prove to the world that portability was possible. A laptop computer was designed to feature everything a desktop computer could, plus run off batteries for an hour or so. Yeah, believe it or not, people were *delighted*.

Calculating laptop weight: The missing pieces

When computer companies specify the weights of their laptops, I'm certain that they do it under ideal conditions, possibly at the North Pole or some other location where the earth's gravity field is at its weakest. The advertised weight is, like they say, "for comparison purposes only."

Commonly left out of the laptop's weight specs is the *power brick,* the AC adapter used to connect the laptop to a wall socket. When the laptop isn't running off batteries, you need the power brick to supply the thing with juice. This means that the power brick is a required accessory — something you have to tote with you if you plan on taking the laptop on an extended trip.

In the old days, what they didn't tell you in the advertisements was that the power brick often weighed half as much as the laptop itself! Either that, or the power brick was more bulky than the laptop, as seen in the figure with the Dell 320LT's obnoxiously big power brick (and heavy 30-minute batteries). Lugging around such items isn't very convenient. Things are better today.

The search for weightlessness

Just because the marketing department labeled the computer a "laptop" didn't mean that it was sleek and lightweight. For a while there, it seemed like anyone could get away with calling a portable PC a laptop, despite the computer weighing up to 20 pounds — which is enough to crush any lap, not to mention kneecaps.

In the fall of 1989, NEC showed that it could think outside the laptop box when it introduced the UltraLite laptop, shown in Figure 1-6.

The UltraLite featured a full-size screen and keyboard, but no disk drives or other moving parts! It used battery-backed-up memory to serve as a *silicon disk.* The silicon disk stored 1 or 2MB of data — which was plenty back in those days.

As was required of all laptops, the UltraLite featured a modem, and it could also talk with a desktop computer via a special cable. Included with the UltraLite was software that would let it easily exchange files and programs with a desktop PC.

Figure 1-6:
The NEC
UltraLite.

The weight? Yes, the UltraLite lived up to its name and weighed in at just under 5 pounds — a feather compared to the obese laptops of the day. And, the battery lasted a whopping two hours, thanks mostly to the UltraLite's lack of moving parts.

From laptop to notebook

The UltraLite marked the line between what was then called a *laptop* to what is today called a *notebook*. Although manufacturers had perverted the term *laptop* to include heavy, bulky portables that were anything but lap-friendly (such as the cannonball-heavy Compaq III), the UltraLite raised the bar and created the notebook category.

Any laptop that weighs under 6 pounds and is less than an inch thick is technically a notebook. Some even lighter units earned the moniker *subnotebook*. Keep in mind that all these terms are for marketing purposes; today, all these computers, regardless of weight, size, or what the brochure says, are called *laptops*.

The modern notebook

As technology careened headlong into the 1990s, it became apparent that users were desperate for three things from their laptop computers — in addition to the basic PC compatibility, portability, and communications features that were long ago deemed must-haves:

- ✔ Light weight
- ✔ Long battery life
- ✔ Full hardware compatibility with desktop systems

Over time, all these qualities were achieved — at a price. Today, the Holy Grail of a lightweight, PC compatible laptop that boasts a long battery life isn't elusive; it's just expensive!

- ✔ **Weight:** Depending on how much you want to pay, your laptop can be anywhere from a half-inch thick to just under an inch thick and weigh in between 2 to 6 pounds, such as the IBM Thinkpad, shown in Figure 1-7. The weight and size also depend on the features you want in your laptop, with more features adding more weight.

Figure 1-7:
The author's
IBM Think-
pad T-41
weighs in
at 4 pounds.

✔ **Battery life:** Although the batteries themselves haven't improved much in the past several years, thanks to power-management hardware and software, modern laptops can extend battery life from the once-standard two hours to about three or four hours.

✔ **Hardware compatibility:** Since the late 1990s, all laptops come with color screens, just like desktop systems do. They also sport CD-ROM or DVD drives, although a floppy drive is seldom found in a modern laptop (and then usually as an external device). Laptops also feature modems, networking (wired and wireless), and expansion options. Special laptop microprocessors and other hardware have been developed over the years, keeping the laptop hardware small and energy efficient.

The future of the laptop

Human laps aren't getting any smaller. Human eyes can only comfortably read text that's so big. Most importantly, human fingers have trouble with keyboards that are too tiny. Because of these limitations, the laptop of the future will probably remain the about same size as a laptop of today. (Even though scientists could make the keyboard and screen smaller, the human form wouldn't appreciate it.)

What about Tablet PCs?

This book doesn't specifically cover Tablet PCs. These computers are essentially laptops without the keyboards; the tablet consists of only the monitor "half" of the laptop, on which you write information using a special pen or stylus. It's an electric triptych!

Although the notion of the Tablet PC sounds intriguing (and I must admit that they are sexy), it's yet another example of the computer industry's thinking that something is "really neat" and designing a gizmo that no one needs or wants. In fact, this is nothing new; back in the early days of laptop computers, various *Pen Computers* (as they were called) were introduced, but also failed to attract users.

So, what happened to the Tablet PC? You can still buy them, but most of them are merely laptops where the lids can close "face up." You can use a stylus to draw directly on the screen, but there's a keyboard handy just in case. People like keyboards! In my world, the keyboard makes the Tablet PC a laptop, and if it's a laptop, it's not really a Tablet PC, is it?

The laptop won't replace the desktop system, although the current trend is to use both a laptop and desktop computer. Smaller devices exist, such as the popular BlackBerry or Palm Treo, but the laptop holds its own as a fully functional, truly portable computer.

Technology continues to make laptop hardware smaller, more energy efficient, and better able to handle the portable environment. But one area that needs vast improvement is battery technology.

The battery of the future is the *fuel cell,* which is like a miniature power plant directly connected to your laptop PC. Fuel cell technology promises power that lasts for weeks instead of hours, which will prove a boon to portable gizmos of every kind — but only when the fuel cell makes sense economically. Although fuel cells are available today, they're just too expensive and bulky for laptops. Scientists and other people in white lab coats are predicting that the first practical fuel cell will be widely available by the end of the decade. Until then, laptop users will have to slug it out with rechargeable batteries and power packs.

(See Chapter 8 for more information on batteries as well as other power-management issues.)

Why You Need a Laptop

Obviously, Adam Osborne was right: Computers need to be portable! The question should really be "Why buy a desktop computer that's stuck in one spot all the time?"

Naturally, a desktop computer is more powerful, expandable, and cheaper than a laptop. *But you can't take it with you!* Well, you could, but hauling around all that desktop stuff would make you look like a dork.

On the other hand, it's impossible to look like a dork with a laptop. Imagine yourself sitting in that trendy coffee shop and sipping some overpriced caffeinated beverage while poring over your e-mail and chatting on a cell phone — that's hip! That's so five-minutes-from-now!

Seriously, you want a laptop for one of the following reasons:

✔ **As your main computer**

Why dither over saving money with a desktop when you really want the portability of a laptop?

A desktop computer cannot pretend to be a laptop, but a laptop can certainly fake being a desktop: You can use a full-size keyboard and monitor with your laptop. You can also connect any number of popular desktop peripherals, such as a printer, scanner, external hard drive, and so on. But, unlike with a desktop system, you're free to disconnect the laptop and wander the world whenever you want.

✔ **As a space-saving computer system**

Unlike with desktops, you don't have to build a tabletop shrine to your laptop computer — that is, you don't need a computer desk. If space is tight in your house, apartment, or dorm room, keep the laptop on the shelf or in a drawer. Then set it up on the kitchen table or coffee table when you're ready to work. Forget about the constant mess and clutter that orbits the typical desktop computer station. Viva Adam Osborne!

✔ **As a second computer**

Why buy a second desktop computer when you can get a laptop and enjoy not only the presence of a second computer but also the ability to make that computer system portable? Furthermore, you can network the two computers, allowing them to share the Internet connection and printers, as well as each other's data and files. And you still have the luxury of having one system that's portable.

✔ **As your on-the-road computer**

Laptops let you take your work on the road. After a few moments of *synch* (transferring current files between your desktop and laptop, covered in Chapter 14), you're off and running to anywhere you like (although being in direct, bright sunlight can make it difficult to see the laptop screen).

Taking that laptop off to school

It was hard to deny being a computer nerd back in the old days. At school, you would see these guys, not known for their muscle, struggling to tote several pounds of serious PC equipment up the hard concrete stairwell to their dorm rooms. Today, *everyone* uses a laptop at school. No one considers it geeky, any more than an iPod is considered geeky. In fact, it's practically an insult if your college-bound high school senior doesn't get a laptop as a graduation present. Some parents. . . .

Laptops allow you to bring a full-powered computer with you anywhere on campus. Students can get work done in a dorm just as easily as they can in the library, under a tree, or anywhere else feet can take you (or where there's

a power outlet to mooch from). Laptops were meant for college.

Most colleges and universities provide a laptop requirements sheet that tells you which type of hardware you should look for when purchasing a laptop for school. That's great, but it's not enough.

Laptops at college are subject to two of the nastiest things to assault computer users: The first consists of various ugly programs that can infiltrate a PC over the Internet; the second is theft. See this book's Chapter 12 for vital information regarding online security, as well as Chapter 16, on preventing theft. That stuff is required reading for both parents and their children taking laptop computers to school.

When you return from your "road warrior" trip, you perform another synch, and both computers get all caught up for the day.

- Laptops let you escape the confines of your office and do work anywhere you like for a few hours. Or, if there's power at your location, you can plug in and work all day.

- The laptop lets you take your work with you when you travel. It lets you experience the reality of using a computer on an airplane (which isn't as smart as it sounds).

Why You Don't Need a Laptop

Laptops aren't cheap. They're also expensive to fix. Forget about upgrading the hardware. They can easily get stolen. The battery life never lives up to the printed specifications. It's tough to get work done on a jet or in a café because people either look over your shoulder or ask you questions about the laptop. Ack! But those are minor quibbles.

Thanks to their light weight, long battery life, and increasing computing power, laptops make ideal computers for just about anyone. If you don't own a laptop today, you will someday.

Chapter 2

Buying a Laptop Just for You

*B*uying a laptop works like buying any big-ticket, pricey item: The more you know about what you're buying, the better chance you have of finding exactly what you need. An educated consumer is a wise and thrifty consumer. Who wants to feel like a clumsy doof when buying something technical, like a computer?

Even if you're an old hand at buying desktop PCs, I recommend that you do a little research and investigation before you go shopping for a new laptop. Many issues are unique to laptops, such as weight, battery life, and wireless networking options. Therefore, I present this chapter to help you make the best decision possible. Here, you can read about the easiest way to buy a laptop, plus which swanky laptop features to consider. The idea is to get a laptop that perfectly fits your needs (not to mention your lap).

For more information on buying computers, including definitions and descriptions of various computer pieces parts, refer to *Buying a Computer For Dummies*, published by Wiley Publishing, Inc., and written by yours truly.

Buy That Laptop!

The best computer you can buy is the one that does what you need it to do. To find that computer, you have to ignore a few things. Above all, avoid discussing brand names. Too many people consider brand name first and don't even know which components they need, how much memory is necessary, which type of microprocessor to buy, or other, more important, factors.

I also highly recommend avoiding the low-price game. An abundance of cheap laptops are out there. In haste, you may buy one — and get stuck with it. More important than price is service and support. Again, this chapter helps steer you in the right direction.

You don't buy a computer for the hardware alone. Low price isn't the reason, either. Instead, the reason you want a computer is to complete some task, to have the computer do work for you, or to help you get something done. When you approach the purchase with that information in mind, you end up getting the best computer possible — not some cheap-o brand name that you have to upgrade in a few months.

The five steps to buying any computer

To get a computer that works perfectly for you, follow these five simple steps:

1. Figure out what you want the computer to do.
2. Find the software to get that job done.
3. Match hardware to the software.
4. Shop for service and support.
5. Buy the computer.

Two items here stand out more than the others. The first — often surprising to most folks — is to look for software *before* hardware (Step 2). That's because it's the software that gets the work done. Surprise! Despite all the flash and glory that the hardware offers, software is more important.

The second item most folks don't expect is found in Step 4: service and support. More important than finding a low price or good deal is to find folks who will give you help when you need it and fix the silly thing in case it breaks. That makes sense, but it's nuts how people forget it.

The hunt for software

Allow me to distill this information for you: If you plan on getting a laptop as an extension of your desktop computer, you'll most likely be running the same software on the laptop as on your desktop. In that case, your laptop's hardware requirements are identical to the desktop system. Bingo! You're done.

If your laptop adventure is new, what you probably need is a basic laptop setup. You want to browse the Internet, plus you want a basic Office suite of applications. That's pretty much what a typical laptop user needs.

Beyond these two examples, you might be running specific software on your laptop. If so, find out what kind of hardware that software requires. For example, if the software needs 256MB of RAM, you have to be sure that your laptop comes with at least that much RAM. If the software needs special graphics power, make a note of it. Ditto for hard drive storage, a CD-ROM, microprocessor power, and other hardware requirements.

How can you tell how much hardware your software needs? Easy! Hardware requirements for all software packages are listed right on the side of the software box. Sometimes it's brief, and sometimes it's detailed, but it's the information you need to help you configure your new computer.

- The most important piece of software you need is the computer's operating system. For this book, I assume that you're using Windows. Windows XP is currently popular, but Windows Vista is coming soon (if it's not here already). So, maybe you want to consider a laptop that runs XP now with an eye toward upgrading to Windows Vista in the future. That's entirely possible.

- Generally speaking, any laptop powerful enough to run Windows XP can run just about any desktop software that's sold.

- Windows Vista can run on any Windows XP system. But, to get the most from Vista, you need more computer memory (RAM), a faster microprocessor, and advanced graphics. This book covers the details.

- You have to refer to the software license agreement to see whether you're allowed to install a single program on both your desktop and laptop computers. Most of the time, this is considered okay by the developer because it's assumed that you won't be using both computers at one time. But some software developers, specifically Microsoft, don't allow multiple installations from the same set of software.

- ✔ Happily, most laptops come with all the software you need. You get an operating system, such as Windows XP or Windows Vista, plus you get Microsoft Office or a similar productivity suite of programs. Perhaps you get other software as well. Be sure to inquire about included or bundled software before you buy a laptop.

- ✔ Hardcore computer gamers prefer desktop systems to laptops, but that doesn't mean that your laptop must be bereft of games. The good news is that laptop manufacturers understand the need to play games, so the newer systems are more than up to the task.

- ✔ Also note that the laptop's LCD monitor doesn't update as fast as a CRT, or traditional monitor. Gamers prefer CRTs.

- ✔ In the realm of graphics applications, diehard graphic artists also prefer CRT, or traditional glass monitors, because they can more accurately reproduce a variety of colors. Note that you can connect such a monitor to a laptop when the need arises. (Refer to Chapter 7.)

Figuring out how much basic laptop hardware you need

The three basic items you want to mull over in matching your laptop's hardware to the software you need are

- ✔ The microprocessor
- ✔ Memory, or RAM
- ✔ Hard drive storage

The *microprocessor* is the laptop's main chip. It's not "the brain." No, your computer's software is the brain. It tells the microprocessor what to do. You want to ensure that you get a microprocessor that's plenty fast enough to deal with the applications you need *tomorrow*. It's worth the extra money to invest in a fast microprocessor now, which extends the useful life of your laptop by ensuring that you can run tomorrow's software before tomorrow comes. Find a laptop with the fastest microprocessor you can afford, and then buy the next-most-expensive microprocessor. You'll be thankful later.

Memory is where the action happens in a computer, where the work gets done. If the software states that it wants more than 256MB of memory, get a laptop with however much RAM the software requires. The more RAM your computer has, the happier it appears to be and the more your software will enjoy the computer.

The *hard drive* is the electronic closet where the laptop stores your stuff. The hard drive must have room for the computer's operating system, all the software you get and later install, all the data files and junk you collect, plus room to grow (lotsa room). Again, the software you plan on using should tell you how much hard drive space it requires. The total space for each application should be added up and then at least doubled, to give you a general figure for how much hard drive storage you need.

- ✔ Laptop microprocessors are more expensive than their desktop counterparts. That's because the laptop microprocessors must be designed to use less power and generate less heat. That takes time, so their development cycle is longer; hence, the added cost.

- ✔ When reading the hardware requirements on a software box, use the recommended values, not the minimum values. For example, a program may request 256MB of RAM but really thirst for 384MB. If so, get 384MB — or more.

- ✔ RAM is where it's at! If you cannot afford a faster microprocessor, you can afford to buy more RAM. Pack your laptop with as much RAM as you can afford now.

- ✔ Buy the fattest hard drive you can afford. Especially if you plan on putting music on your laptop, you need at least an 80GB hard drive, and perhaps more.

- ✔ I recommend a laptop with at least 512MB of RAM in it, if possible. If you can afford 1024MB of RAM, get it. If you can afford 2048MB of RAM, get it, but don't e-mail me about it because it will make me terribly jealous.

- ✔ The things that consume huge amounts of hard drive space are graphics image files (such as digital photographs), music or audio files, and video files. If you plan on collecting any of these files on your laptop, get a larger hard drive!

- ✔ By investing in the latest, fastest microprocessor, lots of RAM, and copious amounts of hard drive space now, you're extending the life of your laptop. That's a good thing. You want your laptop investment to last for years to come. Pay more now, and you'll earn it back down the road, when you're still using your laptop while others are forced to buy a new one.

Finding out what you don't need

Laptops generally don't come with floppy drives. Ditto for Zip disks. If you want such a thing, it can always be added as a peripheral, but, honestly, you don't need it — and you really don't want to be carrying around such a thing with you anyway.

Laptops also lack a desktop PC's internal expansion slots, because most laptops come with all the options preinstalled (another reason for a laptop's high price tag). If you want to play expansion card poker with your computer, you probably want a desktop PC and not a laptop.

Thanks to the laptop's expandability — primarily because of its USB ports — you can add ' most any desktop device as an external peripheral. Don't be fooled! You're buying a laptop for its *portability,* so you want extra options installed *when you buy* the laptop. Adding on extras is possible, but then you're tethering your laptop to other things, which reduces its portability.

More important than buying a floppy drive, consider getting a laptop with a memory card reader. A combination Secure Digital and CompactFlash card reader means that your laptop can immediately read the same media used in digital cameras. You can even use that media as removable storage and as a way to swap information between two computers.

CD/DVD/R/RW/+/-/E]-E]-0

Don't be cheap and try to save money by getting a laptop without a DVD drive. Remember that DVD drives can read CDs as well as DVDs, so a single DVD drive is two drives in one.

Where you can spend or waste money is on the *recordable* CD or DVD options. Some drives play CDs and DVDs and also record CD-R and CD-RW discs. Then there are superdrives that read and write *everything.* Yep, you pay more for them.

Specific laptop issues

In addition to all the regular hardware, you need to consider the following five items when you're choosing a laptop:

- ✔ Weight
- ✔ Size
- ✔ Display size
- ✔ Battery life
- ✔ Battery type

The laptop buzzword jungle

When you go laptop shopping, you're going to discover a bewildering bazaar of various technical terms and such. Most of them are marketing terms, meaning that they were invented by nontechnical types to describe technical things. This is okay because technical people tend to overuse the words *keen* and *neato*. Here's a round-up of some laptop technical terms you may encounter during your shopping exercises:

Celeron M: This is Intel's version of its Celeron microprocessor that's comparable to the Pentium M. In both cases, the M stands for *mobile*. The Celeron M is a low-cost alternative to the Pentium M. It isn't considered part of the Intel Centrino design.

Centrino: Intel uses this term to describe various laptop technology — specifically, stuff designed for a mobile computer that you won't find in a desktop. The Centrino technology includes a special chipset, or the main circuitry on the laptop's motherboard, a specifically designed laptop microprocessor, and wireless networking technology.

Centrino Duo: The Duo suffix describes a newer version of Centrino technology, specifically with an Intel dual-core microprocessor.

Core Duo: This is the Intel replacement microprocessor for the Pentium. The Core Duo chip contains two CPU cores, like getting two microprocessors on one chip.

Core Solo: This is the Intel single-core replacement for the Pentium microprocessor.

DDR: Also known as DDR-SDRAM, it stands for *double data rate*. This type of computer memory is better than plain ol' SDRAM.

Dothan: This name was originally used by Intel to describe the next-generation Pentium M microprocessors. Intel wanted to get away from the number-naming thing, but this notion failed, and the Dothan eventually became known as the Series 700 Pentium M.

GHz: An acronym for *gigahertz*, or billions of cycles per second, this speed measurement is used to gauge microprocessors. The actual speed, of course, varies, and often in mundane tasks, it's difficult to tell the difference between a microprocessor running at 2.0 GHz versus 2.4 GHz. But that doesn't stop the manufacturers from boasting about their chips' speed.

Mobile Sempron. An AMD processor designed for laptop (mobile) computing. It's the economy version of the Turion flavor chip.

Pentium M: The M stands for *mobile*, and the Pentium M chip is the Intel microprocessor specifically designed for use in laptops.

SDRAM: This acronym stands for Synchronous Dynamic Random Access Memory, the most popular type of memory used in computers today.

Turion 64. The AMD version of Intel's Pentium M, a powerful 64-bit mobile processor that comes in single and dual core models. The dual core is named Turion 64 X2. The Turion was formerly named the Mobile Athlon 64.

Weight: Nearly all laptops sold today fall in the range of 4 to 7 pounds. The heavier laptops have more features. The lighter models may have fewer features or merely more advanced features, but they're generally more expensive. Although you pay more for less weight, oddly enough, you pay more for extra weight too, thanks to the added features.

Size: Most laptops are less than 1 inch thick and about as tall and wide as a small coffee table book. They could get smaller than that, but there's a limit based on the size of the keyboard and the size of the display. Speaking of which. . . .

Display: Recently, manufacturers have discovered that people love larger LCD displays on a laptop — despite the larger display adding to the laptop's size and weight (and consuming more battery power). For a laptop being used at one location and only rarely going on the road, a huge display is wonderful. If you want portability, though, and a longer battery life, consider a smaller display.

Battery life: Despite the claims on the brochures, most PC laptops last anywhere from two to three hours unplugged. They last even less if you do a lot with the laptop, which means lots of disk access and networking and stuff that requires copious amounts of electricity.

Battery type: Many types of batteries are available, but what you want in your laptop is a lithium-ion battery. You don't want a nickel-cadmium, or NiCad, battery. You also want to shun the nickel metal hydride (NiMH) battery. Lithium-ion batteries can be recharged at any time and don't have the "memory" problem that NiCads and NiMHs have. They also last longer and keep a more potent charge longer.

- ✔ There's nothing wrong with buying a 7-pound laptop that has all the features you need.

- ✔ See Chapter 8 for more information on battery types and the memory problem.

- ✔ Stuff that's important to the overall weight of the laptop — the power brick and cord, extra batteries, discs, manuals, and so on — aren't included with the basic tonnage calculation. Keep that in mind when weight is important to you.

- ✔ Larger LCDs are sweet, but they use up battery power more quickly, and they add to the system's overall bulk and weight.

- ✔ The larger displays on laptops are designed to be in the same aspect ratio as a DVD movie. Coincidence?

- ✔ The LCD display is only the external half of the laptop's graphics equation. The internal half is a graphics adapter. Choosing the proper graphics adapter for your laptop depends on what your software needs; the side of the software box tells you exactly which graphics standard to get for your laptop. Pay attention to that information when graphics are important to you!

✔ A popular trick that's used to make the battery life seem longer is to specify the time used by two batteries. With some laptops, you can swap a drained battery with a fresh one, thereby extending your portable time. Although there's nothing wrong with that trick, the extended battery time should not be used for comparison.

✔ Avoid any so-called laptop computer that doesn't run off batteries. Spurn it! Point, scream, and run away!

Laptop expansion options

Laptops use a special expansion card system no longer called PCMCIA. It was once called PCMCIA, and you may still hear that term bandied about. But, because no one can remember PCMCIA, let alone what it stands for, it was changed back in the 1990s, renamed first to *Fred* and then to *PC Card*. Despite this, I noticed in Office Depot the other day that some guy called them PCMCIA cards. His name was Fred.

Seriously, PCMCIA was re-dubbed CardBus some time ago. Some folks even refer to it as PC Card. What. Ever. The system, no matter what it's called, uses special expansion slots and cards for adding options to your laptop. The card is about the size of a credit card, though thicker (and without revolving debt). It slides into a special slot on the laptop's side, which is how you can add special options to your laptop. The options include a memory card reader, networking abilities, more storage, and so on.

A newer slide-in laptop expansion standard, one designed by the PCMCIA folks, is ExpressCard. It offers greater expansion options plus a faster communications speed, making it an ideal replacement for the older PCMCIA. The ExpressCard expansion cards can also be lighter, use less power, and overall more handsome than their clunky old PCMCIA ancestors.

Laptops may also use an exchangeable disk system. For example, the CD-ROM or DVD drive might be removable and could be replaced with a second hard drive or a floppy drive. This type of drive swapping is usually specific to certain laptop models; you generally cannot swap drives between two laptops from different manufacturers, unless you're just incredibly lucky.

✔ ExpressCard is a relatively new technology and therefore may not exist on most laptops.

✔ Okay: PCMCIA stands for Personal Computer Memory Card International Association. Big deal!

✔ CardBus = PCMCIA.

- It's often said that PCMCIA stands for People Cannot Memorize Computer Industry Acronyms.

- Better than getting the swappable drive option is simply knowing exactly what you need in a laptop in the first place. Buying a laptop with nonswappable disk drives is cheaper.

- Other laptop expansion options are available through the same type of expansion *ports* available on desktop PCs. These options include standard USB ports as well as older serial and printer ports.

Communications choices

Laptops thirst for communications! Therefore, they must come with internal modems plus networking abilities, either wire-based Ethernet or wireless networking, or often both.

Most laptops are adorned with infrared communications ports, which allow for communications with other infrared devices. Or, I suppose that the infrared ports exist so that you can use your laptop to change channels on the hotel room TV.

- Ethernet is provided on a laptop via internal circuitry and an RJ-45 port (or hole) on the laptop's case. If the laptop doesn't have this circuitry built in, you can add it via a PC Card.

- Wireless networking is done via the 802.11 standard. The most popular version of this standard is 802.11g, though some older systems use 802.11b. (They say that the 802.11g standard is compatible with the older 802.11b.)

- Yes, the 802.11 standards keep marching up the alphabet. Rumor has it that 802.11n is all the rage with the folks in the lab. But don't let that furrow your brow. A good gauge of which wireless standard to get is to look at what's available in the store. According to Fred at Office Depot, it's still 802.11g.

- If the laptop doesn't come with wireless networking built in, it can be added via a PC Card. I recommend getting a card with an external, directional antenna.

- Avoid the temptation to fondle the external antenna or to direct it at others in the cybercafé as though it were a small ray gun.

- If the laptop lacks a modem, you can also add a modem via a PC Card.

- For more on networking, see Chapter 9.

- No, sadly, you cannot use your laptop to change channels on the hotel room TV. I have this information on authority from many who've tried.

Your knees are alive, with The Sound of Music

Laptops almost always come with the cheapest, worst, tiny stereo speakers. Ugh. Fortunately, your laptop may have a headphone jack. It may also have a microphone jack. Remember to check for those things because not every laptop has them. The tinny speakers? Oh, laptops have —'em in spades!

When sound is important to you, look into a laptop that offers decent sound hardware. One way to tell is to see whether the laptop has digital audio output. Don't despair when you can't find anything, though. You can add PC Card sound adapters to your laptop, as well as USB sound solutions, like the Creative SoundBlaster Audigy.

Energy management hardware

Although desktop computers come with some energy management features — the ability to suspend or sleep the computer, or the "hibernate" option — these features are far more necessary on a laptop. Primarily, energy management on the laptop is concerned with controlling the power drain on the battery.

Ensure that your future laptop has the ability to merely sip power when necessary. Chapter 8 has more information on various tricks to make this happen, but it helps to look for such abilities in your laptop before you buy.

When power is really important to you, consider getting one of the power-miser microprocessors, as opposed to the high-speed, top-of-the-line models. This option saves a tad on battery life, but keep in mind that a high-end microprocessor works better for extending the laptop's lifespan.

Docking stations and port replicators

One optional item you can purchase for your laptop is the docking station or port replicator. Despite these items being optional, I highly recommend them.

The docking station or port replicator serves as a base for your laptop when it's not on the road. This item can be used to recharge the laptop's battery, but more importantly, it has connectors that allow you to add desktop options to the laptop. In fact, you can keep the full-size keyboard and monitor connected to the docking station or port replicator and just pop off the laptop when you're ready to go on the road.

 ✔ A port replicator may be nothing more than an extra attachment that plugs into a special expansion jack (or hole) on a laptop. The port replicator then lets you plug in standard desktop peripherals to the laptop.

✔ Docking stations are generally more sophisticated than port replicators. They offer all the connections found on port replicators, and include things like extra memory, optional expansion cards, are more desktop-like features. Docking stations are more expensive than port replicators, and they smell better.

Hunting for Service and Support

Please don't make the mistake of shopping for the cheapest laptop in the world. You'll find it, of course! The same laptop may have multiple prices. The price you get when you're buying directly from the manufacturer is different from the price of the same laptop you find in the Big Box store, and different still from the price in the back of the local computer flyer. Be not tempted!

People who overlook service and support when they buy laptops are doomed to despair. Unlike desktop computers, laptops contain specific, tiny, and expensive hardware. Those items aren't easily swappable components, like similar items in desktop systems. Because of that, buying from an outfit that offers personal support is important.

Support is best offered as a free telephone call for help when you need it.

Service is the art of fixing your laptop. The best service happens when the fix-it guy comes to your home or office. Otherwise, the laptop has to be returned, either directly to the dealer or to the manufacturer.

✔ There's a difference between support for your laptop hardware and support for its software. The software is supported by the software developer, which isn't the same company that makes the laptop hardware. Be aware of the differences before you make the call.

✔ A helpful tool in your support arsenal is my book *Troubleshooting Your PC For Dummies* (Wiley Publishing, Inc.).

✔ There's nothing wrong with mail-in service. Just be aware that you'll be without your "baby" for a few days while it's being fixed.

✔ Some manufacturers offer you only a replacement laptop while yours is being fixed via mail-in service. That's a bonus.

✔ A lack of service and support is one reason that some dealers (and large department stores and discount houses) offer laptops at such ridiculously cheap prices. Don't ever expect the employees in such a place to be able to help you, and the guy who cuts meat in the back can't fix your laptop, either.

Extended warranties: Don't buy a laptop without one!

For the past 175 years or so that I've been writing about buying computers, I've had one consistent recommendation: Avoid the extended warranty! That's because computers are hardy, reliable devices. If a PC can live through the standard warranty period, it will probably live forever or, well, a *long time* (longer than most television situation comedies, at least). And, repairing or replacing any item on a desktop PC is often cheaper than any extended warranty you can find. Laptops, however, are another beast.

Laptops lack the replaceable components of a desktop PC. Often when something breaks on a laptop, the entire unit must be repaired or replaced. That can be expensive. For example, the monitor connector on a laptop may be only a 23-cent part. But, if it breaks, the entire laptop motherboard must be replaced, which costs up to $1,000 — or more. That's also true for other items inside the laptop's case; fixing things just isn't cheap!

Because of the laptop's unique nature, I highly recommend getting a manufacturer's extended warranty. In fact, I *insist* that you get at least a 4- or 5-year warranty to cover everything on your laptop, full replacement, and repair costs. That may set you back $120 or so, but the price is worth it. It's an *investment*.

Beyond the manufacturer's warranty, don't worry. In fact, I strongly recommend that you avoid any other warranties, no matter how tempting they may sound or no matter how persuasive the guy in the blue vest can be. Warranties offered in addition to the manufacturer's warranty are a waste of money. They sell them hard! But that's because such a warranty is pure profit for the store that fools you into buying one.

Where to Buy

Obviously, you want to buy your computer at the location that will give you the best deal plus the service and support you need. Beyond that, I can't be specific (because no one has bought me off — yet). I can, however, highly recommend local dealers over buying from huge discount stores, office supply stores, chain stores, or even the Internet.

Local computer dealers have a reputation that needs to be only as big as the community they serve. Although their prices may not be the lowest, the people you buy from and who offer you service and support are all local. They're people you meet face to face, and are maybe even your neighbors. As such, I believe that you'll find local dealers to be your best choice for buying any computer.

✔ Laptops are more of a commodity than desktop computer systems are. Unlike with the desktop system, you can just plug in a laptop, and it's ready to go; rarely is there anything to configure or set up.

✔ I highly recommend sticking with name-brand laptops made by big companies whose names you recognize. The reason is that laptop technology is not as modular as desktop PC technology. Therefore you need a reliable, well-known name to ensure that you're getting the quality you're paying for. Also it's easier to find service and support for national name brands than for lesser-known equipment.

✔ Beyond the local stores, buy your laptop from any place where you feel comfortable doing business. Don't forget your service and support options!

✔ Buying a laptop on the Internet is safe; just keep in mind where the support comes from!

✔ When you're considering nonlocal dealers, such as Internet or catalog dealers, ensure that they have real street addresses so that you can verify their existence. Companies that list only 800 numbers may be fly-by-night operations, and you may never see your laptop — or your money — again.

✔ Don't ever put money down on a laptop. Laptops come fully assembled from the factory, and there's no need to put money down to "hold" one.

✔ If possible, pay for your laptop by using a credit card. The law offers far more protection to credit card users than to people who pay by check or (don't even think about it) cash.

✔ When you're buying from the Internet or some other nonlocal dealer, verify that it doesn't charge your credit card until the order ships. This is standard practice, but some dealers apparently haven't gotten the word yet.

The Final Step: Buying Your Laptop

When you're ready to buy your laptop, buy it!

Don't sit and wait for a better deal or a lower price. That's because there will *always* be a better deal and a lower price. Hardware gets better and better. The price will always come down. Therefore, when you're ready to buy, take the plunge and buy! Waiting gets you nowhere.

Part II

Discover Your Laptop

All right fellows — basketball today! Get changed and make sure everyone's wearing a mouse pad!

In this part . . .

Wouldn't it be wonderful if your new laptop just
sprang out of the box complete with two or three
cheerful youths in bright, colorful clothing all eager to
help you set everything up and get going? Maybe it works
that way in some optimistic television commercial, but
not in real life.

This part of the book answers the question "You have
your laptop — now what do you do?" The chapters here
provide a general introduction to your laptop and its features, plus important stuff you need to note. Because laptops don't come with manuals or getting-started booklets
any more, consider the chapters in this part as your
handy laptop-survival guide.

Chapter 3

Out of the Box and into Your Lap

Don't be fooled by the box! For some reason, you pay a lot of money to get a thin, wispy laptop — "It practically floats," the salesman promised — and the sucker shows up in a box the size of a dog house. Panic ye not, gentle reader! Most of that box is protective swaddling designed to shield your laptop from the brutality of our modern-day package delivery system. But there's more in that laptop box than your new portable computer and a multitude of foam peanuts.

Opening your laptop's box is the very first step you take on your long portable-computing journey. The second step, however, remains a mystery. Long gone are the days when any computer came with a fat manual, a getting-started booklet, or even a fold-out roadmap showing how to hook things up. Oh, those things might be in the box, and other helpful goodies may be nestled betwixt the foam and the packing tape. How do you know what's what? Why, may I present this handy chapter, specifically designed to help your laptop make it out of the box and into your lap?

Basic Box Unpacking 101

Watching my late grandmother open her presents was an exercise in patience. She carefully plowed the seams on the wrapping, deftly slicing through the Scotch tape with her finger. The festive paper was removed intact, with far more care than it was applied. Having lived through the experience of the Great Depression, Grandma would save the paper wrapping, folding it up and setting it aside for use again later. It drove us grandkids nuts!

Later generations understood that there's no point in being polite or patient when opening anything. Removing wrapping has such a speed these days that it makes me wonder whether future generations will merely whip out a chainsaw and open up their gifts in that quick, rude manner. But I digress.

There's no point in my telling you how to open up the box your laptop comes in. Odds are pretty good that you've already done that. Despite that guess, here are some tips I have regarding proper laptop box-opening etiquette:

- ✔ If you see instructions on how to unpack the box, heed them! I refer specifically to labels like "Open other side" or "Remove first."
- ✔ Be sure to open and free the packing slip (if any) attached to the outside of the box. The slip contains the shipping invoice, which you should look over to confirm that what was shipped is exactly what you ordered. (Often, the invoice is inside the box instead.)
- ✔ Don't destroy the box to open it, and don't throw anything away! If the laptop is a dud, you want to return everything in the original box.
- ✔ Be sure to look for boxes within boxes. Also be on the lookout for things stuck in the sides or ends of the foam packing material.
- ✔ Don't fill out any warranty or registration cards until you're certain that the laptop works.

- ✔ Always open computer equipment boxes with your hands. Never use a box cutter because you could slice into something important.
- ✔ Beware of those big, ugly staples often used to close cardboard boxes. They can go a-flyin' when you rip things open, poking out eyeballs or just lying in wait on the floor for a bare foot to stomp on by.

Making piles for the various things in the box

Laptops, like all computers, come with lots of bits and pieces. Some of that stuff isn't junk, and you want to keep it for as long as you own the laptop. Other stuff is junk, and you can toss it. The problem you face now is that it's difficult to determine what's worth keeping and what to throw away. My advice is to keep everything for now. I suggest creating piles for the stuff that comes with the laptop.

Here's a handy way to approach this unpacking and pre-setup stage of your laptop's introduction to your lap:

1. **Unpack the laptop.**

   Remove the laptop from any plastic bag or shrink-wrap. Don't worry about opening the laptop's lid yet (though the temptation may be great). Just set the thing on a table by itself.

2. **Find all the various hardware pieces that came with the laptop.**

   Look for the power adapter, power cord, battery, extra batteries, phone cord, adapters, cables, connectors, weird, tiny gizmos that you'll probably lose eventually, and other mystery pieces of equipment.

3. **Make a pile for any discs that came with the laptop.**

   These include all CDs and DVDs. Those discs may contain programs that are already installed or ready for installation. Some discs might contain *device drivers* or special software required to run your laptop's hardware. Plus, you may see an operating system disc or system recovery disc. These are all important things!

4. **Make a pile for all the paperwork.**

   There are four categories of paperwork: manuals, warranties, special offers, and weird pieces of paper, the importance of which cannot be determined.

5. **Place all the packing material back into the box.**

   This material includes plastic bags, twist-ties from the cables, and those silica pouches they tell you not to eat (probably because the stuff inside tastes like candy).

Later, after your laptop is all set up and you're starting to get familiar with it, you can do further organization. As you work, you need to keep various items with the laptop at all times — for example, the power cord, extra batteries, and other things, depending on how you use the laptop. You need a place, such as a laptop case, for those items.

Other stuff that came with your laptop you might want to keep for a while, such as the discs and any manuals. Those things don't need to be with the laptop all the time, so setting them in a drawer or shelf is okay.

Only after using the laptop for a while should you consider throwing some stuff away, such as the special-offer cards you don't use. Often times, you can just toss those things in the laptop box. See the next section to find out what to do with the box.

- ✔ If the laptop came with a how-to manual, consider yourself lucky. Most laptops don't come with any how-to material whatsoever.

- ✔ Sometimes, the only manuals that come with the laptop are directories listing the locations where you can get it fixed.

- ✔ Software discs are included even though the software may already be installed on the laptop. Don't toss away the discs! They were given to you so that you can reinstall the software if you need to.

- ✔ See Chapter 15 for information on finding the best laptop case. Even though your laptop may have come with a genuine imitation-leatherette case, you want to see what else is out there.

- ✔ I have a shelf in my office where I keep containers for each computer I own. The container holds all the stuff included with the computer that I want to keep: the manuals, spare parts, and other documentation. I suggest that you have a similar shelf or location for a container or special box for your laptop's extra stuff.

"How long should I keep the box?"

I recommend keeping the box and the packing material for as long as you own the laptop. That way, if you need to ship the laptop to a repair center or return it to the dealer, you have the original box.

When the laptop dies, you can then bury it in its original box and throw them both out at the same time.

- ✔ Many dealers and repair centers don't accept a laptop unless it's packed in the original box.

- ✔ If you don't have the original box, you can order another one — but why pay for that when you can just save the original?

- ✔ Note that many communities have disposal standards for electronic equipment, such as laptops. Check with your municipal refuse-disposal people before blithely throwing a laptop in the garbage.

- ✔ No, you don't need to pack the laptop in a box when you take it on the road; slipping the laptop into a briefcase or any quality carrying case is fine for that. You need the boxes only if you plan on mailing or shipping the laptop.

When to send in the warranty

Wait a week to ensure that the laptop works and that you have everything you ordered. When you're satisfied, fill out and send in the warranty card.

Often times, when you order a computer directly from the manufacturer, you don't need to fill in and return a warranty card.

In some cases, filling out and returning the warranty card sets the start date for the warranty period. Otherwise, the warranty may start on the day the laptop was manufactured, which could have been three months ago! Read the card to be sure.

Setting Up Your Laptop

Features vary from laptop to laptop: Not every laptop has the same keyboard layout; the CD-ROM or DVD drive may eject forward or to the left or right, or it might not even exist; connectors and holes may be on the sides or back or both. The power button? Well, it could be *anywhere!*

Beyond the differences, if you squint your eyes tightly enough, all laptop computers look basically the same. The setup for each one is similar, so this section addresses issues that are the same for all laptop owners.

When you find any specific instructions regarding setup inside the laptop box or — should you be so lucky — if you find a manual, heed its instructions first. Then look back here for a gentle review.

Do you need to charge the battery?

When you're setting up your laptop, the holiest piece of hardware is the battery. Om! It either came preinstalled (and perhaps even nonremovable) inside the laptop or must be installed separately.

Install or set up the battery per any directions that came with the laptop. Yes, this is one of those rare instances when the instructions are actually included with the laptop. The instructions may tell you how to install the battery or which doodah to remove to make the battery work or other important battery preparations.

- ✔ You can use your laptop without the battery, but before you do that, I recommend properly setting up the battery to ensure that it works.

- ✔ Some batteries come DOA and must be charged before use. This is normally done by installing the battery inside the laptop and then plugging the laptop's power brick into both the wall and the laptop. Battery charging takes place automatically.

- ✔ It usually takes a few hours to charge a laptop's battery. The length of time depends on the type of battery and power management hardware and on whether you're using the laptop at the time.

- ✔ If the battery is already charged, install it — and you're ready to go! Literally!

- ✔ The manufacturer may claim that the battery is fully charged, but don't be surprised when it isn't. No big deal: Just install the battery and plug in the laptop. It will charge.

- ✔ I usually let my laptop's batteries charge overnight.

- ✔ Be sure to put any extra or spare batteries in storage when they're not in use. Chapter 8 discusses battery storage.

- ✔ Also refer to Chapter 8 for more information on managing your laptop's battery and power management in general.

"Is some assembly required?"

Beyond that battery, you may be required to add some features to your laptop. Pray that such a thing doesn't happen to you! I've known some laptops to arrive without memory, disk drives, and other options installed. When that's the case, it's up to you to properly install those items. I wish you the best of luck!

- ✔ Most laptops come fully assembled. In fact, installing extra features isn't an option for many laptops.

- ✔ Fortunately, installing options such as memory or a network adapter are one-time affairs. Follow the directions closely. Read them over first before attempting the installation. In most cases, the operation proceeds smoothly. It also helps that most things are inserted in only one direction so that you cannot goof things up.

- ✔ Beware of electrostatic discharge (ESD). That tiny little spark you generate on a dry day can permanently damage your laptop. When you're installing options, always keep one hand touching the laptop's metal chassis to help lessen the potential of the dreaded ESD.

✔ If your laptop came with a docking station or port replicator, don't worry about setting it up or using it just yet. The laptop works fine without that optional feature, so I recommend using the laptop for a while before you mount the docking station or port replicator.

Finding a place for the laptop

Laptops can go anywhere or be put anywhere. With a fully charged battery, your laptop has a home wherever you go! Beyond that, you can place your laptop anywhere you like: on the kitchen table, the coffee table, a real desk, or a computer desk or in bed with you.

I recommend keeping the laptop on a flat, steady surface. Try to keep it away from, or out of spilling range of, any drinks or food you might be consuming.

When I use my laptop around the house, I like to keep it plugged in. For example, when I'm browsing the Internet while I'm watching a football game on TV, I put the laptop on the coffee table and plug it in just behind the couch. I keep the beer and Doritos well away from the laptop.

If your laptop doesn't have a permanent home, create a consistent storage place for it. I've seen laptops slid into bookcases between the Steinbeck and Grafton novels. You can keep the laptop in a drawer or cupboard, or in the box with the rest of the laptop stuff. Keeping it in the same place means that you can always find it when you need it.

Avoid putting the laptop in a spot where it can overheat. Today's laptops get hot all by themselves. Anything you can do to help keep the laptop cool is good.

When the laptop has a docking station or port replicator, try to keep that part in the same place all the time. Set up a desk and put the docking station or port replicator in one spot. You might also keep various peripherals — such as a printer, big keyboard, mouse, full-size monitor, scanner, and other toys — ready to go and plugged in. Call this location your *Laptop Shrine*.

One great way to set up a laptop is to place it on an elevated platform above the desktop. Then use an external keyboard to type on, and rest the keyboard on the desktop itself. That way, the laptop's screen is at eye level, which naturally makes you sit with better posture and gives you less neck strain than keeping the laptop down on the desktop itself.

✔ Although you can use the laptop anywhere, be aware of ergonomics! For example, when you're using the laptop on a coffee table, if you start to feel a pain in your back from hunching over, stop! Find a better, more comfortable place to work.

✔ See Chapter 7 for more information on attaching devices to your laptop.

The last thing to do: Plug it in!

When you choose your laptop's final resting place — even if it's final only until you find a new resting place — plug it in, as illustrated in Figure 3-1.

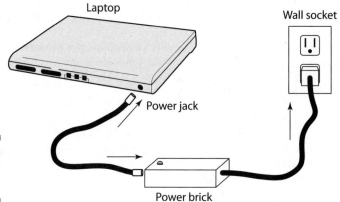

Figure 3-1:
Plugging in
your laptop.

Attach the power cord to the laptop's back or side. On a newer laptop, the power cord connector may be color-coded yellow; the yellow hole is where the power cord plugs in. Otherwise, the power connector should be unique; it plugs in to no other hole on the laptop.

Attach the power cord to the power brick, if necessary. Plug the power brick into the wall. Note that the power brick may also contain the plug that connects directly to the wall.

That's it. The laptop is now ready for use.

"Should I plug the laptop into a UPS?"

I advise my desktop computer readers in *PCs For Dummies* (Wiley Publishing, Inc.) to consider investing in a UPS, or Uninterruptible Power Supply, specifically one with both surge and spike protection. This device serves to protect the computer from nasty things that can come through the power lines as well as to provide emergency power if the electricity goes bye-bye.

A UPS for a laptop is unnecessary. The main reason is that your laptop already has a battery for backup power. If you're running your laptop from an electrical outlet and the electricity goes off (or some doofus unplugs it), the laptop quickly and happily switches its power source over to the internal battery. Nothing is lost!

- ✔ Note that although you don't need a UPS for a laptop, I still highly recommend plugging your portable baby into a power strip with surge protection and line filtering. They help keep the power your laptop uses clean and steady.

- ✔ It's a wise idea to use a UPS for any external storage devices connected to the laptop. For example, plug an external disk drive into a UPS. You also do well to plug your DSL or cable modem into a UPS as well as the router. There's no need to plug a scanner or printer into a UPS.

- ✔ Generally speaking, if there's a lightning storm nearby, don't plug your laptop into the wall unless you're using a spike protection filter. If not, just run the laptop from its battery until the storm passes.

What to Do Next

My guess is that after setting up your laptop, you'll want to turn it on and see how it works. That's covered in Chapter 4, which also contains details on using the Windows operating system on a laptop. That chapter also describes the many different ways to turn your laptop computer off — which can be confusing if you've never used a battery-powered computer.

On the subject of batteries, I also recommend that you read Chapter 8 to bone up on how to treat your laptop's battery in a fair and just manner.

And, before taking your laptop on the road, read Chapter 15, which covers a few nifty things you might want to consider before you venture out into the cold, cruel world with your new computer companion.

Chapter 4

An Entire Chapter About Turning a Laptop On and Off

Are you old enough to remember when electronic gizmos came with *real* on-off switches? If so, you're probably *really* old. Back in the days when PCs were called *microcomputers*, the beast truly did sport an on-off switch, as did your TV, dishwasher, and maybe even your car. Today, things are on all the time, though the manufacturer has begrudgingly succumbed to human nature and supplied each gizmo with a *power button*.

Unlike a plain, familiar on-off switch, the power button no longer turns the computer on and off. Well, it can be trusted to turn the thing on, but what about turning it off? That's an entirely different matter, one that requires an entire chapter to explain.

Turning On a Laptop

Despite having only 3 seconds of memory, a goldfish can be trained to turn on a laptop computer: Just push the power button. The only thing that's preventing legions of goldfish from escaping the confines of their aquariums and powering up laptops across the globe is that it takes considerably longer than 3 seconds to even *find* the power button on most laptops. May the hunt begin!

It's a *power button,* not an on-off switch.

Before you turn on the power!

Ensure that your laptop is set up in the proper location and position for working. Yes, this even includes putting it on your lap — if you dare! More importantly, if there's a power source nearby, plug in the laptop! Always use that juice whenever you can. Save the battery for later.

- ✔ Don't be a high-tech dweeb and turn your laptop on *before* you enter the cybercafé. Seeing someone use a laptop in a coffee house is cool. It's very *in*. Seeing someone standing in line to order coffee while holding an open laptop and talking on a cell phone is wretchedly pathetic.

- ✔ If the laptop has a docking station or port replicator, attach it per the instructions.

- ✔ Refer to Chapter 3 for more information on laptop setup.

- ✔ See Part IV of this book for information on taking your laptop on the road.

Open the lid

Believe it or not, the laptop must be in an open position for you to use it. It's difficult to see the screen and nearly impossible to use the keyboard with the lid closed. Many have tried. They all have failed and, after giving up in frustration, returned the laptop to the store and written the whole thing off as a high-tech folly.

Here's the catch: The lid has a catch, or possibly two! The catch is either a button that you push in or a little slider that you push sideways to release the lid. After you release the catch (or catches), the laptop's lid pops up slightly. You can then raise it up to an angle best suited for viewing; use Figure 4-1 as your guide.

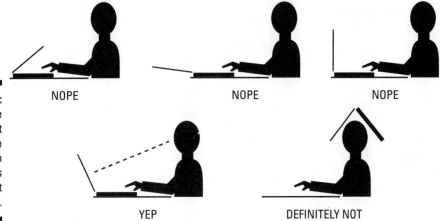

Figure 4-1:
Adjust the lid so that you view the screen at an angle that's just right for you.

✔ If your laptop has one catch that you must release to open the lid, the catch is probably in the middle. If your laptop has two catch release buttons, they're on the front corners of the laptop's lid. The catches are either on the front or sides. Figure 4-2 offers some hints.

✔ The front side of the laptop is the side without all the connectors (although, in the future, laptops may have connectors on the front).

✔ It's possible to configure the laptop to be on without opening the lid — for example, when you're using a docking station or an external monitor. See Chapter 7 for the details.

✔ Some laptops allow you to play a music CD when the lid is closed, even sporting special buttons to control the CD player.

✔ Be aware that your laptop's cooling system is designed on the assumption that the lid will be open. Many laptop users who keep their systems on while closed have cooked their displays. Beware!

"Where is the power button?"

Laptop designers have grown adept at hiding or masking the power button. The most recent trend is to put the power button under the laptop's lid; you must open up the laptop to find and press the power button, turning the laptop on.

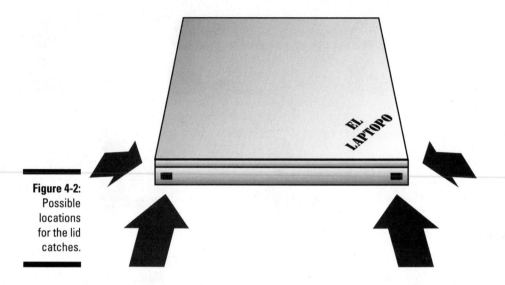

Figure 4-2:
Possible
locations
for the lid
catches.

✔ Older laptops may have the power button anywhere, usually along one of the laptop's sides: front, left, right, or back.

✔ The power button may be a spring-slide switch that you must push in one direction and then release.

✔ Some power buttons are tiny push buttons, or what I call *pray-and-press* buttons. There's no click or bump to the button's feel; you just press it in with your finger and pray that the laptop obeys you.

✔ You can put a red sticker dot by or near the power button's location, in case it's easy to overlook. Even so, I find that a few times after opening the case and turning the system on, I remember where the button is. Of course, this doesn't help you use anyone else's laptop, because the power button is never in the same location twice.

"What is the moon button for?"

The moon icon labels a *sleep* button. This might be in addition to the power button, although on most modern laptops the sleep button and power button are one and the same.

The moon icon is still used on many laptops to indicate when the computer is in sleep, or standby, operation. So, you may find that symbol on your laptop row-of-symbols and lights thing, but not associated with any specific button.

- ✔ Sleep, or suspend, mode is covered later in this chapter, in the section "The bliss of sleep mode."

- ✔ See Chapter 5 for more information about the symbols you find on your laptop.

Random power-button symbols

Blessed is the laptop owner whose laptop's power button has a symbol on it. And wise is he who recognizes the symbol as that of the power button. Let it be so. Amen.

Figure 4-3 displays a sordid sampling of laptop computer power-button symbols.

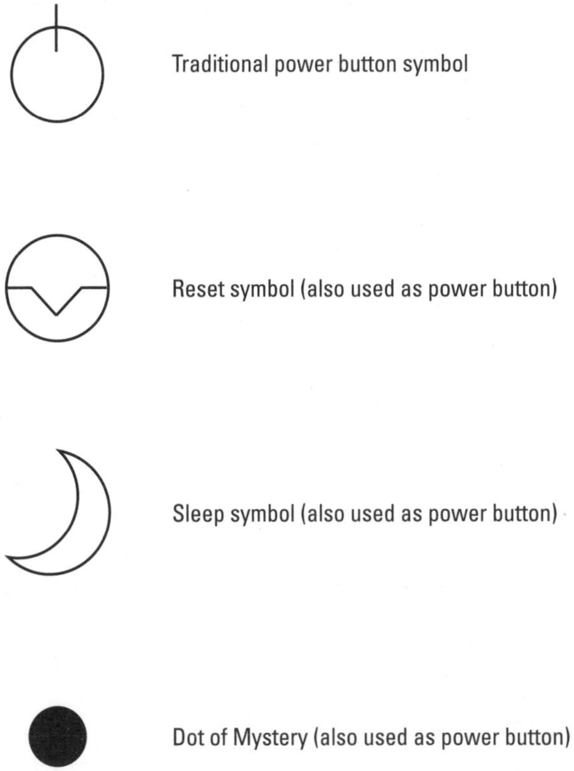

Traditional power button symbol

Reset symbol (also used as power button)

Sleep symbol (also used as power button)

Figure 4-3:
Power
button
symbols
common
and
obscure.

Dot of Mystery (also used as power button)

Nerdy terms for starting a computer

Despite years of effort to come up with better words, the computer industry continues to use ancient and primitive jargon to say "starting a computer." Among the lingo, you will find

Boot: The oldest and most mysterious computer term; it basically means to turn the thing on, or to "pull it up by its bootstraps." In fact, *bootstrap* is an even older version of this term.

Cold boot: To turn the computer on when it has been off for a while. See *warm boot*.

Cycle power: To turn the computer off, wait a few seconds, and then turn it on again. This is often required when you're trying to fix something.

Das Boot: Not a computer term at all, but rather the title of a German film about a U-boat in World War II.

Power up / power on: More human terms for turning the computer on.

Restart / reboot / reset: To shut down a computer and then start it up again without turning off the power.

Start / turn on / switch on: Again, more human terms for turning the computer on.

Warm boot: Another term for a restart, reboot, or reset.

Punch the power button

To turn on your laptop, press the power button. Power on!

- ✔ Refer to the previous sections if you need help finding the button.
- ✔ If nothing happens, the battery is most likely dead: Plug the laptop into a wall socket by using its AC adapter cord (or module or power-brick thing).
- ✔ Be sure to check all the power cables! The power brick may wiggle loose from the wall socket cable.
- ✔ When everything is plugged in and nothing happens, you have a problem. Contact your dealer or laptop manufacturer for assistance.

A Brief Foray into Windows

When your laptop starts up, you see some initial messages, and perhaps a logo or graphic, and then the computer's operating system — its main program — comes to life. For PC laptops, this program is Windows.

The version of Windows used on laptops is identical to the one used on desktop computers. Some extra options are included for laptops, specifically for power management and battery monitoring. Plus, some other utilities and fun junk may have been installed by the laptop manufacturer. Otherwise, it's the same Windows you know and despise.

✔ This book covers both Windows Vista and Windows XP. The differences between the two are noted in the text.

✔ Chapter 6 covers a few of the places in Windows that laptop computer owners should be familiar with.

✔ Some messages may appear before Windows starts, especially when the laptop was improperly shut down or the laptop's battery expired the last time you used it. These messages are all normal, and the laptop recovers from such things rather nicely.

✔ For more information on Windows, visit a bookstore near you and purchase a good Windows book. (The last time I looked, there were no books specific to Windows on laptops.)

TECHNICAL STUFF

The laptop's Setup program

All modern PCs, laptops included, have a special Startup or Setup program. This program is not a part of your computer's operating system (Windows). Instead, it's built in to the computer's circuitry, or _chipset,_ and it might also be referred to as the BIOS Setup program.

What the setup program does is configure your laptop's hardware. It keeps track of such things as how much memory (RAM) is installed, the type of hard drive, whether or not you have a CD-ROM or DVD drive, plus other hardware options. The Setup program also keeps track of the time with the computer's internal clock as well as other random things.

Be sure that you know how to get into your laptop's Setup program. The method used to access it differs from computer to computer. Commonly, to get into the Setup program, you press a specific key or key combination on the keyboard when the computer first starts (and before Windows starts). On most laptops, the special key is Del or F1. If your laptop uses a different key, be sure to make a note of it on this book's Cheat Sheet.

One important item to know about in the Setup program is the security system, which usually includes a password. I don't recommend setting that password at this time (when you're just getting used to your laptop). Instead, see Chapter 16, which covers laptop security, for more information.

Windows for the first time

When you first turn on a brand-new laptop, Windows goes through some gyrations and prompts you to set up Windows on your computer. You're asked certain questions, such as which time zone you live in and what's your name and your company name. This is designed to finish the installation of Windows, which was begun back at the factory, before your laptop shipped.

Heed the instructions on the screen! It's painless, and it's over with quickly.

When you're asked to create user accounts, just create one for yourself. Don't bother creating one just yet for each member of the whole fam-damily as well as your pets. You can do that later, and then only when other people *really* need to use the computer.

 ✔ The main Windows account is known as the *administrator*. That account is the one used to modify the computer, add new software, and do other administrative chores. Even when you don't intend it, when you're the only person using the computer, *you* are the administrator.

 ✔ Do not forget the administrator's password! Refer to the sidebar "Passwords" for more information.

 ✔ You don't have to use your own name for your account in Windows. For example, I type in the name I've given the computer rather than type my own name. A friend of mine is fond of typing in "Al Gore" as his name. It really doesn't make any difference.

 ✔ Entering an organization name is optional, though it's fun to specify fictitious organizations or something juvenile, like Central Intelligence Agency.

Special-deal software

After setting up Windows for the first time, you may encounter some dealer- or manufacturer-specific program or registration routine. For example, my laptop came with some help thingy from the manufacturer, something I could optionally sign up for. I opted not to and just canceled out of the program.

You can always save software registration for later, but don't forget about it! Generally, you find the registration program's icon on either the desktop or the Start menu.

Passwords

Windows lets you slap a password on your account and then requires you to type that password before you can use Windows. Though this is optional, and seems kind of silly when you're the only one around to use the computer, I highly recommend it. Even if you pick a silly, easy password, do it! The future of computers is all about security. I predict that in a few years, passwords will no longer be optional, so get used to the password thing now!

Of course, the natural problem with passwords is that people forget them. So, the idea is to do two things: First, choose a password that you can easily remember, and, second, write that password down in an obvious location but in a secure manner.

For example, a good password contains a combination of numbers and letters. For example, if you once lived at 4870 Elsa Road, `elsa4870` would be a suitable password. Another technique is to use two obnoxiously unrelated words and connect them with a number, such as `stinky7teeth` or `pirate3diaper`.

When you have a good password, write it down in a handy, obvious place. Just write it in a manner that doesn't say "My password is." For example, write the password on a recipe card or in your address book or portfolio. Stick it in a list of otherwise innocent information, a place where you can recognize it but a snoop would easily miss it.

See Chapter 16 for more information on passwords and Windows security issues.

No, you don't have to sign up for AOL or MSN or NetZero or whatever other advertisements are included with the laptop. Feel free to skip over those programs or just delete the icons if you couldn't care less.

Windows starts every time you start your laptop

After the initial setup, and every time you start your laptop after that, you're greeted with the graphical fun and folly of the Windows operating system. It may start right up, or you may have to log in first.

If you set up your account with a password, you're prompted to enter the password before you enter Windows.

On laptops with multiple accounts, you have to choose your account name and then enter the password before you can behold the glory that is Windows.

✔ *Log on* is the term used to identify yourself to the warden, er, to Windows. That way, multiple people can use the same computer and keep their stuff separate. It also helps the computer keep track of personal things, such as passwords, e-mail, and other junk.

✔ The term *log on* means to identify yourself. A *logon* is the name of your account or the word you use to log on.

✔ The terms *log in* and *login* can be used instead of *log on* and *logon.* They did that just to keep you confused.

✔ By the way, it's *log,* as in *to write down.* It has nothing to do with timber.

Behold the desktop

Eventually the Windows desktop appears on your laptop's screen, similar to what you see in Figure 4-4, which shows the Windows XP desktop. The Windows Vista desktop looks different, but the important things noted in Figure 4-4 are found in the same locations. Here's what you need to find:

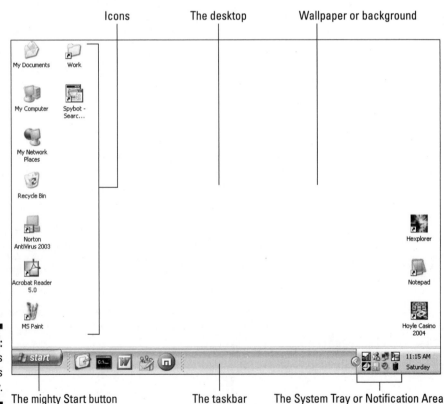

Figure 4-4:
Windows
XP in all its
glory.

- ✔ **The desktop:** This is your home plate, the starting point for all your adventures in Windows.

- ✔ **Desktop background:** The desktop is the image you see on the desktop, or it may just be a solid color. The desktop background, also known as *wallpaper,* is optional and can be changed in the Control Panel. (More on that in Chapter 6.)

- ✔ **Icons:** These tiny pictures represent files, folders, or programs inside Windows.

 - ✔ **The mighty Start button:** This button pops up a menu that contains options for controlling the computer or for starting programs. In Windows Vista, the Start button doesn't have the word *Start* on it.

- ✔ **The taskbar:** This doohickey displays a host of buttons that are used to switch between windows and programs opened on the desktop.

- ✔ **The system tray, or notification area:** This annoying little thing contains teensy icons that can help you do things on the computer, alert you to certain happenings, and show the time and day.

Take a moment to find each of those items on your laptop screen right now. Don't touch the display to point them out! Just find them and point (and maybe even say "Oh, there it is!").

Various Options for Turning Off (or Not) the Laptop

Turning on a computer is easy. After you find the switch, it's click (or press), and the thing fires up and is ever so happy to please you. But turning the computer off? That ain't so easy. That's because you have many options for turning a laptop off, leaving it on, putting it to sleep, or even sending it off to the electronic cave for some well-earned hibernation.

You also have the option of hurling the laptop, discus-like, out the window and feeling the satisfaction of seeing it land and splinter into a zillion pieces. But that technique isn't really necessary to teach.

This section unravels the mysterious answer to the question "How do I turn my laptop computer off?"

Properly shutting down your laptop

Here are the not-so-obvious steps you need to take to properly shut down Windows and turn off your laptop when you're done for the day:

1. **Save your work and close all your programs.**

   The generic Save command is Ctrl+S. The command to close most windows is Ctrl+W, although often the weirdly obscure Alt+F4 is needed.

2. **Click the Start button.**

   Up pops the Start menu thing.

   At this point, things are different between Windows Vista and Windows XP.

3a. **In Windows Vista, click the right-pointing triangle next to the padlock icon.**

   A pop-up menu appears with various shutdown options, as shown in Figure 4-5. Skip to Step 4a.

Figure 4-5: Windows Vista shutdown options.

3b. **In Windows XP, click the Turn Off Computer button.**

   A colorful Turn Off Computer box-thing appears, as shown in Figure 4-6. Skip down to Step 4b.

Figure 4-6: Options for turning off a computer in Windows XP.

4a. Choose the Shut Down menu item.

4b. Click the Turn Off button.

The laptop turns itself off.

Yes, that's correct: The laptop turns itself off. When the screen goes dark and the power lamp is dimmed, you can shut the laptop's lid and put away the laptop.

Note that Windows XP offers you a cancel button (refer to Figure 4-6) so that you can change your mind before Step 4. In Windows Vista, choosing the Shut Down menu item immediately shuts down the computer — unless:

When you still have unsaved files, first, you didn't follow all the instructions, and, second, you have an opportunity to save them before the laptop shuts down.

But — honestly! — merely shutting down a laptop is so trite. There are far more interesting ways to end your laptop session, as covered in the sections that follow.

"I need to restart Windows"

Occasionally, you're directed to reset the laptop, which is often referred to as "restarting Windows." To do so, heed these steps:

1. **Save your work and close all your programs.**

2. **Click the Start button.**

3a. **In Windows Vista, click the triangle next to the Padlock icon and choose Restart from the pop-up menu.**

3b. **In Windows XP, click the Turn Off Computer button, and then click the Restart button in the Turn Off Computer window.**

The laptop seems to be turning itself off, but just before it does, it starts right back up again. Amazing.

Sometimes, restarting Windows is automatic, such as when installing some software, some hardware helpers called *device drivers*, and when performing Windows Updates. You're generally given a choice: "Would you like to restart Windows now?" If so, click the Yes button, and things happen automatically. When the process stalls, such as when you have an open and (gasp!) unsaved document, you have to interrupt things, take care of business, and then manually restart Windows according to the preceding steps.

The bliss of sleep mode

All laptops have a special low-power mode. In this mode, the computer is still on but power to certain areas is shut off. That way, you can keep the laptop ready for an extended period without wasting a lot of battery juice. This low-power mode is officially called Stand By mode, but many people refer to it as sleep mode.

Your laptop can slumber in sleep mode for quite some time, much longer than it would otherwise stay alive when it's turned on. The amount of time the laptop stays in Sleep mode depends on various power settings in Windows. You can direct Windows to sleep for maybe 30 minutes and then have the laptop automatically turn itself off or switch into Hibernation mode (covered later in this chapter).

The method for putting your laptop to sleep varies, depending on whether your laptop has a sleep button and which version of Windows you're using. The following sections describe the details.

- ✔ There's no need to be quiet while your laptop is sleeping.

- ✔ The moon lamp might be on when the laptop is in Stand By mode. See Chapter 5 for information on this and other lights on your laptop.

- ✔ I recommend that you save your work before your laptop enters Stand By mode.

- ✔ If you're going to quit all your programs before putting your laptop into Stand By mode, just shut down the laptop instead. Honestly, the laptop mysteriously benefits from being turned off every once in a while.

- ✔ See Chapter 8 for information on checking how much charge is left in your laptop's battery.

- ✔ The laptop may beep just before it goes to sleep. That's okay.

- ✔ Sometimes, Stand By mode gets "lost." When that happens, it's typically a software issue. Either you need to turn off the laptop and then turn it back on again, or your laptop's power-management software needs updating. Check your laptop manufacturer's Web site for the latter.

Putting your laptop to sleep by using the sleep button

When your laptop is blessed with a sleep button, pressing it puts the laptop to sleep instantly. But, hang on! The sleep button's function can be changed, so pressing that button may not always put the laptop to sleep. Before you use this method, see the section "Changing the Whole On-Off Scheme of Things," later in this chapter.

It just goes to sleep by itself!

Windows configures itself so that the laptop automatically goes into Stand By mode when you're using battery power. An activity timer keeps track of what the laptop is doing. When there hasn't been any keyboard or mouse activity for a set amount of time, the laptop is automatically put to sleep. (The time interval can be adjusted.) The idea here is to save power; when the computer thinks that you're bored or off for a walk (or dead), it slips off to sleep to conserve power.

The Power Options icon in the Control Panel sets the inactivity timer value. See Chapter 8 for the details.

Putting your laptop to sleep (Stand By) in Windows Vista

To "sleep" your laptop when Windows Vista is the operating system, heed these steps:

1. **Click the Start button.**
2. **Click the triangle next to the Padlock icon.**
3. **Choose Sleep from the pop-up menu.**

   Refer to Figure 4-5.

Putting your laptop to sleep (Stand By) in Windows XP

To put your laptop to sleep in Windows XP, follow these steps:

1. **Click the Start button.**
2. **Click the Turn Off Computer button.**

3. **Click the Stand By button.**

Waking up from sleep (Stand By) mode

To revive a snoozing laptop, simply press a key on the keyboard or tap on the mouse pad. That wakes the sucker up, bringing it back to active duty.

After waking up the laptop, you may have to log in to Windows again. That's okay — in fact, it's what you want; it's very insecure not to have the Windows logon appear when the laptop wakes up from Sleep mode. (See Chapter 16 for more information on wake-up passwords.)

- ✔ If your laptop doesn't wake up after you press a key, press the power button to wake it up again.

- ✔ If you closed the lid to put the laptop into Stand By mode, opening the lid wakes it up. See the later section "Changing the Whole On-Off Scheme of Things."

- ✔ The key you press to wake up the laptop isn't passed along to whatever program is running. So, if the screen says "Destroy all your data files? Y/N" and you press the Y key to wake up the laptop, nothing dastardly happens. Even so:

- ✔ I generally push the Ctrl key on the keyboard to wake up my sleeping laptop.

- ✔ Sometimes, you have to press the power or sleep button to wake up a snoozing laptop.

- ✔ One reason a laptop may not wake up is that the battery is probably dead. Check the laptop's power-on lights. If they're off, the battery is dead.

- ✔ If the laptop still doesn't wake up, you may have a problem with the system's power management software. Try pressing (and holding) the power button until the unit turns either off or on again. Then try starting up the laptop as you normally would. Ask your dealer or laptop manufacturer for updated power management software.

Hibernation is better than sleep

Hibernation is a useful power management feature that's often sadly ignored despite its great benefits. When you hibernate a laptop, you're essentially turning it off. So, unlike Stand By (sleep) mode, a hibernated laptop isn't using any battery power at all — that laptop is off!

The secret behind hibernation is that before you turn off the laptop, everything you're doing with the computer is saved. (The contents of memory are saved to the hard disk.) When the computer is turned on again, it recovers from hibernating by reloading all the saved information and restoring your laptop to exactly the same condition it was in before it was hibernated.

Briefly, hibernation works like this:

1. **You activate the hibernation feature.**

   Hibernation is activated differently depending on how it's set up. (This topic is covered later in this chapter.)

2. **The laptop hums as everything in memory is saved to disk.**

3. **The laptop turns itself off.**

    It's really and truly off: The battery isn't being used, and it's safe to store the laptop or put it away until you need to use it again.

To recover from Hibernation mode, turn the laptop on, although in some cases the laptop may recover from hibernation when you press a key or touch the mouse pad. I generally try that trick first, before I punch the power button.

Obviously, hibernation plays a key role in prolonging your laptop's battery power.

✔ I prefer to put my laptop into hibernation when I know that I won't be using it for longer than a half-hour or so.

✔ Unlike when you put your laptop in Stand By mode, you can leave your laptop in a hibernated state for as long as you wish. Even if the batteries eventually drain, the system returns to where you left it after the computer is plugged in and started again.

✔ Note that Hibernation mode requires hard drive space. When hard drive space runs low, it's possible that Hibernation mode won't work. Be aware of that.

Hibernating a laptop in Windows Vista

To hibernate your Windows Vista laptop, do this:

1. **Save your stuff.**

    I know: The documentation claims that your stuff is "saved" by the hibernation processor. Uh-huh. Better be on the safe side and save anyway, before you hibernate. Note that there's no reason to quit your programs or close open windows.

2. **Click the Start button.**

3. **Choose Hibernate from the pop-up menu (refer to Figure 4-5).**

    The laptop powers off into Hibernation mode, as described earlier in this chapter.

Turning on Hibernation mode in Windows XP

Hibernation mode must be activated before you can use it in Windows XP. Follow these steps:

1. **From the Start menu, choose Control Panel.**

2. **Open the Power Options icon in the Control Panel.**

   See Chapter 6 for more information if this Control Panel stuff has you perplexed.

3. **In the Power Options Properties dialog box, look for and click on the Hibernation tab.**

   If you don't see a Hibernation tab, there's your answer: The laptop isn't capable of hibernating. Oh, well. (You might want to also check the laptop's Setup program to see whether hibernation can be activated there. Refer to the sidebar "The laptop's Setup program," earlier in this chapter.)

4. **Select the Enable Hibernation option by clicking the check box to place a check mark in the box.**

5. **Review other options, if they're available.**

6. **Click OK to confirm the changes and close the Power Options Properties dialog box.**

   Optionally, close the Control Panel window as well.

Some laptops may require you to restart Windows for this change to take effect. If so, refer to the earlier section "I need to restart Windows.'"

Hibernating in Windows XP

Here's how to hibernate your laptop:

1. **Save your work.**

   Do this as a precaution; you should always save your stuff. Even so, there is no need to quit any applications now.

2. **Click the Start button.**

3. **Click the Turn Off Computer button.**

   The Turn Off Computer box-thing appears. (Refer to Figure 4-6.)

4. **Press the Shift key.**

   Notice that the caption beneath the Stand By button changes to read "Hibernate." Keep that Shift key down!

   If the caption doesn't change, your laptop lacks the Hibernation feature (or it hasn't been enabled).

5. **Click the Hibernate button.**

   The laptop hums for a few moments, and then it hibernates and turns itself off.

The Windows Vista power button

The Start menu in Windows Vista has a power button right next to the pop-up menu for the various turn-off-your-laptop options. When you click this button, it instantly tosses the laptop into Hibernation or Sleep mode, which can be handy.

So, which mode is it? That depends; the function on the Windows Vista power button can be changed. Refer to the section "Power button functions in Windows Vista," later in this chapter.

Shutting down when the laptop doesn't want to

Unlike with a desktop computer, you just can't yank that power cord from the wall on a laptop. The reason that it doesn't work is that with the AC power gone, the laptop immediately starts using its battery. This can be very disconcerting when the system is locked up and you really, badly, want to turn the sucker off.

If the computer just utterly seems to be ignoring you, press and hold the power button. Keep holding it down, usually for 5 to 10 seconds. Eventually, the laptop turns itself off.

See Part V of this book for laptop troubleshooting information.

Changing the Whole On-Off Scheme of Things

Your laptop doesn't have an on-off switch — it has a *power button*. Although that may seem confusing, it actually has one nice benefit: *You* control what happens when you press the power button. Ah, to be in charge . . . .

You can not only control the power button's function, but you can also dictate to Mr. Laptop what happens when the power is on and you close the laptop's lid. If that weren't enough, if your laptop sports a sleep button, well, you can control what happens when it's pressed as well.

The secret to your power isn't a magic ring or special incantation. Nope, the answer lies in opening the Power Options icon in the Control Panel. After the Power Options window or dialog box is open, read the sections that follow for specific information on modifying your laptop's behavior.

✔ See Chapter 6 for more information on the Control Panel.

✔ When the laptop is off, pressing the power button turns it back on again. There's no way to change that, nor would you really want to.

Power button functions in Windows Vista

Windows Vista placed all the power button and lid-closing functions in one handy spot. To get there from the Power Options window, click on the link Choose What Power Buttons Do, located on the left side of the window. You see a special System Settings window, as shown in Figure 4-7.

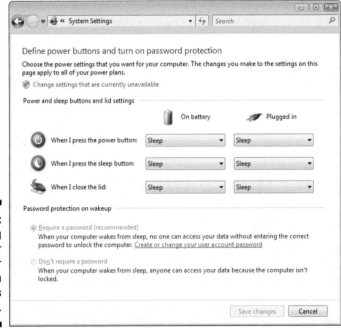

Figure 4-7: Controlling the power button (or buttons) in Windows Vista.

Each button has two options, depending on whether the laptop is running from battery power ("On battery") or is plugged in. There are four settings for each option:

Do nothing: Pressing the button or closing the lid doesn't change anything. If the laptop is on, it stays on.

Sleep: The laptop immediately enters Stand By mode, saving vital battery power.

Hibernate: The laptop hibernates, saving important information to disk and then turning itself off.

Shut down: The laptop turns itself off.

My recommended options are shown in Figure 4-7; I prefer to have the power button hibernate the laptop when I close the lid on battery power. Otherwise, I have my laptop sleep.

To change the function on the Start menu's power button, obey these steps:

1. **Open the Control Panel's Power Options icon.**

   See Chapter 6 for more information about the Control Panel.

2. **Click on the link that says Change Plan Settings.**

   The link appears multiple times in the window; you can click on any of the links.

3. **Locate and click on the link that says Change Advanced Power Settings.**

   The Power Options dialog box appears — a treasure trove of various power-saving settings in Windows Vista.

4. **Scroll through the list and locate the item labeled Power Buttons and Lid.**

5. **Click on the + (plus sign) to open the Power Buttons and Lid branch-thing.**

6. **Click on the + to open the item labeled Start Menu Power Button.**

   Two items appear, one for when the laptop is on battery power and the other for when the laptop is plugged in.

7. **Choose an option for the Start menu power button.**

   Click on the current setting (shown in blue text) to see a pop-up menu of options, as shown in Figure 4-8. On my laptop, three options are available: Sleep, Hibernate, and Shut Down. Whichever option you pick becomes the new Start menu power-button setting.

8. **Click OK to close the Power Options dialog box, and then optionally close the Control Panel window.**

The Start menu's power button thing now functions as you've dictated.

Figure 4-8:
Controlling
the
Windows
Vista Start
menu power
button.

✓ You may prefer to have Shut Down chosen when you press the power button. You can also shut down by using the Start menu as described in this chapter's earlier section "Properly shutting down your laptop."

✓ Be careful to note the password-protection options at the bottom of the window (refer to Figure 4-7). I recommend requiring a password to be entered when the laptop revives itself. The password would be the same one used to log into Windows (not the BIOS password or your Internet password). Quite honestly, I cannot think of any situation where you would not want a password prompt for your laptop.

Power button functions in Windows XP

In Windows XP, the power button controls are also found dwelling in the Control Panel's Power Options icon. When you open that icon, click the Advanced tab in the Power Options Properties dialog box. What you see looks something like Figure 4-9.

Figure 4-9:
Lording it
over the
power
button.

You can control three items: the power button, the sleep button, and the laptop's lid-closing action. For each item, you have five choices for what to do:

Do nothing: Nothing happens. This option is preset on every Congressman's laptop.

Ask me what to do: Although this option isn't available to those snooty Windows Vista users, choosing it directs Windows to display the Turn Off Computer message (refer to Figure 4-6). You can choose what to do from that menu.

Stand by: The computer goes into Stand By mode.

Hibernate: The computer hibernates.

Shut down: The computer shuts down Windows and then turns itself off.

For each of the power buttons (and lid), choose an appropriate action. My choices are shown in Figure 4-9, although I do change my mind from time to time.

Note that not all the options listed in this section may be available. It all depends on your laptop's design and whether the manufacturer has enabled certain functions. In other words, don't get all bent out of shape and yell at me just because I list an option that isn't on your laptop!

The "Ask me what to do" option is obviously not available for when you close the laptop's lid.

Now, if only your refrigerator had an option that would let you know, once and for all, whether the light remains on when you close the refrigerator door.

Chapter 5

Basic Laptop Hardware

. . . .

In This Chapter

▶ Recognizing things on your laptop

▶ Discovering connectors and holes

▶ Recognizing mystery symbols

▶ Using your keyboard

▶ Understanding laptop pointing devices

▶ Cleaning your laptop

. . . .

*F*or being billed as tiny and lightweight, your laptop is festooned with bumps, holes, lights, and buttons all along its inside, outside, length, breadth, and width. It's a carnival of craziness! There's so much to behold that I've devoted this entire chapter to exploring the various features found on and about the typical PC laptop. So grab your laptop in one hand and this book in the other, and be prepared to take your basic laptop hardware tour.

 ✔ *Hardware* is the computer's physical part, the stuff you can touch. The *software* consists of instructions that make the hardware do stuff.

 ✔ Not every laptop has all the gizmos and grottoes mentioned in this chapter. Some laptops have even more! Consider your exploration a generic survey. For some items specific to your own laptop, the mysteries of what they do might never be solved!

Your 'Round-the-Laptop Tour

Rules? We don't need no stinkin' rules!

When it comes to designing a laptop, the rules are simple: There are no rules. Or, it's just that the rules are so vaguely defined that they seem to make no sense to anyone.

For example, I've used laptops where the disc ejects on the right side and laptops where the disc ejects on the front. The only place I've not seen discs eject from is the back of the laptop, which makes sense, or the left side, which is just another universal snub at all left-handed people.

This section mulls over some of the many electronic barnacles you'll find clinging to or embedded in your laptop's sides (and perhaps even bottom).

A place for your CD/DVD

Please fetch your laptop and locate the spot where the CD or DVD is inserted.

Note that there are two types of CD/DVD drives. The first is the slot type: The disc is inserted into a slot. At some point, the computer "grabs" the disc and pulls it all the way in. The second type of drive is the tray: You push a button, and a disc tray pops out of the laptop's body, or the tray might pop out when you use an Eject command in Windows. You pull the tray out the rest of the way and snap the CD or DVD into the tray. Then you gently push the tray back inside the laptop.

CD drives can be labeled as CD, Compact Disc, or CD-RW or CD/R-RW or some combination of those. The word *disc* can also appear on the drive.

DVD drives use the DVD logo (see the margin).

Combination CD/DVD drives might use some mishmash of the logos.

And, of course, some drives might not use any labeling.

> ✔ Be aware of the method by which discs are inserted into the drive: either slide in or pop-out tray. Either way, you need room to insert or remove the disc.

> ✔ For the pop-out tray, be sure that you find and recognize the tiny button you press to eject the disc.

> ✔ It's a good idea to use the Eject command in Windows to properly remove a disc. Refer to Chapter 6, in the section "Storage and Disk Drives."

Does Mr. Laptop have a floppy drive?

No, your laptop doesn't have a floppy drive. If it does, it's most likely a relic laptop, back from the days when people lived in fear of something called "DOS." Modern laptops don't come with floppy drives, although you can readily add a USB floppy drive when you really, *really* need one.

And that's all I want to say about floppy drives.

A home for Mr. PC Card

Locate on your laptop the spot where PC Cards are inserted. It might be a gaping hole on the side of the laptop, a tiny "garage door" that's covering the hole, or a hole that's hidden behind a panel.

 I've often seen the PC Card dock labeled with the icon shown in the margin, although I'm not sure if this is a universal hieroglyph.

Note that some laptops sport a depot for two PC Cards, stacked one atop the other. Some laptops might have room for only one PC Card.

A PC Card is inserted into the slot "holy" end first. In fact, it fits in only one way. Push the card in all the way until it fully docks with the connectors deep down inside the laptop.

To remove the card, locate the eject button alongside the slot, right next to the door. (See Figure 5-1.) Press the eject button all the way in, and the card pops out a little bit. You can then pinch the card between your thumb and forefinger and pull it out the rest of the way.

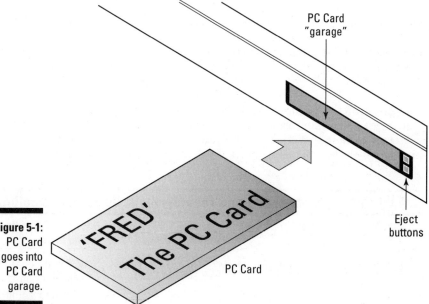

Figure 5-1: PC Card goes into PC Card garage.

PC Card "garage"

Eject buttons

'FRED' The PC Card

PC Card

An equal number of eject buttons appears alongside the spot where the card slides in.

  ✔ Be sure to read the instructions before inserting a PC Card the first time. Some cards might require that the laptop be turned off before inserting the card.

  ✔ Hole too small for a PC Card? Then what you've found is most likely a memory card reader, a hole that accepts Compact Flash, Secure Digital (SD), and other memory cards often used in digital cameras.

  ✔ Note that an eject button pops out a ways from the laptop's case. Remember to push it back into the case when you're done with the PC Card. That way, the knob doesn't snag on anything and possibly break off.

Mystery things called ports

Laptop PCs come with just about all the expandability options found in desktop computers. These options are generally referred to as *ports*. They consist of connectors, holes, and plug-in-type things you use to add features and attach cables to your laptop, which increases its potential while limiting its mobility.

Each of these ports is configured in a certain pattern — a hole or a connector with a specific shape and size. Each one is also labeled with an appropriate hieroglyph, and is often color coded. It's really difficult to plug the wrong connector into the wrong hole, although I'm certain that there are people out there who try.

Table 5-1 lists the pictures, symbols, colors, and duties of the various ports you might find lurking around your laptop. Try to locate each one on your own laptop. Note that some can be hidden behind doors or panels, and also that not every laptop manufacturer uses the color-coding scheme.

Table 5-1	Laptop Ports and Their Symbols, Designs, and Colors			
Port Name	*Configuration*	*Symbol*	*Color*	*What You Can Do with It*
Custom	Nonspecific	?	None	Most likely, connect a docking station or external disk drive or some other form of expansion

Port Name	Configuration	Symbol	Color	What You Can Do with It
Digital video			White	Connect a high-performance, external digital (LCD) monitor or TV
Headphone			Forest green	Plug in head-phones, which automatically disables the laptop's speakers
IEEE			None	Connect high-speed peripherals; also called the 1394 or FireWire port
Infrared			None	Communicate with other infrared devices
Keyboard			Purple	Add a full-size, external keyboard
Line in			Gray	Plug in an external audio device
Line out			Lime	Send sound to audio out/ speakers
Mic			Pink	Connect a micro phone
Modem/phone			None	Attach a modem for online communications or send or receive faxes

(continued)

Table 5-1: *(continued)*

Port Name	Configuration	Symbol	Color	What You Can Do with It
Monitor			Blue	Connecting an external monitor or video display for presentations
Mouse			Green	Attach an external mouse
Power			Yellow	Plug the laptop into an AC power socket
Printer			Violet	Attach a printer to your laptop
RJ-45/Ethernet			None	Add your laptop to an Ethernet network or connect to the Internet
Serial			Cyan	Add a mouse or use for desktop-laptop communications; an older port
S-video out			None	Attach a desktop video projector or attach the laptop to a TV or VCR
USB			None	Add a variety of components to the laptop, including printers and disk drives

✔ Despair not when your laptop lacks most of these ports. Ports can be added to most laptops by using a port replicator or docking station. See Chapter 21 for more information.

✔ Yes, the mouse hole and keyboard ports look alike. Use the pictograph next to the ports and the color codes to tell which is which. You can also use USB keyboards and mice, in which case any USB port works to connect the gizmo.

✔ The RJ-45/Ethernet port might also have the icon shown in the margin labeling its trapezoidal crack.

✔ By the way, that Ethernet port and the modem port look awfully similar. Happily, one (the Ethernet port) is larger than the other (the modem port).

✔ The power jack might look different from what's shown in Table 5-1. Be sure that you don't plug the power cable into a microphone port!

✔ The IEEE symbol might be different on some laptops. Apparently, the Y type of symbol isn't universal.

✔ If your laptop has S-video out, note that the S-video connection is video only, not sound.

A place for the old ball and chain

Some laptops have a special "belt loop," though which you can snake a security cable. The belt loop's real name is the Universal Security Slot, or USS. A common icon for the USS is shown in the margin.

✔ Note that the security cable must be attached to something solid and immovable to prevent the laptop from being stolen. Just threading a cable through the security hole doesn't do the trick.

✔ See Chapter 16 for more information on laptop security.

The thing's gotta breathe

As you conclude your journey around the perimeter of your laptop, note where the breathing slots are. They might not be obvious; they might not even be there. If they are, note their location and try to keep the vents clear.

Look at the Pretty Lights!

What would a computer be if it weren't for all the blinking lights? Even before real computers were popular, those monster computers of science fiction came equipped with banks and banks of blinking lights. Although I'm certain that a modern laptop could easily replace all the bat-computers in Batman's batcave, it just wouldn't be visually impressive — and believable to a 1960s television audience.

Your laptop most likely has many more lights than the typical desktop computer. I'm trying to think of a reason for this, but it honestly baffles me. Suffice it to say that Table 5-2 lists some of the common lights, lamps, and bright, blinking things you might find on your laptop along with what they do or why they're necessary.

Table 5-2	Pretty Laptop Lights
Symbol	*What It Could Possibly Mean*
☾	The laptop is in Stand By, or sleep, mode.
🔋 +	The laptop is running on battery power. This lamp can change color when the laptop is charging.
Ⓥ	The laptop is on.
⌽	The hard drive is being accessed.
🄰 A	The Caps Lock state is on. There might also be a light on the Caps Lock key.
🄰 1	The Num Lock state is on. There might also be a light on the Num Lock key.
((•))	Wireless networking activity is taking place.
✳	Bluetooth wireless activity is taking place.

Other pretty lights doubtless exist, some specific to your laptop's manufacturer. Thanks to that International Symbol Law, most of the symbols are pretty common. In fact, consider checking with Table 5-2 to see whether any of those symbols appears on the laptop's pretty light strip as well.

Some lights can blink or change color. For example, the battery indicator might change from green to amber to red as the battery drains. The hard drive or wireless lights might flicker as access is being made.

When the laptop is off, or even in Hibernation mode, none of the lights is lit. (See Chapter 4 for hibernation information.)

This Isn't Your Daddy's Keyboard

The full-size PC keyboard is an aircraft carrier! It's one huge boat! The thing was designed to be separate from the computer — a novelty back in 1981 — so that you could place the keyboard wherever you felt comfortable, even in your lap. But, golly! That keyboard is way too huge, even for the roomiest of laps.

The PC keyboard is big because it sports a lot of keys — 105 of them at least (not counting specific Internet buttons and volume controls). Pretty much all the keys on a desktop computer keyboard are used, too, which means that they must also be found on a laptop's keyboard. Aye, and therein lies the rub. A laptop cannot have a huge, honking keyboard! So sacrifices and work-arounds were devised.

This section mulls over the laptop's keyboard. Follow along with your own laptop as you read each section, and note how to use your laptop's keyboard and where the important keys dwell.

The general keyboard layout

Figure 5-2 illustrates a typical laptop keyboard layout, where all the common keys found on the whopping desktop keyboard have been miniaturized to laptop size. The design intends to let you type without the risk of fire from your fingers rubbing together.

As with a desktop keyboard, you should be able to identify the following basic items on your laptop keyboard:

✔ **Alphanumeric, or "typewriter," keys:** These are the basic typing keys, each of which is labeled with a character (a letter, number, or punctuation symbol). When you're typing on the computer, pressing a key produces its character on the screen.

Figure 5-2:
Typical
laptop
keyboard
layout.

✔ **Shift keys:** The keyboard sports various shift keys used either alone or in combination with other keys. These include Shift, Alt, Ctrl, and the special Windows keys Win and Context. The Win key appears in the bottom row between the Fn and Alt keys in Figure 5-2; the Context key appears between Alt and Ctrl. Also note the Esc (or Escape) key, found at the beginning of the top row of keys.

✔ **Function keys:** These keys are labeled F1 through F12 and are found on the top row of the keyboard, right above the number keys.

✔ **Cursor-control keys:** These keys can be anywhere around the keyboard, although in Figure 5-2 they're on the top and bottom right. They include the four directional arrow keys, usually found in an inverted T pattern, as well as the Insert (or Ins), Delete (or Del), Home, End, PgUp (or Page Up), PgDn (or Page Down) keys.

✔ **Numeric keypad:** This is covered in the next section.

Because typing is most important, a laptop's keyboard features alphanumeric keys that are often the same size and with the same *travel,* or feel, as on a desktop computer keyboard. Beyond that, the keys get *smaller.* Those are the keys you generally don't type on, the Chiclet-size keys that include the function keys and the cursor-control keys.

The text on some keys is color coded. That generally tells you which keys are used in conjunction with each other. For example, if the Alt key is green and the Num Lock key is green, it means that the Alt+Num Lock key combination is required in order to use Num Lock. (See the section "The Fn key is the Fun key!" later in this chapter.)

At one point in the computer's history, the function keys were programmable; you could tell the computer what to do when each key was pressed. In

Windows, however, the function keys have taken on specific functions. For example, F1 is the Help key.

The cursor-control keys are used to move the text cursor when you're editing text in Windows. They can also be used to help navigate through the Web. The keys can take on other functions in other programs as well.

Some keys are labeled with images or icons rather than with text. For example, I've seen the Caps Lock key labeled with the letter *A* and a padlock symbol. (I've never seen Caps Lock with a tiny cap on it.)

Your keyboard might have more or fewer keys than those shown in Figure 5-2, and the arrangement might be different.

Where did the numeric keypad go?

The first thing the laptop designers decided to sacrifice on their keyboards was the numeric keypad. Rather than just saw off that end of the keyboard, laptops since the Model 100 have used a combination of numeric keypad/alphabetic keyboard.

This combination can be seen on your laptop by examining the 7, 8, and 9 keys. Note that these are also the top three keys on the numeric keypad. Because of this, a shadow keypad is created using the right side of the alpha keyboard, illustrated in Figure 5-3. The trick, of course, is knowing how to turn the thing on and off.

Figure 5-3:
The hidden numeric keypad.

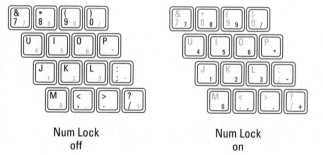

Num Lock off　　　　　Num Lock on

Attempt these steps to turn the Num Lock key on or off:

1. **Open a program you can type in, such as Notepad or your word processor.**

2. **Type** I just love Kimmy **in Notepad.**

   You discover in a few steps why you adore Kimmy.

3. **Find the Num Lock light on your laptop's strip of lights.**

   The light is your confirmation that you're in Num Lock mode and can use the embedded numeric keypad. (See Table 5-2.)

4. **Find the Num Lock key on your laptop's keyboard.**

   Somewhere on your keyboard is a Num Lock key. It might be called NumLock, or NumLk, or Num, or it might even be labeled with a symbol, as shown in the margin. Locate that key.

5. **Attempt to activate Num Lock.**

   Press the Num Lock key. If nothing happens, try Shift+Num Lock.

   If the text *Num Lock* is shown in a different color, find the matching-color key, such as Alt or Fn. Then press that key in combination with Num Lock.

   You're successful when the Num Lock light comes on. At that point, the keyboard has switched into numeric keypad mode.

6. **Try to type** I just love Kimmy **again.**

   It doesn't work. You get something like `14st 36ve 500y`. That's because most of the keys on the right side of the keyboard now have their numeric keypad abilities activated. It's great for entering numbers or working a spreadsheet, but rather frustrating at other times.

7. **Deactivate Num Lock.**

   Press whatever key combination you used to turn it on.

8. **Close the program.**

   There's no need to save the document.

Try to remember which key combination you used to activate the numeric keypad. Write it down on this book's Cheat Sheet, lest you forget.

The Fn key is the Fun key!

To make up for a lack of keys, early laptops came with a special function key, the Fn key. This was used in combination with other keys like a Shift key, giving those keys multiple purposes.

For example, in Figure 5-4, you see the keyboard from the old Compaq SLT. Its Fn (function) key is located in the lower-left corner, enclosed in a rectangle. Other keys with rectangles are activated when they're pressed with the Fn key. So the arrow keys (in the lower-right corner) double as other cursor-movement keys. Notice how the embedded numeric keypad also becomes an embedded cursor-movement pad as well. What a nightmare!

Figure 5-4:
The Compaq
SLT
keyboard
(1987).

Most modern laptops retain the Fn key, but it's used primarily to activate *special* laptop functions. These functions share other keys on the keyboard, typically the Function keys. They're marked by special icons and are color coded to match the Fn key.

Sadly, there's no standard for naming these Fn keys and their functions. But, among the many laptops out there, you find Fn key combinations that do the following:

✔ Turn the laptop's internal speaker volume up and down

✔ Mute the laptop's internal speaker

✔ Increase or decrease the monitor's brightness or contrast

✔ Activate an external monitor for giving a presentation

- ✔ Activate Stand By mode
- ✔ Hibernate the laptop
- ✔ Eject a CD/DVD
- ✔ Lock the keyboard

Take a moment to peruse your laptop and look over the available Fn keys.

Some Fn keys can be rather fun. For example, on my IBM laptop, Fn+PgUp is used to turn on a tiny keyboard light in the laptop's lid.

Mind these specific keys

In addition to the standard keyboard, or perhaps right along with it, your laptop may have some custom keys or buttons next to the keyboard. These are totally specific to the manufacturer, and you might never end up using them. But they're keys nonetheless.

The most common location for these keys is above the keyboard, although I've seen them on the left and right sides as well. Some keys can be used to pick up e-mail, browse the Web, connect to a digital camera, or contact the vendor for tech support. I've also seen keys that control the display or speaker volume.

Use these keys if you will, but keep in mind that their functions are specific to your laptop. Don't expect to find similar keys on a desktop computer or even on a laptop from another manufacturer.

The special keys are controlled using specific software that must be loaded into Windows. If there's a problem with this software, or if you end up using an operating system other than Windows, don't be surprised when the special keys no longer function.

This Isn't Your Momma's Mouse

The marriage of mouse and laptop is an old idea. Even back before Windows, laptop users were aware of how handy a computer mouse could be. The problem was, unlike now, laptop users wouldn't accept a standard desktop mouse as a solution.

Figure 5-5 shows one funky solution to the laptop mouse problem. It's a "thumb-ball" mouse. It plugged into the laptop's serial port and attached to either the lid or the side of the keyboard, giving the laptop user a primitive pointing device. Yes, using it was as awkward as combing your hair with a spoon, but it was something.

Today, nearly all laptops use something called a touch pad or mouse pad as a pointing device. The following sections describe the various options.

Figure 5-5:
An early-
model
Microsoft
thumb-ball
mouse.

The mouse pad

It took laptop developers years to come up with the current solution: the mouse pad. Originally called a *touch pad,* the mouse pad allows you to control the mouse by gliding a thumb or finger along a flat surface. Buttons nearby emulate the left and right buttons on your typical bar-of-soap mouse. (See Figure 5-6.)

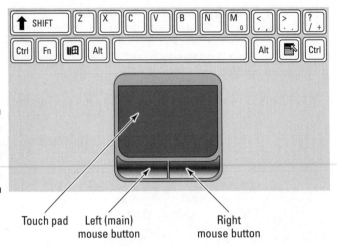

Figure 5-6:
The touch
pad mouse
thing.

Touch pad   Left (main)
mouse button

Right
mouse button

There's an art to using the mouse pad:

✔ It helps to use your forefinger to move the mouse. Use your thumb to click the left-right buttons on the bottom of the mouse pad.

✔ A light touch is all that's required.

✔ You must be careful not to touch it in more than one spot. If you do, the pointer jumps about on the screen as though it were being electrocuted. Touch the mouse pad in only one spot and with one finger.

✔ The most difficult mouse operation is the *drag*. That's where you have to hold down a button while moving the pointer. With practice, this can be done — but you must practice! (It's another excuse to play FreeCell.)

✔ Try to avoid accidentally hitting the right mouse button when you mean to hit the left one. This causes context menus to pop up in Windows — very frustrating.

✔ Some mouse pads let you tap the pad to simulate a mouse click. You can check the Mouse icon in the Control Panel to enable or disable this feature; see the section "Controlling the mouse," later in this chapter, for more information.

Note that I like to refer to the mouse pad as such. Others may use the term *touch pad*. That's because a "mouse pad" can also mean a special mat on which you use a desktop computer's mouse. Whatever.

Where is the wheel button?

Most modern computer mice come with a *wheel button*. The button sits in the middle, between the mouse's left and right buttons, and is used to scroll, pan, or click for various effects. People love the wheel button, and obviously they want it on their laptops. Well, tough!

Sadly, there isn't a standard wheel-button replacement on the common laptop mouse pad. Some manufacturers provide a button with similar features, but if you want a wheel button, you just have to end up using an external "wheel" mouse with your laptop. (That's not a bad idea, anyway.)

The IBM "happy stick" keyboard mouse

Popular on some IBM laptop models is a joystick-like mouse that looks like a pencil eraser jammed between the keyboard's G, H and B keys. IBM calls it the TrackPoint, although I prefer to call it a happy stick. Regardless, the gizmo is actually quite handy to use.

The idea behind the happy stick is that you can manipulate it by using the index finger of either hand. You can then use your thumb (on either hand) to click the left or right "mouse" buttons, as shown in Figure 5-7.

Figure 5-7:
The
TrackPoint.

Note that a middle button exists in Figure 5-7. That's the "wheel" button, and it can be used with the happy stick to scroll information in a window. Although it's not a full replacement for the wheel button on a mouse, it's a pretty neat trick.

✔ As with the mouse pad, using the happy stick takes some training and getting used to.

✔ Some IBM models come with both a happy stick and a touch pad. You can use either one.

✔ As of 2005, IBM sold its laptop business to Lenovo, so technically, I should refer to the IBM Happy Stick as the Lenovo Happy Stick. Same thing.

Controlling the mouse

The laptop's mouse hardware yields to the Mouse icon in the Windows Control Panel. By opening that icon, you find the controls for configuring and setting up your laptop's pointing device.

In addition to the standard mouse information, you might find a custom tab in the Mouse Properties dialog box, similar to the one shown in Figure 5-8. That's where you can configure the laptop's touch pad or custom pointing device. In Figure 5-8, the IBM TrackPoint and touch pad mouse options are set.

Figure 5-8:
Setting
custom
mouse
options.

✔ If you're a southpaw, use the Buttons tab in the Mouse Properties dialog box to switch the functions of the left and right mouse buttons. Be aware, however, that most manuals refer to the main mouse button as being on the *left!*

✔ You can use the Pointers tab in the Mouse Properties dialog box to change the way the mouse pointer looks on the screen. That can be a fun waste of time.

✔ Items on the Pointer Options tab can be used to help you locate a lost mouse pointer. Settings such as Pointer Trails and Show Location can be used to help find hard-to-see mouse pointers on the laptop's display.

✔ Note that it's possible to disable your laptop's mouse pad. Some laptops, such as some models of the HP Pavilion, might even have a mouse pad on/off switch. This is entirely acceptable if you plan on using an external mouse. (See the next section.)

✔ See Chapter 6 for more information on the Control Panel.

Get a real mouse!

The best solution for using a mouse on a laptop is to *get a real mouse.* No, not the furry rodent kind. Silly. A desktop computer mouse.

Now you can readily use a desktop computer mouse on your laptop instead of or along with the touch pad. Yes, it's one more thing to carry. But because desktop computer mice are so familiar and people are used to them, it often makes sense for the laptop to have a "big computer" mouse. Then again, you can find smaller laptop mice, such as the wireless model shown in Figure 5-9.

In Figure 5-9, you see a wireless USB mouse, the Microsoft Wireless Notebook Laser Mouse 6000. It's smaller and lighter than a desktop mouse, plus it has no tangly wires to mess with. Sadly, you cannot use the Laser Mouse 6000 to dispense with your enemies; the laser isn't that powerful.

✔ Beyond the Laser Mouse 6000 are other specialty laptop mice — some wired, some wireless, some with retractable cords.

✔ I often pause and wonder what happened to the Laser Mouse models 1 through 5999.

✔ Buy your laptop a nice wheel mouse, and you'll never again moan about your laptop missing a wheel button.

✔ I've seen people on airplanes use real mice. Even in that cramped space, people find a place to roll about the mouse. Pant legs work.

Figure 5-9:
Would
Goldfinger
use this
Laser
Mouse
against
James
Bond?

✔ There's no need to disable the mouse pad when you use an external mouse. Consider the mouse pad a bonus! You might be able to disable it if you desire to do so; refer to the previous section.

✔ Be careful when you install the software for your external mouse. Sometimes, doing so disables the software controlling the laptop's touch pad. Follow the installation advice that comes with the external mouse.

✔ Note that not all laptops come with a mouse port! If so, get a USB mouse and plug it into your laptop's USB port.

Keeping It Clean

After that you've been around your laptop a few times, you should do some cleanup. Look at all those tiny footprints! Look at those fingerprints! Yikes! If only your mother could see it. . . .

Laptops are really robust beasts. They can go through a lot without cleaning. When your mind does turn to it, heed this section.

✔ Turn off the laptop before you start cleaning it.

✔ You need a sponge or lint-free cloth as your cleaning tool.

- ✔ Isopropyl (rubbing) alcohol is also a good cleansing agent.

- ✔ If your laptop manufacturer has any specific cleaning instructions, directions, or warnings, please refer to them first before following the instructions offered here.

Sprucing up the case

The best way to give the case a bath is with a damp sponge. You can use standard dishwashing liquid, by mixing it at about 1 part detergent to 5 parts water. Soak the sponge in the mixture, and then wring the sponge clean. Use it to gently wipe the laptop's case.

When you're done with the sponge, wipe off any excess moisture or dust by using a lint-free cloth.

- ✔ Ensure that the sponge is dry enough that it doesn't drip liquid into the laptop.

- ✔ You might also want to use cotton swabs to clean some of the gunk from the cracks.

- ✔ Do not clean inside any disk openings or the PC Card slots. Never spray any liquids into those openings, either.

- ✔ Avoid using detergent that contains strong chemicals (acid or alkaline). Don't use abrasive powders.

Grooming the keyboard

Every so often, I vacuum my laptop keyboard. I use the little portable vacuums, either with the tiny (toothbrush-size) brush or the upholstery-cleaning attachment. This effectively sucks up all the crud in the keyboard. It's amazing to watch.

Some people prefer to clean the keyboard by using a can of compressed air. I don't recommend this because the air can blow the crud in your keyboard further inside the laptop. Instead, use a vacuum.

Remember to have the computer turned *off* when you do this!

To clean the tops of the keys, use isopropyl alcohol. Soak it up into a soft, dust-free cloth, or use a cotton swab and gently rub the key tops. Try not to drip any alcohol inside the keyboard.

Never use a spray cleaner directly on the keyboard.

Consider washing your hands from time to time.

Cleansing the screen

I've found the techniques used for cleaning an LCD screen, whether it's for a desktop or laptop computer, to be filled with controversy! Generally, no one recommends using any liquids because they can damage the LCD's delicate surface. Even so, you've gotta have something to rub with if you ever plan on getting that sneeze residue off the thing!

First, for general cleaning, get a soft, lint-free cloth. Use it to wipe the dust off the monitor.

Second, dampen a sponge or lint-free cloth with water. Be sure to wring out all the excess moisture. Rub the screen's surface gently, and don't get any excess liquid on or inside the monitor.

Let the monitor dry completely before closing the lid!

- ✔ Often times, the keyboard creates "stains" on the screen. They're hard to avoid and even harder to clean off. To help prevent the stains, consider storing the soft, lint-free cloth that you use to clean the monitor inside the laptop, between the keyboard and screen.

- ✔ Office-supply stores carry special LCD screen cleaners as well as the lint-free wipes that you can use to clean your screen and the rest of your laptop.

- ✔ One product I can recommend is Klear Screen, from Meridrew Enterprises (www.klearscreen.com). No, it's not cheap. You want *good*, not cheap.

- ✔ Avoid using alcohol or ammonia-based cleaners on your laptop screen! They can damage the LCD screen.

- ✔ Never squirt any cleaner directly on a laptop's screen.

Chapter 6

Exploring Windows on Your Laptop

. . . .

. . . .

A computer system consists of both hardware and software. Although the hardware is pretty to look at, it's really the software that provides the computer's brains and makes all that hardware worthy. Software is in charge. And, the main piece of software in charge of all other software is the operating system. For your laptop, that operating system is Microsoft Windows.

This chapter is about Windows, specifically how Windows comes into play on a laptop computer. Information on both Windows Vista and Windows XP is covered here, though keep in mind that this isn't a book about Windows — merely how Windows comes into play on your laptop.

Places to Know and Go in Windows

A lot of effort is put into making Windows look easy to use, and for the most part, it is. But Windows itself is one vast, complex program. For example, although the concept of copying a file seems easy, Windows provides at least one dozen ways for copying files. That's overwhelming. It's boggling! And it's something most folks overlook.

Rather than tell you *everything* (and risk your being bored), I decided to do a quick summary of those places in Windows where you'll spend most of your time, specifically with your laptop. This is the "Places to See and Things to Do" Windows tour.

The desktop

The desktop is the main thing you see when you use Windows. It contains icons, the taskbar, the Start button, and other things. Review Figure 4-4, over in Chapter 4, if you need to know what's what.

The Start thing

To get things done on the laptop, you need to run programs. These can be started from icons that appear on the desktop or, more likely, from the Start button and its slab-o-stuff to choose which programs to run.

You can see the Start slab after clicking the Start button with the mouse. The Start menu looks subtly different between Windows Vista and Windows XP, but the important things remain the same, as noted in Figure 6-1.

Click the Start button with the mouse, or press the Windows key on your laptop's keyboard (if your laptop has the Windows key).

Find the following goodies on the left side of Start-thing menu:

- **The pin-on area:** The top-left half of the slab contains programs permanently attached, or *pinned*, to the Start menu.

- **Recently Used Programs area:** Just below the pin-on area, on the left side of the Start menu, you find the names and icons of programs you've used recently.

- **The All Programs menu:** Below the Recently Used Programs area is the All Programs link. Clicking that item displays a list of programs installed on your computer, all organized into menus and submenus. If your laptop is brand-new, you see only Windows own programs plus any software that's been preinstalled on your laptop.

Recently Used Programs area

Pin-on area   Account image

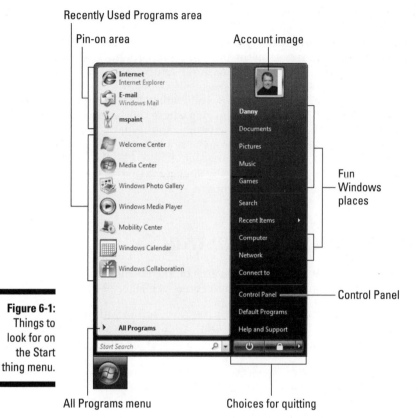

Figure 6-1:
Things to
look for on
the Start
thing menu.

All Programs menu   Choices for quitting

Find these items lurking on the right side of the Start menu panel:

✔ **Fun Windows places to visit:** The items on the right side of the Start
menu represent places to go in Windows, where you can carry out interesting (or not) tasks and play or dawdle. These include locations where
you find the stuff you create as well as general computer and networking
items.

✔ **The Control Panel:** One of the most important places to visit is the
Control Panel, which is accessed by choosing the Control Panel item
from the right side of the Start menu's palette. You visit the Control
Panel often as you set up various options for your laptop. (See "Visiting
the Control Panel" later in this chapter.)

Finally, in the bottom-right area of the Start button's menu, you find:

> ✔ **Choices for quitting:** The mysterious options for ending your computer-time fun and folly appear in the bottom right corner of the Start panel. I prefer a Stop button, but Bill Gates never returns my calls.

You discover more about using Windows and what all this stuff means elsewhere in this chapter. For now, just knowing where things are is all you need to know. Take care: The Start menu is customizable. What you see may differ from what's shown in Figure 6-1 and from what's listed in this section.

You can make the Start menu go away by clicking the mouse on the desktop or by pressing the Esc key on the keyboard.

Goodies on the system tray

The *system tray* is that obnoxious little area on the far-right end of the taskbar. It's also known as the *notification area* (see Figure 6-2).

People are of two minds about the system tray. Some ignore it. The rest allow it to bug the living heck out of them. They obsess over it. Really, it's just a tiny place for storing programs that may, from time to time, need your attention.

 The icons on the system tray also give you quick access to many common places in Windows. For example, if the twin networking-buddies icon indicates that your network isn't working, you can double-click the icon to get to a networking dialog box and address the issue.

 If any of the items on the system tray annoys you, try right-clicking them. Often, this produces a context menu where you can choose an Exit or Quit command. If not, try finding a Properties command, or access the window that controls the little icon. You usually find a turn-me-off item there.

Storage and Disk Drives

When it comes down to the basics, your computer is really about information input, output, and storage. The input is done through the keyboard, mouse, network connection, modem, and other input devices. Output is done through the monitor, speaker, printer, network connection, modem, and other output devices. Storage is the realm of the disk drive.

To see the gamut of storage devices available to your computer, you use a special window. In Windows Vista, it's the Computer window. In Windows XP, it's the My Computer window. You can open this window by choosing either Computer or My Computer from the Start menu.

The window that's displayed lists all the hard drives, removable disk drives, and any network drives you may have attached to your computer. In Figure 6-3, you see how Windows Vista displays the hard drive, the DVD/CD-ROM drive, as well as a network drive.

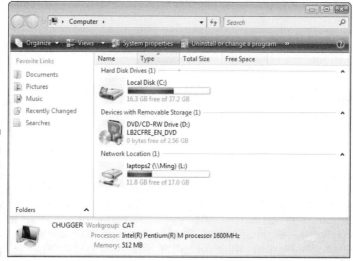

Figure 6-3:
Various places to store stuff, as shown by Windows Vista.

✔ The Computer/My Computer window is your gateway to the laptop's disk drives. When you're told to "examine drive C," for example, you open the Computer/My Computer window.

✔ For more information on the various types of disk drives available, as well as good background computer knowledge, refer to my book *PCs For Dummies*, published by Wiley and available at fine bookstores.

✔ You might also be able to access the Computer/My Computer window from an aptly named icon resting on the Windows desktop. Open the icon to see the window. (You can add the Computer/My Computer icon to the desktop easily: Refer to the following section, and use the same instructions as you do for placing the Account or My Documents folder on the desktop.)

✔ The Computer/My Computer window might also display things such as a scanner or digital camera, as well as other toys attached to your computer.

✔ The icon for the CD or DVD drive may change, depending on whether you have a disc in the drive and what's on the disc.

A Place for Your Stuff

Most of the stuff stored on your computer is placed on the hard drive. This includes the Windows operating system, plus all the applications and other software installed on your computer. In addition, you need a location to save your own stuff, the files you create, documents you write, music you listen to, videos you collect, plus all that porn — I mean, all those interesting pictures you've saved from the Internet, such as the bunny with the pancake on its head. All that stuff has to go somewhere.

In Windows Vista, you have your account's main folder, named after your login ID. The technical name is *Local User Storage*, but it's really a home for your stuff on the computer. I call it your Account folder. To open the Account folder, choose it from the Start menu. It's always the top item on the right side of the Start menu, just below your account's picture (see Figure 6-1).

Obviously, the folder you open is important because it contains all your stuff, all the *junk* you create and hoard on the laptop. Knowing how to open the folder is vital, just as much so as finding your clothes closet in the morning before you get dressed. Well, unless you're a nudist or you sleep in your clothes. But that's not my point. The point is to use the account or My Documents folder for storing your stuff. That way, you always know where your stuff is.

✔ A *folder* is a storage container for files. *Files* are those things you create using your software: documents, graphics, and so on. Files go in folders. This is all basic Computer Knowledge, stuff you probably ignored in school or assumed that you knew already.

✔ Windows Vista has a Documents folder, which is designed specifically for documents (word processing, lists, and such). It's different from the My Documents folder in Windows XP, which acts more like a home folder for all types of files.

✔ Most of the Save As dialog boxes use the Account/My Documents folder as the first choice for where to save your stuff.

✔ Your programs *do not* reside in the My Documents folder. No, they go in the Program Files folder. See the section "Where Your Programs Lurk," later in this chapter.

Placing the Account folder from the desktop in Windows Vista

It's handy to keep a shortcut to your Account folder on the desktop because this folder is where all the stuff in your computer is kept. To do so, follow these easy and painless steps:

1. **Click the Start button.**

2. **Right-click your account folder in the upper-right part of the menu.**

   The account folder has the same name as your login ID. That's Danny, for my account.

3. **From the pop-up menu, choose Show on Desktop.**

   If there is already a check mark by the Show on Desktop item, then you don't need to choose it; you're done!

4. **Press the Esc key to banish the Start menu.**

You should then see your account folder's icon on the desktop, given the same name as your account. The icon lacks the traditional shortcut arrow in the lower-left corner, but it's still a shortcut.

You can use these same steps to put any folder from the Start menu's right side onto the desktop, such as Computer, Network, Pictures, or any other folder. Simply repeat the preceding steps, choosing the appropriate folder from the Start button's menu in Step 2.

Placing the My Documents folder on the desktop in Windows XP

When the My Documents folder doesn't appear on the desktop, follow these steps to display it:

1. **Open the Display Properties icon in the Control Panel.**

   Look elsewhere in this chapter for information on the Control Panel.

2. **In the Display Properties dialog box, click the Desktop tab.**

3. **Click the Customize Desktop button.**

4. **In the Desktop Items dialog box, on the General tab, put a check mark by the My Documents item.**

5. **Click OK to close each dialog box.**

   The My Documents icon now appears on the desktop.

Network things you're connected to

When the laptop is connected to a network, it can access other computers on that network, including any resources (folders, printers, and so on) shared by those computers. The place to go for that type of networking action is the Network window in Windows Vista or the My Network Places window in Windows XP.

To display the folder full o' networking goodness, open the appropriate icon in either Windows Vista or Windows XP. The icon can be found on the desktop or on the Start menu. You can also find Network or My Network Places on any folder list or menu.

Figure 6-4 displays the Network window in Windows Vista. Each icon shown represents a computer elsewhere on the network. The display in Windows XP lists computer resources, or shared folders and printers.

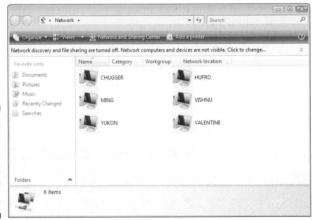

Figure 6-4:
Things
you're
connected
to on the
network.

Other, special folders for your stuff

The key to not losing your sanity in Windows is to organize your stuff. You get a head start on that because Windows comes out of the box with certain folders designated to hold certain types of files. In Windows Vista, these folders are found in your Account folder. In Windows XP, they're found in the My Documents folder. Here are a smattering:

> **Music / My Music:** A place to store all audio files, especially songs copied from the Internet.

> **Pictures / My Pictures:** The folder where your graphics go. Most graphical applications automatically store your images in this folder.

> **Videos / My Videos:** A special folder for storing digital video on your computer.

Windows Vista has even more custom folders: Downloads, Contacts, Saved Games, and so on. You can create similar folders in Windows XP, and you can even prefix them with "My," if you want to be consistent.

Where Your Programs Lurk

The hard drive stores everything, including all the software you install. Fortunately, software installation is automatic, so you rarely — if ever — need to tell Mr. Laptop where to put new software. No, in fact, the only time you really choose where to put something is when you create or store something yourself. For that, you use either your Account or My Documents folder, as described earlier in this chapter.

"Where is Windows?"

Windows installs itself on your hard drive in a folder named Windows or WinNT. The folder name depends on which version of Windows you're using.

Windows (the operating system) doesn't want you to view Windows (the folder). When you try, you may see a message that says something along the lines of "Whoa!" If you persist, you might get to see the folder. But like looking at any piece of art: don't touch! Don't delete! Don't tell!

"Where are the programs and other software?"

Windows places the programs and other software you install on the laptop into a folder named Program Files. As with the Windows folder, this folder is found by opening the C disk drive from the Computer / My Computer window.

As with the Windows folder, do not modify or change or add anything to the Program Files folder. Installing and removing software is done in a specific way in Windows, as described in the sections that follow. Do not manually delete or add programs on your own!

Installing new software

The easiest way to install new software on your laptop is to stick the software's CD into your laptop's CD-ROM or DVD drive. After inserting the disc, just sit back and watch as the installation program runs. Follow the directions on the screen. Soon, you're done.

✔ If the program doesn't automatically install after you insert the CD, open the Computer / My Computer window. Double-click the CD drive's icon. Look for any SETUP or INSTALL program icon. Double-click that icon to open the installer program and set up the software.

✔ Programs you download (receive) from the Internet should be saved (not "run") to the Downloads folder. When the download is complete, you can open that folder to run the program file, which installs the software.

✔ Windows Vista may beg your permission to run or install certain types of software; click the Allow button in the User Account Control dialog box to proceed.

Note that some older programs don't install or work properly on Windows Vista.

✔ Some programs require that you restart Windows before installation is complete.

✔ The reason you occasionally have to quit all other running programs is that such programs may interfere with the installation process. Also, if the computer automatically restarts when the installation is over, you can lose unsaved data in any running program.

Removing old software

Because software is installed all over the hard drive, it's a bad idea to just up and delete a program. No matter how satisfying that may seem, it's just a better idea to properly uninstall those programs you no longer use.

Uninstalling programs works differently, depending on your version of Windows. Read the proper sections that follow for specific info.

✔ Uninstalling a program erases its files from the laptop's hard drive. The uninstall program also resets certain options deep inside Windows, by trying to change things back to how they were before the program was first installed.

✔ Not every uninstall operation is successful. Sometimes, pieces of the program, or its files, remain behind. This is normal, sadly, and there is little you can do about it.

✔ Removing a program *does not* remove its associated data files. For example, removing a graphics program does not delete all the graphics images you created with that program. After all, you created and own those files, and only you can remove them.

✔ Removing programs frees up space on your hard drive.

✔ You can also remove various Windows components (games, the Notepad program, and so on) that you never use, which frees up hard drive space. Refer to a good Windows reference for more information.

✔ Occasionally, you can find an Uninstall command on the All Programs menu (from the Start thing). Such a command sits on the same menu as the program itself. Very handy.

Uninstalling programs in Windows Vista

To rid yourself of unwanted software, obey these steps:

1. **Open the Control Panel.**

   Directions are found elsewhere in this chapter.

2. **Open the Programs and Features icon.**

   You see a list of installed programs.

3. **Click to select the program you want to remove.**

4. **Click the Uninstall or Uninstall/Change button that appears.**

What happens after you click the button depends on the software you installed. Each program has its own Uninstall procedure, and most are easy to follow. Note that some applications, such as Microsoft Office, run a special program that lets you change the installation as well as remove programs. My advice: Read the screen directions *carefully*.

Close the window when you're done.

Removing a program in Windows XP

Uninstalling software is in the realm of the Control Panel's Add or Remove Programs icon. Here's how it works:

1. **Open the Control Panel's Add or Remove Programs icon.**

A list of installed programs appears, similar to the ones shown in Figure 6-5.

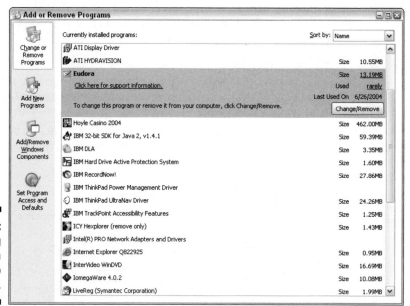

Figure 6-5:
Hunting down a program to remove.

2. **Click to select the program you want to remove in the list.**

You see some bonus information displayed, including the amount of space the program occupies (13.19MB in Figure 6-5) and how often the program has been used ("rarely" in Figure 6-5).

3. **Click the Change/Remove button to remove that program.**

   At this point, Windows turns control over to the Uninstall program that came with whatever program you're trying to uninstall. Carefully heed the directions on the screen.

   And the program is gone.

Visiting the Control Panel

In Windows, you can work, you can play, or you can dink. *Dinking* is the art of adjusting and fine-tuning Windows, by changing the appearance of this and the performance of that. It's playing with a purpose, and that play takes place in a land called the Control Panel.

The most consistent way to get to the Control Panel is to choose the Control Panel item from the Start menu. Additionally, links to the Control Panel are found in most windows, plus you can always choose Control Panel from any folder list displayed in a window.

The Control Panel

There are two ways to view the Control Panel: the easy way or the best way.

The easy way, also known as Category view, is how Windows normally displays the Control Panel. Yeah, this way is all graphical and fun, but it takes far more steps to get things done there. On a laptop, time is battery power, so you probably want to switch to Classic view, which is what I recommend.

What did they preinstall this time?

Most laptops come with a host of software pre-installed. Don't feel compelled to use it. In fact, if that software annoys you, refer to the sections nearby for the steps required to uninstall it. There's no point in keeping anything on your laptop's hard drive that you don't plan on using.

For example, if your laptop came with a wireless mapping tool and you don't ever plan on using it — or don't even know what the heck it is — freely delete it. One of my laptops came with a program to digitally call a cab in New York City. Feel free to delete any laptop tutorials or sample programs after you've seen them.

Remember: It's *your* laptop!

Figure 6-6 shows the Control Panel's Classic view as it appears in Windows XP. In this mode, all the Control Panel icons are visible at once, making each one equally and quickly accessible.

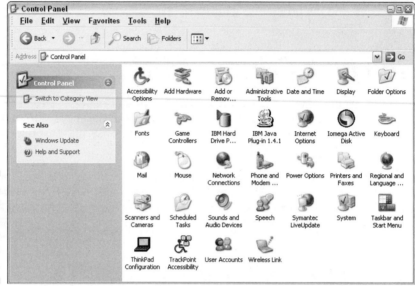

Figure 6-6:
The Control Panel works best in Classic view.

To switch to Classic view, click the Switch to Classic View link on the left side of the Control Panel window.

- ✔ Note that some of the icons you see in your laptop's Control Panel contents will be different from what's shown in Figure 6-6.

- ✔ Some laptop manufacturers include custom Control Panel icons, as do various hardware vendors. These icons are used to control hardware that's specific to your laptop, such as the IBM ThinkPad Configuration or the Iomega Active Disk icons shown in Figure 6-6.

- ✔ Of all the icons in the Control Panel, only a handful play roles specific to a laptop computer. For information on icons not mentioned here, please refer to a good Windows reference.

The optional Start menu approach

When finding the Control Panel takes too much time (and time is battery power on a laptop), you might consider another approach to accessing the Control Panel: the Start menu Control Panel menu, shown in Figure 6-7.

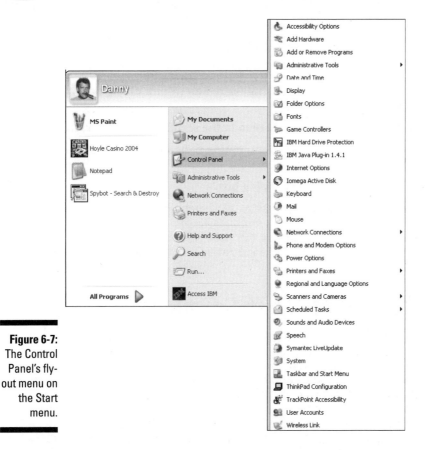

Figure 6-7:
The Control Panel's fly-out menu on the Start menu.

By changing the Control Panel item on the Start menu into its own menu, you save time in choosing Control Panel options. Simply pop up the Start menu, and then use the mouse to choose Control Panel and then the individual icon for your specific dinking needs.

The following steps configure the Control Panel as a pop-up menu on the Start menu:

1. **Right-click the Start button.**
2. **Choose Properties from the Start button's pop-up menu.**

   The Taskbar and Start Menu Properties dialog box appears.
3. **Click the Start Menu tab.**
4. **Click the Customize button, by the Start Menu option.**
5a. **In Windows Vista, skip to step 6.**
5b. **For Windows XP, in the Customize Start Menu dialog box, click the Advanced tab.**
6. **Locate the Control Panel item in the scrolling list of Start menu items.**
7. **Select the Display as a Menu option beneath the Control Panel heading.**
8. **Click OK to close each dialog box.**

   The Control Panel now lives as a submenu on the Start-panel thing.

Prove that it worked by clicking the Start button and finding the Control Panel item. It now has a triangle indicating that it's a menu.

What you see on the display

Display

To mess with the screen, to control the way Windows looks as well as how your laptop's monitor is configured, you need to visit the Personalization icon in the Windows Vista Control Panel or the Display icon in the Windows XP Control Panel. Oddly enough, the same icon is used in both versions of Windows (see the margin).

To set the screen resolution and colors and work with multiple monitors, in Windows Vista use the Personalization icon and open the Display Settings item. In Windows XP, open the Display icon and click the Settings tab. The window for both versions of Windows looks similar and is shown in Figure 6-8.

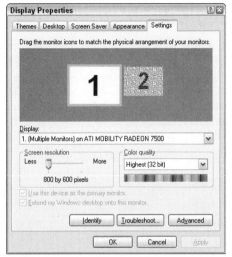

Figure 6-8:
The Settings
tab of the
Display
Properties
dialog box.

Display Settings is where you go to set up the laptop for giving a presentation. As shown in Figure 6-8, it's where you configure the projector, which is treated like a second monitor. (Also see Chapter 17.)

✔ The quickest and handiest way to get to the Personalization or Display Properties dialog box is to right-click a blank part of the desktop and choose Properties from the pop-up menu.

✔ Your laptop's display has certain modes and resolutions that work best — for example, 800 x 600 or 1024 x 768. These and other resolutions are known as the *native* settings for the monitor. Although other resolutions might be possible, the results don't look good and can wreak havoc on the display.

✔ It may seem trivial, but by not setting a background image or wallpaper, Windows spends less time updating the screen. And, time is battery life! To set a blank background image in Windows Vista, choose Desktop Background and select a solid color. In Windows XP, click the Background tab in the Display Properties dialog box in Windows XP and choose "(None)" as the background from the scrolling list.

✔ You might also consider setting a lower resolution and number of colors for your monitor. The higher resolution and color settings require more video memory, which means more work for the computer, more power, and less battery life.

Windows Mobility Center

A special Control Panel icon unique to Windows Vista is the Windows Mobility Center. It presents laptop users with a slate of common places to visit and things to adjust to help hone your laptop's performance, as shown in Figure 6-9. Note that the items shown can be adjusted from elsewhere, and many of the buttons simply display other Control Panel windows. But the Windows Mobility Center remains a handy place to know and visit for your laptop.

Figure 6-9: The Windows Vista laptop Mobility Center.

Networking stuff

The Control Panel sports a few icons to help you deal with networking on your laptop. Windows Vista uses the Network and Sharing Center icon. Windows XP has the Network Connections icon.

- ✔ **Network Sharing Center:** The main networking icon for Windows Vista. Figure 6-10 shows this handy window. You can also get to this window by clicking the Network Center link or button in any other window.

- ✔ **Network Connections:** In Windows XP, this Control Panel icon displays a list of networking items in the computer, including wired and wireless connections, the Internet, dialup, and other networking options.

For both Windows Vista and Windows XP, you can quickly get to the networking hardware center by double-clicking the wee li'l Networking Guys icon on the system tray or notification area. The icon looks like two computer monitors, one overlapping another.

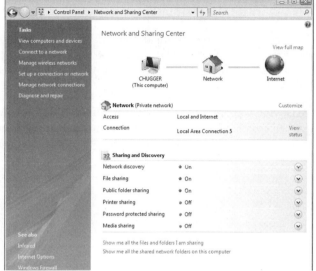

Figure 6-10:
The
Windows
Vista
Network
Center
window.

Power options

The Power Options icon is your main location for adjusting how your laptop uses the battery. The settings in the Power Options Properties dialog box enable you to control how the laptop goes to sleep and hibernates, control the power button's function, and control the settings for bossing the battery itself. See Chapter 8 for more information.

System

The System icon opens a window or dialog box that serves as a central location for gathering information about your laptop's hardware, controlling that hardware, and performing minor troubleshooting.

✔ If the Computer/My Computer icon dwells on the desktop, you can quickly get to the System Properties window or dialog box by right-clicking that icon and choosing Properties from the context menu.

✔ The keyboard shortcut for displaying the System window or dialog box is Win+Break or Alt+Fn+Break or even Alt+Pause, depending on your laptop's keyboard.

The Device Manager

The Device Manager is a window listing all the hardware in your laptop, and it's extremely useful for troubleshooting. In fact, a quick glance at the Device Manager window is all it takes to determine whether any hardware is behaving badly inside the computer.

To display the Device Manager in Windows Vista, open the Device Manager icon in the Control Panel. A User Account Control warning may appear; click the Continue button. The Device Manager window then appears, as shown in Figure 6-11.

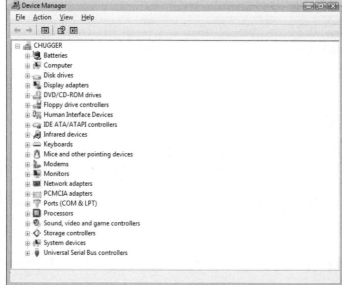

Figure 6-11:
The Device
Manager
lists your
laptop's
hardware.

In Windows XP, show the Device Manager window by first opening the System Properties dialog box (see the previous section). Then click the Hardware tab and click the Device Manager button.

Phone and modem options

The Phone and Modem Options icon is used to not only set up the modem but also configure phone dialing for when you're away from your home or office. This is a necessary thing to do on the road and is covered in Chapter 11.

Printers / Printers and faxes

Although your laptop may only occasionally dally with a printer, the software side of connecting the printer to your laptop is handled by the Control Panel's Printers icon, called Printers and Faxes in Windows XP.

To add a printer to your laptop, click the Add a Printer link in the window. Follow the directions and steps in the wizard to add your printer. Also refer to your printer's documentation; note that some printers must be connected before their software is installed; for other printers, the software must be installed first.

> ✔ Windows Vista is cautious about adding network printers. You may see a dialog box warning you that the printer driver software contains viruses and is just plain nasty. Although that's true, it's rare; if you practice safe-computing habits on your computer network, adding the printer driver software is okay.

> ✔ Also note that Windows Vista has dropped faxing as an option in the Printers window. That's fine: I recommend third-party fax software or the various Internet fax services as a better alternative anyway.

Infrared / Wireless link

Your laptop may sport an oddball infrared communications port. If so, you see a special icon in the Control Panel to help you configure and potentially use that port. In Windows Vista, the icon is called Infrared. In Windows XP, Wireless Link is the icon's title.

You can use the infrared port to transfer files between two computers or to upload pictures from a digital camera to your computer. Note that both devices must have and support the same kind of infrared port — and use the same type of protocols — for this to happen.

> ✔ Also read Chapter 16 for some security issues regarding the infrared port.

> ✔ Okay, I may be a bit harsh to us the term *oddball,* but this is my book. So there!

User Accounts

To modify your account, login picture, and password, as well as to manage others who use your laptop (heaven forbid!), open the Control Panel's User Accounts icon. Opening the icon displays a window listing all the accounts for users on your laptop, plus links and fun stuff for changing the accounts.

Chapter 7

Expanding Your Laptop's Universe

· ·

In This Chapter

▶ Understanding the USB port

▶ Connecting a USB device

▶ Using a USB storage gizmo

▶ Working with PC Cards

▶ Adding an extra keyboard

▶ Connecting an external monitor

▶ Going beyond the laptop's mouse pad

▶ Printing from your laptop

▶ Printing when you don't have a printer

· ·

*P*ursuing a life of wild and free computing on the road with your laptop shouldn't involve being tied down with a lot of accessories. How could you possibly pursue the desires of life, liberty, and happiness when your laptop is tethered to various external devices and gizmos, veritable anchors to drag upon your freedom? Indeed, having a laptop means that you can whip it out, flip it open, and start your work without spending a fortnight arranging, assembling, and connecting peripherals. Surely everyone else at the cybercafé would snicker at you if you even attempted such a thing!

There must be a balance between the need for portability and the advantages that external gizmos offer a computer. Even when you heed this book's advice (from Chapter 2) and get yourself the perfect laptop, there still stands a chance that you'll want a few extra gizmos, some items to expand the laptop's universe. This chapter describes the best ways to add more power and potential to your laptop without trying to compromise computer portability.

Going Beyond Your Lap

Thanks to their expandability options, laptops can sport just as many peripherals and add-ons as desktops — externally. Internally, expansion options are anywhere from proprietary to non-existent. The real question, of course, is "How much are you willing to carry?"

The miraculous expandability options of the USB port

Once upon a time, a portable computer needed to sport two COM ports, one printer port, plus other obscure ports, each designed for a specific hardware. The miracle of the USB port is that it allows for a variety of gizmos to be attached without the requirement of a specific port or bulky connector.

USB stands for University of Santa Barbara. For your laptop, USB refers to the Universal Serial Bus. The key word is *universal*, which means that this standard supports a vast array of gizmos. I've listed the common ones in Table 7-1, and those devices are covered later in this chapter. In Table 7-2, you find some uncommon USB gizmos — things that surprised even me! Check them out when you have time.

Table 7-1	Typical, Plain, Boring Uses for the USB Port
Device	*Typical Boring Usage*
External storage	Includes external hard drives, CD/R, DVD, and flash memory storage options, covered in the section "The joys of external USB storage," later in this chapter.
Printer	Prints stuff on paper. See the section "The Laptop and the Printer," later in this chapter.
Scanner	Sucks images from flat surfaces and reproduces them as graphics inside the computer. (This topic isn't covered anywhere else in this book, mostly because scanners aren't portable.)
Network adapter	Simply provides, through the USB port, another way to add networking to your laptop (although I recommend a PC Card network adapter over USB because the PC Card adapters fit better).

Device	Typical Boring Usage
MP3 player	Beams music between the laptop and the player. Note, though, that a laptop by itself with a set of headphones works like an MP3 player.
Digital camera	Lets you grab photos from the camera's memory card and store them on the laptop. This can also be done directly, by removing the camera's digital storage media, which is covered in the section "The joys of external USB storage," later in this chapter.

Table 7-2	More Unusual Ways to Use the USB Port
Device	*Unusual Thing It Does*
Legacy adapter	Allows you to connect ancient *(legacy)* serial, parallel, joystick, and other devices to your laptop. This adapter saves you from buying a port replicator and allows you to continue to use older hardware with your newer laptop.
Mouse and keyboard connector	Lets you connect an external mouse or keyboard, or both, to a laptop lacking a specific mouse or keyboard port (assuming that the mouse and keyboard don't have USB-specific connections).
Numeric keypad	Causes you to forget, when numbers are your game, about using the laptop's silly numeric-keypad thing. Instead, buy an external numeric keypad and let your fingers fly.
Sound hardware	Laptops lack internal expansion options to add high-quality sound hardware, so the next-best thing is to get external sound hardware provided by the USB port. For example, the Sound Blaster Audigy can be added via the USB port to give your laptop full 5.1 Dolby surround sound. (No word on how best to lug around the six speakers.)
Speakers	Lets your hear sound. To go along with the USB sound expansion, you can get some mini-USB-powered speakers for your laptop. Get the type with the handy tote-strap.
Video camera	Takes care of all your on-the-road videoconferencing needs. (These devices may also be referred to as *Webcams,* although a Webcam is generally connected to the Internet full time.)

(continued)

Table 7-2 (continued)

Device	Unusual Thing It Does
Little light	Imagine! Plugs in and is powered by the USB port. Furthermore, imagine it with a stiff-yet-twistable neck so that you can see the keyboard when you use your laptop in the dark.
Game controller	Control your little man, pilot your space ship, or wield that sword of magic. Most of the hot new game controllers are USB-based.
Laptop cooler	Acts like a fancy pad on which to sit your laptop. It contains a tiny, quiet fan that helps keep your laptop cool, and it runs from the power supplied by the USB port. (Also see Figure 21-1, in Chapter 21.)
Mobile phone recharger	Lets you transfer some of the laptop's power to your mobile phone. Some may consider the use of this interesting USB gizmo to do that as robbing Peter to pay Paul, but I'm not really here to comment on the gizmos; I just list 'em.
Security device	Uses the USB port to power an alarm on a cable lock or plugs in to the USB port and unlocks (or unscrambles) the laptop's data.
Bluetooth communications device	Allows your computer system to chat with other Bluetooth-enabled devices. If your laptop isn't equipped with Bluetooth wireless communications, such a gizmo can be added via the USB port.

Doing the USB thing

Your laptop may have one or two USB ports on its sides or rear. Refer to Chapter 5 for more information. Into those ports you either plug a USB device directly or attach a USB device by using a cable.

For example, a memory card reader or flash memory disk drive may plug directly into your laptop, as shown in Figure 7-1.

Other devices use a USB cable to attach themselves to the laptop. For example, a USB printer or external hard drive connects to your laptop by using a USB cable.

Figure 7-1: A JumpDrive looks more like a diving board when it's attached to this laptop.

Note that the same USB ports and the same cables are used for a variety of devices. As long as the devices are all standard USB, you can add them to any laptop with USB ports.

- ✔ If your laptop lacks USB ports, they can be added by using either a port replicator or (better) a PC Card with USB ports. See the section "Using the PC Card," later in this chapter.

- ✔ USB cables come in a variety of lengths.

- ✔ Not every USB device needs a cable.

- ✔ Computer stores, as well as most office-supply stores, keep a variety of USB cables in stock.

- ✔ USB cables cannot be longer than 12 feet. Any longer and the signal degrades. Note that for some devices, as well as for your laptop, shorter cables are best.

- ✔ USB devices, even the cables, have the USB symbol on them.

✔ The current USB standard is version 2.0, often written as USB 2.0. This standard is faster than the original USB, although it's still compatible with older USB devices. USB 2.0 allows for high-speed devices, such as external disk drives and CD/DVD players, to be connected to USB ports. Ensure that your laptop has the USB 2.0 standard and that all USB devices support that standard. That way, you get the most from your equipment.

What are the A and B ends of a USB cable?

USB cables have two ends, and each end can be different. On one end of the cable is the A connector. The other end, most likely, has the B connector.

The A connector is rectangular. It's what plugs into the computer. This connector is often called the *upstream* end.

The B connector has a D shape to it. This type of hole and cable connector are fitted on USB devices. It's called the *downstream* end.

For example, to connect a USB printer, you plug the A end of the cable into your laptop and the B end into the printer. Ta-da!

✔ When you get a USB cable, you want a USB A-to-B cable.

✔ If you want a USB *extension* cable, you want a USB A-to-A cable, or one that's labeled as an extension.

✔ You can get other cable ends as well, although they're specific to the devices they plug into. For example, my MP3 player uses a special USB cable with an A connector on one end and a specific dongle on the other end that plugs only into the MP3 player.

Plug in that USB gizmo

USB devices are a snap to connect — literally. You don't need to turn off the computer, run a special program, or wave a magic wand. Just plug in the USB gadget, and you're ready to roll.

✔ Some devices are recognized the second they're plugged in. A flash drive, for example, may be instantly *mounted* on your computer, with its disk drive-like icon appearing in the My Computer window, ready for access. See the section "The joys of external USB storage," later in this chapter, for more information.

✔ If the USB device has its own power switch, you must switch the thing on before the computer will recognize it.

✔ It's a Bad Thing to remove a USB storage device (disk drive or flash memory card) while your laptop is in Stand By (Sleep) mode or Hibernation mode or turned off. Wait until the laptop is on again before removing the device. Otherwise, you can lose or scramble your files.

✔ Some devices, such as a scanner or printer, may involve extra setup. Be sure to read the manual that came with the device to determine whether you need to install special software before plugging in the device or turning it on.

✔ Although you can just unplug a device, it's best to properly *unmount* it. See the section "Removing USB external storage," later in this chapter, for more information.

✔ The ability to plug and unplug USB devices without having to turn the computer off or on is known as *hot swapping*. It sounds risqué, but it's not.

USB-powered devices

Quite a few USB doohickeys are self-powered. That is, they draw the electricity that they need from the laptop's USB port. The good news is that you don't need an extra cable, power supply, wall socket, or battery for that device. The bad news is that it sucks up even more of the laptop's precious juice even faster.

I tend to lean toward using USB-powered devices. They're more portable because you don't have to worry about taking along power cables or batteries. Anything that lightens your load is good.

✔ When you're looking for a USB peripheral for your laptop, get the USB-powered version.

✔ Most flash memory devices are USB-powered.

✔ Those cooling fan pads you can get for your laptop are also USB-powered.

✔ Not all USB ports provide the proper power to run some USB-powered devices. Generally speaking, you must plug the USB-powered device into the laptop itself or into a powered hub for it to work.

Here a hub, there a hub

It may not seem practical, but your laptop can have up to 127 USB devices attached to it at any given time. Yes, all at once. That's one of the keys to the USB port's expandability. The way to add ports is by connecting a USB *hub* to the computer.

A USB hub is really nothing more than a gizmo with more USB ports on it. You plug the hub into your laptop's USB port. Then you can plug anywhere from two to four to eight USB devices into the hub.

✔ Some devices cannot be run from hubs, such as certain high-speed hard drives. In that case, the device must be plugged directly into the computer's USB port. Don't fret: A warning message comes up and instructs you what to do when such a thing happens.

✔ Keep your eye out for *pass-through* USB devices. This USB thingamabob sports an extra USB port somewhere on its body, so you can plug the USB device into your laptop and then plug another USB device into the first device. That way, you don't run out of USB ports.

✔ There are two types of hubs: powered and unpowered. The powered hub must be plugged in or derive its power from the computer. Powered hubs are necessary in order to supply more power to some USB devices.

✔ Obviously, a USB hub is probably not something you would want to pack in your laptop's case. The more cables the computer has, the less portable it becomes.

✔ Note that smaller, more portable, laptop-size USB hubs are available. They're very quaint — and more portable than the desktop, or full-size, USB hubs.

✔ One of the best ways to add more USB ports to your laptop is to get them on a PC Card.

✔ Each USB port on your laptop is considered a *root port*. The 127-device limitation is per root port, so if your laptop has two USB root ports, it can access up to 254 USB devices.

The joys of external USB storage

One of the most common thingies to add to a laptop is a USB storage device, such as a flash memory card reader or USB flash drive.

Both these devices meld into your computer system just like any other disk drive. Or, you can attach a real external hard drive or CD-ROM to your laptop's USB port, if those devices are USB-happy and properly powered. Here's how it works:

1. **Insert the USB mass storage device into your laptop's USB port.**

   I am assuming that your computer is on and working.

   You may hear an audible alert, a signal letting you know that Windows has found and detected the device.

2. **If a dialog box appears (see Figure 7-2), choose from the list what you want to do with the device.**

   The list, shown in Figure 7-2 for both Windows Vista and Windows XP, allows you to customize how you view the files on the USB drive, depending on the drive's contents.

Figure 7-2: Options for reading a freshly inserted USB disk (Vista on the left, XP on the right).

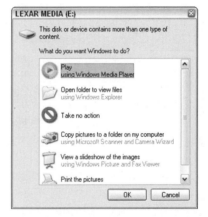

IEEE 1394 or FireWire gizmos

USB was one of two standards that emerged to replace the morass of expansion options and ports that plagued the PC for many years. The second standard is IEEE 1394, or IEEE, for short. Apple Computer refers to it as the *FireWire* standard, which is a cool but extremely scary-sounding name.

At one time, USB was considered the expansion option of choice for connecting items such as keyboards, mice, speakers, printers, and other low-speed devices. IEEE, or FireWire, was preferred for external storage or transferring video files because it was so much faster than USB. But that changed with the USB 2.0 standard, which is

essentially as fast and as good as IEEE (although not quite yet for digital video). That's why you don't find many IEEE ports on PC laptops.

Technically, IEEE works just like USB. You can plug and unplug cables, ports, hubs, and devices at your whim. Some devices — scanners and disk drives — may even support both USB and IEEE ports (although you can't use them both at the same time).

If your laptop didn't come with an IEEE port and you need one, you can add it by using a PC Card. Especially if you plan on transferring movies from a digital video camera, IEEE is your best option.

No matter what you choose to do with the removable drive, you can still see it listed along with other disk drives in your computer system. That view comes from the Computer / My Computer window; refer to Chapter 6 for information on how to display that location. Figure 7-3 shows the removable drive in Windows XP, where it's labeled Lexar Media and given drive letter E.

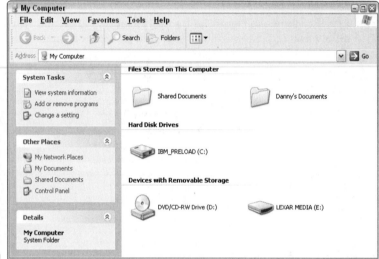

Figure 7-3:
The removable drive (Lexar Media), ready for file and folder action (XP)!

You can leave the USB drive attached to your computer as long as you like. Refer to the next section for proper instructions on removing — or *unmounting* — the drive.

 ✔ *Mass storage* means that some gadget that can store information just like a hard drive, CD, DVD, or silicon disk (flash memory, memory card, and that ilk).

 ✔ A flash memory card reader can be used to read a Secure Digital or Compact Flash memory card. These cards are used in digital cameras to store images. To transfer the images from your camera to the laptop, you just remove the memory card from the camera and insert it into the laptop's card reader.

 ✔ Your digital camera most likely stores its images on the memory card in the camera's folder, inside the DCIM folder. That's odd, but it's how most digital cameras do things.

Removing USB external storage

Yeah, you can just yank the USB drive out of the USB port. Unplug the thing! It works — it's just not proper. Plus, by doing so, you run the risk of losing some important data or seeing the fabled *Blue Screen of Death!* Better not risk it.

Just as there's a proper way to shut down your laptop, there's a proper way to remove any external storage you have plugged in. Here it is:

1. **Locate the Safely Remove Hardware icon on the system tray.**

   The icon is pictured in the margin, and it's different for Windows Vista and Windows XP. Not to mention that the icon isn't the easiest thing to see.

2. **Click the Safely Remove Hardware icon.**

   A pop-up menu appears (after a brief pause), listing the removable storage devices attached to your computer, as shown in Figure 7-4.

Figure 7-4:
A list of removable devices attached to the laptop.

> Safely remove USB Mass Storage Device - Drive(E:)
> Safely remove TOSHIBA DVD-ROM SD-R9012 - Drive(D:)

3. **Click the device you want to remove.**

   For example, I clicked the item Safely Remove USB Mass Storage Device — Drive (E:), shown in Figure 7-4. Note that the description varies, but you can pretty much guess which device it is you want to disconnect.

   If all goes well, you see an announcement that the device can be safely removed.

4. **Unplug or remove the device.**

The whole idea here is that you don't want to yank a storage device from your laptop before your software is done using it. Despite the fact that USB hardware can be hot-swapped, unplugging something that's in use means that you can lose files — A bad thing.

✔ If you see a warning that the device cannot be removed, or "stopped," click the OK button. Locate whichever programs have open data files on the drive, save those files, and then close the programs. That should allow the drive to be removed.

✔ If you double-click the Safely Remove Hardware icon, the Safely Remove Hardware dialog box appears. It's basically a more detailed way to do the same thing described in the preceding set of steps.

✔ Refer to Chapter 6 for more information about the system tray.

Plugging In the PC Card

I'm honestly surprised that the PC Card is still around. For years it was the only way you could expand a laptop, by adding everything from mini-hard drives to network adapters to extra ports. But, because USB options are just far more numerous and flexible, I predicted that the PC Card would eventually disappear, an ugly pock gone from the laptop's face. I was wrong.

Venture into any computer- or office-supply store and you still find an array of PC Cards. Most offer networking options, which I feel is the best way to add such options to a laptop. But other PC Cards are available, many of which help expand your laptop's universe.

Park a PC Card in the PC garage

This is cinchy. Just stick the PC Card into the slot. It slides in only one way: The narrow edge with the holes goes in first. If the computer is on, Windows recognizes the card instantly, similar to what's shown in Figure 7-5. At that point, you can start using the card or whatever other features with which it just blessed your laptop.

Figure 7-5:
You just can't hide the installation of new hardware from Windows.

ⓘ **Found New Hardware** ✕

VIA OHCI Compliant IEEE 1394 Host Controller

✔ Some cards may require extra software to make them go. It says so in the card's manual. Other cards, like many USB devices, can just be plugged in, and they're off and running.

✔ The most common type of PC Card that's available is a wireless networking card. Installing the card is only half the battle; the rest involves properly configuring your laptop to connect to a wireless network. See Chapter 9 for the gory details.

✔ The device installed in Figure 7-5 is an IEEE 1394 (or FireWire) port expansion card.

Using the PC Card

After the PC Card is inserted and properly set up, you can use its features. In fact, you can keep the card inside your PC for as long as you need those features.

Note that some cards jut out from the PC Card slots. Some may have pop-out connectors. Be careful with those! They can get caught on things, so you might consider removing the PC Card before you put the laptop back into its case and potentially break off an expensive gizmo.

✔ If you're adding USB or IEEE 1394 expansion with a PC Card, you can start using those ports right away. Refer to the sections on using USB devices, earlier in this chapter, for more information.

✔ Adding a network device allows you to use that device — if the networking options have been properly configured (as covered in Chapter 9). After you've set up networking, you can remove and reinsert the networking PC Card as often as you like.

✔ Removable storage devices can be used after they're inserted and recognized by Windows. Be sure to properly remove the device, as covered in the following section.

Backing a PC Card out of the PC garage

Although all PC Cards can easily be pinched and yanked out of their cozy sockets, that's not the best way to treat your PC's hardware. Instead, follow these steps:

1. **Click the Safely Remove Hardware icon on the system tray.**

   Refer to the section "Removing USB external storage," earlier in this chapter, for the details.

2. **Choose the device you want to remove.**

   A message appears, telling you that the device can be safely removed.

3. **Pull the PC Card out from its slot.**

   Some cards need a bit of help here. You have to find a small button to the right of the card. Pushing the button in a little makes it pop out about a half-inch or so. Then press the button back into the laptop to help push out the PC Card.

Store the PC Card in a proper place, such as in your laptop bag or in a drawer or cubbyhole with the rest of your laptop gear. The idea here is to keep the PC Card from being stepped on or crushed by a 20-ounce ceramic coffee mug.

Adding Some Big-Boy Toys

If you plan to park your laptop in one place all the time, you probably want to upgrade its teensy portable features with some more-robust desktop counterparts. Specifically, I speak of the keyboard, monitor, and mouse. Any of these desktop-size items can be added to and used with a laptop rather than their feeble laptop counterparts. Use one. Use them all. It's quite easy.

  ✔ Keyboards and mice don't need separate power supplies to work, but monitors do!

  ✔ If you really want a larger monitor with your laptop, and you want to take it with you, consider upgrading to one of the many large-format or wide-screen laptops with those sexy, humongous screens. They might not be as portable as smaller laptops, but *yowza!*

"I want an external keyboard!"

If you miss the full size and action of a real PC keyboard, get one! Just plug it into your laptop, either into the keyboard port or a USB port, whichever is available. You can start using the keyboard the second it's plugged in.

Note that adding an external keyboard often doesn't disable the laptop's internal keyboard. You can use both! But you're probably not crazy enough to do that.

When you're done using the full-size keyboard, simply unplug it.

✔ If all you're yearning for is to have a separate numeric keypad, consider getting only that item. You can pick up a USB numeric keypad, which is just the keypad and not the entire keyboard, at most computer stores and office-supply stores.

✔ Sometimes, the only way you can add a non-USB keyboard to your laptop is by getting a port replicator or docking station.

✔ The standard color for a PC's keyboard connector — the hole somewhere on your laptop for plugging in the keyboard — is purple.

Connecting a second monitor or video projector

Most modern laptops are automatically equipped to handle two monitors: the laptop's own LCD and an external monitor. This is because many laptops are often used for storing and showing presentations, and it just makes sense to have the laptop all ready to go in that respect.

To add the external monitor, locate the monitor connector on your PC's rump. Plug in the monitor, and you're ready to go. You can use that monitor in conjunction with your laptop's LCD or as your laptop's only display.

✔ On some laptops, the same image appears on both the LCD and the external monitor.

✔ If you want to use the external monitor exclusively, just close your laptop's lid. Most laptops are smart enough to see the external monitor and let you start using it, and also keep the laptop's power on while the lid is closed. When you open the laptop's lid, control returns to the laptop's LCD.

✔ Note that if you close the lid, it helps to have an external mouse or keyboard connected to the laptop so that you can still use your software.

✔ To activate the external monitor, you may have to press a special key or key combination on your laptop's keyboard.

✔ The monitor connector can also be an S-video connector. It allows you to connect your laptop to not only an external monitor but also many TV sets, VCRs, and DVD players. Refer to Table 5-1, in Chapter 5, for more information.

Two eyeballs, two monitors

Your head has two eyeballs, so why not give your laptop two monitors? Yep, this is obviously something you do for the laptop at its home base — unless the second monitor has a carrying handle. Because today's laptop are designed to work with video protectors, they can access two monitors at a time. It's an amazing thing to behold if you've never beheld it before.

After connecting the second monitor, follow these steps:

1a. **In Windows Vista, open the Personalization icon in the Control Panel.**

1b. **In Windows XP, open the Display Properties dialog box in the Control Panel.**

> Refer to Chapter 6 for more details on the Control Panel.

2a. **In Windows Vista, open the Display Settings item.**

2b. **In Windows XP, click the Settings tab in the Display Properties dialog box.**

> On either operating system, you see the two monitors displayed in the top of the dialog box.

3. **Click the second monitor.**

4. **Choose the Extend My Windows Desktop onto This Monitor option.**

5. **Click the Apply button.**

6. **Adjust the monitors' positions in the area near the top of the dialog box.**

> You can drag around the number-one or number-two monitor to help align the two desktops. Use the mouse to grab and drag each monitor into a proper position relative to each other.

7. **Click OK when you're done.**

The laptop's LCD is always the first display. It shows the taskbar and Start button. Although you can drag windows and icons to the second display, they all hop back to the first display the next time you restart Windows.

Gotta getta mouse

A computer mouse is perhaps the best companion you can buy for your laptop. Not that flat, odd, mouse pad thing! I'm talking about a real computer mouse. Just grab your favorite desktop mouse and plug it into your laptop. It makes for a much more enjoyable laptop experience — even if you often have to use your thigh to roll the mouse around.

Mice makers are aware of laptop owners' fondness for "real" computer mice, so the makers have a whole line of options available to you. You don't have to get a full-size desktop computer mouse. No, you can opt for one of those new mini-mice for laptops. Although they work just like desktop mice, they're about half the size. Some are even wireless. They're all better than using that silly touch pad.

Also see the section in Chapter 5 about getting a real mouse.

The Laptop and the Printer

When Adam Osborne originally proposed the portable computer, portable printing wasn't part of the big picture. He was right! How many times have you been in the cybercafé and seen someone printing from a laptop? Never! That's because printing is something that can be done later. You can transfer your on-the-road files to your desktop system or wait until your laptop is docked to print.

There are portable printers, of course. I've used the Canon Bubble Jet portable printer with my laptop. It's not that heavy, it has full color, it's fairly fast, and it uses flashlight batteries. So, there are some on-the-road printing options, if you want them.

Whether you're printing on the road or at home, this section describes how to set up and use a printer — or even a printer alternative — with your laptop computer.

Setting up the printer

USB printers are the way to go. In fact, most laptops lack a printer port, or the port can be found only on a port replicator or docking station. Anyway, the only time you truly need the printer port is for older printers anyway. So I just assume that you have a USB printer and that it utterly delights you.

To connect the printer, follow these steps:

1. **Plug in the printer, and ensure that it's turned off.**

   Also, set up the printer with ink and paper and all that other good stuff, according to the directions that came with the printer.

2. **Connect a USB cable to the printer and to your laptop.**

   Or, if you just cannot stand my advice, plug a standard printer cable into the printer's rump or into your laptop's very expensive port replicator or docking station.

3. Turn on the printer.

Windows should instantly recognize the printer, similar to what's shown in Figure 7-6. Then, because you're using a USB printer, it knows the printer's name and brand, and it even completely installs software for you, setting everything up just so.

When you're using the older printer-port type of printer, you'll probably have to use some kind of software installation disk that will just drive you nuts. Good luck!

Figure 7-6:
Amazingly,
Windows
recognizes
a USB
printer.
Wow.

After the printer has been set up and recognized by Windows, you can either print or save some energy and turn the printer off. You can even disconnect it when you don't need it. Reconnecting the printer simply reactivates its support in Windows.

✔ The printer port may not be available on your laptop. You may need a port replicator or docking station to access the old-fashioned, silly printer port.

✔ Leave your printer turned off when you're not using it.

✔ You can unplug the printer's USB cable without having to use the Safely Remove Hardware icon on the system tray. Just unplug the cable, and Windows bids adieu to your printer.

✔ No, it's not a good idea to unplug or turn off your printer while it's printing.

✔ If you're having trouble adding your printer, open the Control Panel and double-click the Printers or Printers and Faxes icon to display the list of printers available to your computer. The Add a Printer or Add Printer task can be clicked to run the Add Printer Wizard, which helps you complete the printer setup task.

✔ Printers work by using a *driver,* which is a software program that controls the printer. Windows knows about many printers and comes with their driver software ready to be installed. For other printers, you need to find a CD with the driver software that came with the printer, or you have to visit the printer manufacturer's Web site to download the latest driver.

Printing in Windows

To print a document, e-mail message, or anything else in Windows, you use the File➪Print command. It displays the Print dialog box, which can also be summoned by using the Ctrl+P keyboard shortcut. An example of this dialog box is shown in Figure 7-7.

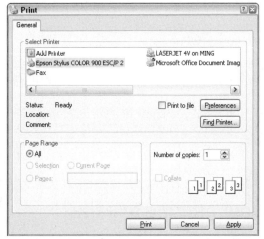

Figure 7-7:
An example
of the Print
dialog box.

Here are the quick steps you can take to work through this dialog box:

1. **Choose your printer from the list of printers.**

   This list is also where you select Fax, Microsoft Fax, or your computer's fax software to send a fax.

   Note that some printers visible in the window are network printers, available only when your computer is plugged into the network. Printing to them is fine; the document waits until you reconnect to the network before it prints.

2. **Select the range of pages to print.**

3. **Select the number of copies.**

4. **Click the Properties or Preferences button to set individual printer settings.**

   For example, if you want to print in black ink only on a color printer, you set that option by clicking the Properties or Preferences button and then setting the printer's color in the dialog box that appears.

5. **Click the Print button to print your document.**

Refer to Chapter 6 for information on setting a default printer as well as where to find the Printers and Faxes window.

Options for when you don't have a printer

Only the truly clever can print when a printer isn't available. For the rest of us, I offer these suggestions:

- ✔ Most hotels have business centers where you can temporarily connect to a printer and get your stuff on paper.

- ✔ Some office-supply stores offer printing services. Print shops and places such as Kinko's also have printers available for rent by the hour or by the sheet.

- ✔ Fax machines are printers. If you know of a fax machine nearby, just send your document as a fax. Note that plain-paper faxes are preferred; avoid wax-paper faxes, if possible. Note that faxes don't print in color.

What about printing to a file?

Once upon a time, you could save printer information to disk, just like you do with a file. Then you printed that file by sending it directly to the printer, either by using a DOS command or dragging that file onto your printer's icon. This worked well in earlier versions of Windows but doesn't work in Windows Vista or Windows XP — despite the Print to File option still being available in the Print dialog box.

A great alternative for the old Print to File option is to create an Adobe Acrobat, or PDF, document instead. For this, you need to buy the Adobe Acrobat Writer software or an equivalent. The Acrobat Writer software appears on your laptop's list of printers. When you select it for printing, the result is a PDF document that's readable on just about any computer.

Chapter 8

Power Management Madness

*T*he last tether to be snipped in the world of portable computing was the power cable. Sure, the marketing guys were pleased with a portable computer that merely had a carrying handle screwed to the case. Naturally, the sales force was eager to sell the portable computer with all its desktop counterparts crammed into one case. But the engineers weren't happy until they discovered a way to make the portable computer run from battery power.

In the laptop computer wars, weight and size are mere battles. Victory cannot be declared until the battery is perfected. Indeed, things are getting smaller and lighter all the time, but, comparatively, the battery technology used today is only slightly better than the batteries powering those original lunch bucket computers of the late 1980s.

Toss away all the software. Disregard all the hardware. Your laptop computer's soul lies somewhere near the battery compartment, and that battery is this chapter's subject. Call it *power management.* That's the goal of using any battery; use it as you need it, but always with the intent to stretch that power as far as you can.

The Battery Will Get a Charge Out of This!

The battery is what separates you and your laptop from that power outlet on the wall. In the laptop world, battery power means *freedom*. Most people understand that, but relatively few really know what the battery thing is all about.

Mention batteries, and people think of those clunky cylinder batteries, used since the 1950s, to power flashlights and toys. Even then, how much do you know about batteries? No, I'm not about to entertain you with a humorous chemistry metaphor. It's not important to know why batteries work — only that you understand how they work. Indeed, when you use a computer laptop, there are batteries of battery issues to understand.

Types of batteries

A battery by any other name would still shock you if you put it in your mouth.

Just as a good gardener knows that there is more than one type of rose, so is there more than one type of battery. They all provide electricity ("direct current," if this were a physics class). Yet between each battery type are plusses and minuses — and not just on the battery's connectors.

Alkaline: This is the most common type of battery, normally used in flashlights, portable radios, remote controls, smoke alarms, and kids' toys. The advantage here is that you can find these standard-size batteries anywhere. A few portable computing devices (printers, handhelds) use them, but laptops do not. The reason is that this type of battery isn't rechargeable. You use an alkaline battery, and then you throw it out (properly, according to the environmentally safe battery-disposal rules of your jurisdiction).

Lead acid: If ever two words could make an environmentalist blanch, they're *lead* and *acid*. Shocking as it may seem, millions of us drive around every day with a quantity of lead and acid nearby; those two chemicals supply the robust power of a car battery. Lead acid batteries are durable, long-lasting, and rechargeable, but they're also heavy and, well, *full of lead and acid!* Yikes!

More commonly, in a laptop computer, you'll find one of the following types of batteries:

Lithium-ion: This is the type of battery you want to have in your laptop. This type is lightweight and performs better than the other types of batteries. Unlike NiCad or NiMH batteries, lithium-ion batteries don't have The Dreaded Memory Effect. (See the upcoming sidebar, "The Dreaded Memory Effect.") There's usually a rapid-charging option with lithium-ion batteries, which is good when you're in a time crunch. Finally, this type of battery is more environmentally friendly than the other types. And, it has a cool, *Star Trek*–sounding name.

Nickel-cadmium (NiCad): Of all the rechargeable types of consumer-electronics batteries, the NiCad is the oldest. It's frowned on now, mostly because it suffered terribly from The Dreaded Memory Effect. Even so, NiCads offer great performance, and they dominated the portable power storage market until the better battery technologies came along.

Nickel-metal hydride (NiMH): This type of battery was one of the first successful alternatives to the NiCad. A NiMH battery is longer-lasting than a NiCad, but, sadly, it suffers from The Dreaded Memory Effect just as badly as the NiCad.

- ✔ Of all these batteries, odds are very good that your laptop has the lithium-ion type. That's pretty much state of the art.

- ✔ If you haven't yet purchased a laptop, ensure that you get one that has a lithium-ion battery.

- ✔ Lithium-ion is often abbreviated as LION. Because that's also the word for a big, ferocious kitty cat, I use "lithium-ion" in this book.

- ✔ You can confirm which type of battery your laptop has by looking at its label. See the next section.

- ✔ A few laptops out there are still using NiMH batteries. This is fine, of course, but you might want to check to see whether there's a battery upgrade option to the lithium-ion type.

- ✔ Your laptop might actually have a secondary, alkaline battery inside. It's used to power the laptop's internal clock, which keeps track of the time even when the laptop is unplugged or the battery has drained.

- ✔ The laptop might even have a second (or third) battery that keeps things powered for the minute or so that it takes you to swap out a spent main battery with a fresh one. See the section "Love that spare battery," later in this chapter.

- ✔ Refer to the nearby sidebar "The Dreaded Memory Effect" for information on, well, The Dreaded Memory Effect.

- ✔ Using unapproved batteries in your laptop may lead to bad things, such as, oh, the laptop exploding.

✔ Another thing to look for is a *smart* battery — specifically, a Smart Battery System (SBS). SBS refers to special circuitry that communicates with the laptop, to let it know the battery's condition so that you get better power control. Such batteries last longer because of better power management. (Smart batteries are typically lithium-ion.)

Finding your laptop's battery

Take a moment to locate your laptop's battery. Odds are good that it loads into the bottom of the laptop, though many laptops have their batteries inserted through a hole or door in the side.

The battery may be labeled, describing what type of battery it is (see the previous section) as well as other information about the charge it holds, its serial number, its replacement information, and so on. Note that often this information may be printed on the laptop case instead of, or in addition to, on the battery.

✔ Know where your battery is stored in your laptop. You may need to remove or replace it in the future.

✔ Most laptops use a few sliding locks or clips to help keep the battery in place. Don't force a battery into or out of your laptop.

✔ Batteries get warm as they're being used. That's simply their nature. However:

✔ Watch out if the battery gets too hot! For example, the battery can get too hot to touch or hold for more than a few seconds. That could be a sign of a malfunctioning battery, and such a thing is *dangerous*. Phone your dealer or laptop manufacturer immediately if you suspect that the battery is running hot.

Monitoring the battery

The laptop's battery drains as you use it, which is to be expected. In modern laptops, you should plan for at least two or three hours of active computer use under battery power. The rate of drain varies, however, depending on what you're doing with the laptop. And, naturally, depending on what you're doing, that time may pass rather quickly.

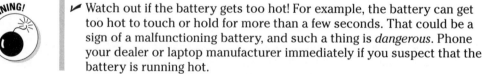

Fuel cells

Laptops of the future, as well as other portable devices, won't use batteries anymore. Instead, they'll be equipped with something called a fuel cell.

Fuel cells use a magical combination of chemistry and physics to provide power for much longer periods than typical batteries do. When the fuel cell gets low, you simply add more fuel to it — similar to filling a gas tank. Then the fuel cell is ready to go, powering your portable electronic device until it needs refilling again.

Certain types of fuel cells are available today, but they're still too large and bulky to be used with laptop computers. The present time schedule states that by the year 2010, fuel cells will be small, light, and compact enough for use in laptop computers. When that time comes, power management on your laptop will become a different creature, and battery-saving tips and techniques will become a thing of the past.

You can monitor the battery by viewing the tiny battery icon on the system tray. The icon graphically shows how much power is left; the icon's color "drains" out as you use the laptop. Often, that display is too tiny, so what you can do is point the mouse at the icon to see a pop-up bubble explain how much juice you have left, similar to what's shown in Figure 8-1.

Figure 8-1:
Nearly two hours are left on the battery.

In Figure 8-1, Windows Vista shows that one hour, forty-five minutes remain for battery life, and the battery has about 94 percent of its power remaining. The display for Windows XP is just as informative, though visually different.

✔ Your laptop manufacturer may have also included other battery tools, such as a battery monitor window, a special keyboard shortcut to display battery status, specific battery icons in the Control Panel, and so on

✔ The battery icon may not appear in the notification area when your laptop is being AC powered. Indeed, a power plug or other icon may show up in its place.

- ✔ On some laptops, a different icon may appear in the notification area when the laptop is AC powered.

- ✔ The battery icon on your laptop's row-o-lights may also indicate how much charge is left by changing color or even the amount of light showing through. Refer to Chapter 5 for more information on finding the battery light or icon on your laptop.

- ✔ *AC powered* means being powered by electricity from a wall socket.

- ✔ *DC powered* means being powered by the battery.

- ✔ Smart-battery technology is responsible for the ability of Windows to determine how much power is left in the battery. Be aware, however, that such a thing is an *estimate*. Different things can affect battery life, so don't bet real money on how much longer your laptop can survive on the battery.

Displaying the battery icon in Windows Vista

To ensure that the battery icon shows up in the notification area, heed these steps:

1. **Open the Control Panel's Taskbar and Start Menu icon.**

   Refer to Chapter 6 for more information on the Control Panel.

2. **Click the Notification Area tab.**

3. **Put a check mark by the Power item.**

4. **Click OK.**

You can also monitor battery usage from the Control Panel's Windows Mobility Center in Windows Vista.

Displaying the battery icon in Windows XP

Here are the steps to get the battery icon to show up on the system tray:

1. **Open the Control Panel's Power Options icon.**

   Chapter 6 contains information about the Windows Control Panel and its various icons..

2. **Click the Advanced tab.**

3. **Put a check mark by the Always Show Icon on the Taskbar option.**

4. **Click OK.**

You can also monitor battery usage from the Control Panel's Power Options icon, on the Power Meter tab in Windows XP.

The Dreaded Memory Effect

In the old days of the NiCad, and even NiMH, batteries, the mantra was that you had to fully discharge the battery, all the way down to empty, before you even considered recharging the thing. This was true and necessary: If you didn't fully drain the battery, it began to lose its potency over time.

What happened, especially with the NiCad battery, was that the battery would "remember" how long it was used. So, if the battery held one hour of power when it was fully charged and you recharged it after only 30 minutes of use, the former one-hour battery would become a 30-minute battery. That's The Dreaded Memory Effect.

To avoid The Dreaded Memory Effect and to prolong the life of their batteries, NiCad users would insist on fully draining their batteries each and every time they were used. Laptop owners would have to wait until their machines completely shut down before recharging. (NiCads aren't "smart" batteries.) Even so, some users would give up, and eventually their rechargeable one-hour NiCads would last for only ten minutes of power — not enough.

Today's lithium-ion batteries don't have The Dreaded Memory Effect. You can use them for a minute, and then recharge them, and the battery is still as good as it was when you bought it. So, boldly use your battery without fear. And the next time someone mentions The Dreaded Memory Effect, giggle with a smug laugh of confidence, secure in the knowledge that you're safe from the power problems of the past.

What happens when the power gets low

You know that feeling you get immediately after a power outage? You know, when everything in the room goes dark or turns off? It's startling! Well, the idea behind using your laptop is to avoid that feeling when the battery's power starts to go.

Thanks to smart-battery technology, your laptop computer gives you a good deal of warning before the battery poops out. You get enough time to finish what you're working on, save, close programs, and shut down the computer properly.

Figure 8-2 shows the low-battery bubble warnings that Windows Vista and Windows XP pop up. But that's only the initial warning. A second warning appears just before the battery dies. It should say "I told you so," but it really just warns you that a power-off situation is imminent. At that point, the laptop ignores you and either shuts down or goes into hibernation.

Figure 8-2:
Oops!
Quitting
time!

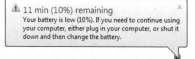

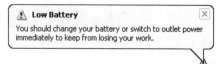

Figure 8-2:
Oops!
Quitting
time!

The warnings that appear, the time-to-zero notices, and the list of things the laptop actually does just before the battery poops out are all adjustable. Of course, you don't have to adjust anything because the standard settings provided by Windows seem ample. If you're willing to mess around, though, refer to the sections that follow for the details.

Adjusting battery warnings in Windows Vista

Windows Vista stores all battery warnings and timeout values in one handy location. That's the good news. The bad news is that it's not the easiest place to get to. Here's how I do it:

1. **Open the Control Panel's Power Options icon.**

   Refer to Chapter 6 if you're bewildered by the words *Control* and *Panel*.

2. **Beneath whichever power plan you selected, click the link that says Change Plan Settings.**

3. **Locate and click the link that says Change Advanced Power Settings.**

   Finally, the Power Options dialog box shows up, which you might have played with over in Chapter 4. Yeah, it's *the* happening place for all things having to do with power management in Windows Vista.

4. **Scroll through the list and locate the item labeled Battery.**

   It's the last item in the list on my screen.

5. **Click the + (plus sign) by Battery to display various battery notification and action options.**

   The five items are listed here. Note that my order is chronological, which is not how the items may appear on the screen:

   A. **Low battery notification:** Sets a warning for a low-battery level, before the situation gets critical. Values are On to set the low warning and Off to ignore it.

B. **Low battery level:** Determines what exactly is the low-battery level as a percentage of battery power. This value should be generous, well above the critical level (see item D).

C. **Low battery action:** Tells the laptop what to do when the battery charge gets to the low-battery level. Your options are Do Nothing, Hibernate, Shut Down, and Sleep.

D. **Critical battery level:** Sets the battery power level at which the crucial action takes place. This is the last-gasp thing Windows can do for your laptop just before the power goes out. The level is set as a percentage of battery power.

E. **Critical battery action:** Directs the laptop to sleep, hibernate, or shut down when the critical battery level is reached.

Each item has two subitems, one for settings when the laptop is plugged in and a second for when the laptop is on battery power.

6. **Set each item according to your needs.**

   Click the colored text next to either the On Battery item or Plugged In item to see a pop-up menu. Choose the setting you want from the pop-up menu.

   I set the Low battery action to Do Nothing and the Critical battery action to Hibernate.

7. **Click OK to confirm your settings; close the remaining dialog boxes.**

These settings don't affect the low-battery display in the notification area. The battery icon continues to drain and appears in yellow with a warning flag, and then the pop-up message appears (refer to Figure 8-2) at the critical point.

Setting battery timeouts in Windows XP

In Windows XP, you see two warnings, low and critical, which can be set on the Alarms tab of the Power Options dialog box, shown in Figure 8-3.

Activate the Low Battery Alarm by putting a check mark by the Activate Low Battery Alarm When Power Level Reaches option, as shown in Figure 8-4. Use the mouse to adjust the slider and set the percentage of battery life that remains when the Low Battery Alarm kicks in. You can further use the Alarm Action button to tell Windows what to do: Pop up a warning, beep, or shut down.

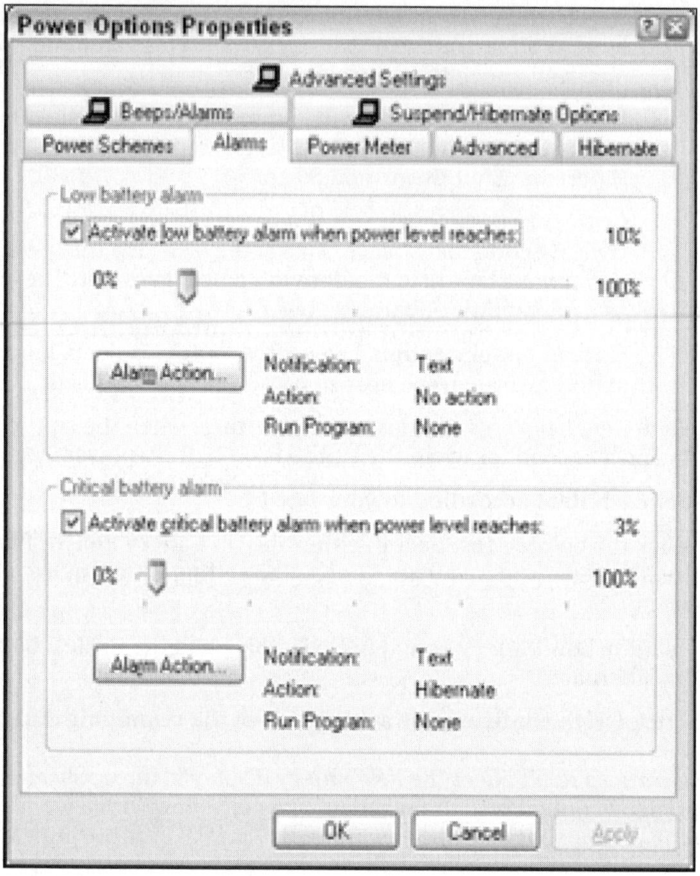

Figure 8-3:
Setting the
power-
low/power-
gone
warnings
and alarms.

The second warning (refer to Figure 8-3) is the Critical Battery Alarm. I highly recommend activating this option and setting the slider to something low, such as the 3 percent shown in Figure 8-3. Click the Alarm Action button to see which options to take when the power gets low, as shown in Figure 8-4. The

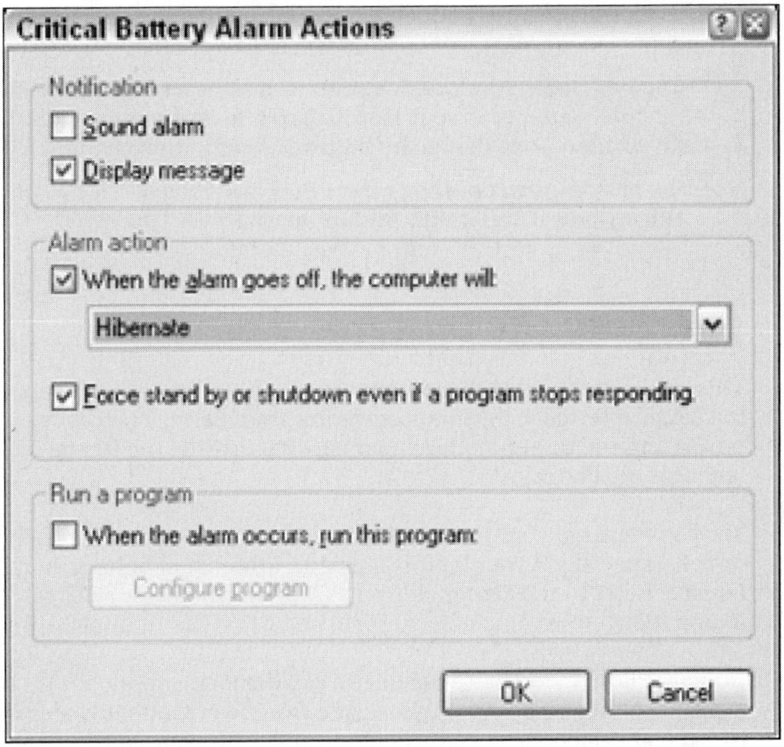

Critical Battery Alarm Actions

Notification
☐ Sound alarm
☑ Display message

Alarm action
☑ When the alarm goes off, the computer will:

Hibernate ⌄

☑ Force stand by or shutdown even if a program stops responding.

Run a program
☐ When the alarm occurs, run this program:

Configure program

OK   Cancel

Figure 8-4:
Options for
when the
battery gets
critically
low.

computer can sound an alarm or display a message when the power gets critical. More importantly, you can direct the computer to hibernate, stand by, or shut down completely, as shown in the Alarm Action area of the dialog box.

Also notice the Run a Program area. If necessary, you can configure a certain program to run when the power gets low, such as a utility to immediately back up your work files to a flash memory card, send remaining e-mail, or take a number of other actions.

✔ That critical-battery notice is serious. Computer time is over! If you ignore the warning, your laptop will stop working. And so will you.

✔ When the low-battery notice sounds or appears and you're blessed with a second battery for your laptop, pop it in and keep working! Refer to the section "Love that spare battery," later in this chapter.

✔ The best thing to do when power gets low: Plug in! This is why I always take my power cable with my laptop wherever I go.

Charging the battery

This is easy to do: Plug the laptop into a wall socket, and the battery begins to charge. Internally, the laptop switches from battery (DC) power to AC power, and the power-management hardware inside the laptop begins to recharge the battery.

You can recharge your laptop's battery whether the battery is fully drained or not. Especially if your laptop is using a lithium-ion battery, it makes no difference. Refer to the earlier sidebar "The Dreaded Memory Effect" for more information.

Note that lithium-ion batteries have a rapid-charging option. This option is available either on a custom tab inside the Power Options dialog box or through special battery software that came with your laptop. In a pinch, a rapid charge can save time. Otherwise, you want a nice, full, slow charge for your laptop's battery.

✔ I leave my laptop plugged into the wall whenever I can.

✔ There's no need to fully drain your laptop's lithium-ion battery every time you use it.

✔ NiCad and NiMH batteries benefit from being fully drained before they're recharged. That type of battery lasts longer and retains most of its potency if you fully drain it.

✔ Your laptop may come with — or have available — an external charging unit. You can use it to charge extra laptop batteries, if you have them.

✔ The battery continues to charge even when the laptop is turned off.

✔ It's been said that if you're using a laptop while you're charging the battery, it takes longer to recharge the batteries than when the laptop is turned off. This might have been true once, but it's no longer true; feel free to use your laptop while the battery is charging.

✔ Never short a battery to fully drain it. By *short,* I mean that you connect the two terminals (positive and negative) directly so that the battery simply drains. This is very bad. It can cause a fire. Don't do it.

Love that spare battery

One option you probably ignored when you bought your laptop was getting a second or spare battery. This item is a must for someone who is seriously on the road or in a remote location, where a long time is spent away from the power socket.

Before you use a spare battery, ensure that it's fully charged. Either charge it in the laptop, or use an external charger (if available). Put the fully charged spare battery in your laptop case or in any nonconducting (nonmetallic) container. Then head out on the road.

If your laptop has some type of quick-swapping ability, when the power gets low you can just eject your laptop's original, spent battery and quickly insert the spare battery. But be sure that your laptop can survive such a heart transplant before you attempt it! Perform a test swap in a noncritical situation, just to be sure.

If your laptop doesn't have the ability to hot-swap batteries, just turn off (or hibernate) the laptop when the original battery is nearly spent. Remove the old battery, insert the fresh one, and then turn the laptop on again.

✔ If you plan on pulling this trick often, get a laptop that supports hot-swapping batteries in the first place.

✔ I recommend labeling the batteries with a Sharpie so that you don't get the two (or more) confused and accidentally insert a dead battery.

✔ You can buy a spare battery from your dealer or from stores that sell extra batteries, such as iGo (www.1800batteries.com) or Batteries.com (www.batteries.com).

✔ Be wary of generic batteries! Always try to get a manufacturer's (or manufacturer-approved) battery for your laptop. Get anything less, and you run the risk of setting your laptop ablaze! It's happened!

Don't fall off the battery cycle!

The act of draining and recharging a battery is known as a *cycling*. If you drain and then recharge a battery three times, you just *cycled* the battery three times, or *thrice,* as my eighth-grade English teacher would have said.

Cycling the battery plays an important role in keeping it conditioned. For example, when you first get a lithium-ion battery-powered laptop, I recommend conditioning the battery: Cycle it three or four times. That means use it, drain it, and then recharge it over and over again for three or four cycles.

To prolong the life of a NiMH battery, I recommend fully discharging it every three to five cycles. So, after you use, drain, and recharge the NiMH battery about four times (or so), do a complete drain, and then recharge it again. That should help the battery last a bit longer.

Should you keep the battery in the laptop when you use AC power all the time?

Quite a few folks use laptops as their primary computers. If that's the case with you, and you keep the laptop plugged in all the time, there's no need for the battery to be in the laptop.

In situations where you never use the laptop's battery, such as when it's more or less permanently docked, remove the battery. The laptop runs just fine without it, and by removing it, you keep the battery in good condition for when you do need it.

To store the battery when it's not in use, place it in a nonmetallic (or nonconducting) container. Keep it in a cool, dry place. Over time, the battery drains. That's just the way nature works. When the battery has been in storage a while, don't be surprised if it's dead when you retrieve it. You can recharge it by inserting it into your laptop and charging it as described earlier in this chapter. The battery should work just fine.

If you occasionally take your wall-bound laptop out on the road, I recommend not removing the battery. Instead, every week or so, unplug the laptop and let the battery cycle. That keeps the battery healthy and reliable over the long haul.

✔ Yeah, some laptops may refuse to run from AC power when the battery is missing. I've not heard of any, but they may exist. If so, keep the battery in the laptop and understand that if you don't cycle it every so often, the battery eventually goes bad.

✔ If you remove the battery, consider plugging the laptop into a UPS (Uninterruptible Power Supply). The laptop's battery acts as a UPS, by keeping the computer powered during brief outages and blackouts. If you remove the battery, consider a UPS as an alternative — just as you would for a desktop computer. Refer to my book *PCs For Dummies* (Wiley Publishing) for more information on using a UPS.

RIP, battery

Eventually, your laptop's battery will die. It's inevitable. Just as humans are subject to death and taxes, batteries are subject to death. (Fortunately, the government hasn't figured out how to plunder tax money from a battery. Yet.)

You can tell when your battery is about to die by observing one unique trait: It suddenly becomes useless. It no longer holds a charge, and what charge it does hold is quick and unreliable.

Don't mourn a dead battery! Toss it out!

Note that batteries are considered to be toxic waste in most communities. You must properly dispose of or recycle dead computer batteries according to the rules of your community or jurisdiction. Never just chuck an old computer battery in the trash.

And don't get all Viking on me and try to burn your battery, either. That's just a bad thing.

You can buy replacement batteries from your laptop manufacturer or use a dealer- or manufacturer-recommended replacement. Be careful of replacement batteries that aren't certified by their manufacturers! Those batteries can damage your laptop. Yeah, they aren't cheap, either!

Managing Your Laptop's Power

You can do certain things to help your laptop's battery last a bit longer. On the short list are things that consume a lot of power:

- ✔ The hard drive
- ✔ The CD/DVD drive
- ✔ The floppy drive (if you have one)
- ✔ The modem
- ✔ The wireless network adapter
- ✔ The network interface
- ✔ The display

Each of these devices consumes power when it's in use. Obviously, by not using these devices or by rationing their use, you can save a modicum of power.

For example, by setting a lower resolution and fewer colors on the display, you cause the computer to use fewer video resources, although those overall savings are minor. For more savings, consider not using the CD/DVD drive, which requires real power to keep it spinning (such as when you're watching a DVD movie).

The real control happens by setting timeouts in the Control Panel's Power Options window or dialog box.

In Windows Vista, use the Power Options dialog box to choose a plan: Balanced, Power Saver, or High Performance. Note that Power Saver gives you the longest battery life. (You can tune the options and settings by clicking the colored text labeled Change Plan Settings.)

In Windows XP, use the Power Schemes tab in the Power Options dialog box, as shown in Figure 8-5. That's where you can disable or time-out certain laptop features and help extend battery life in a dramatic way.

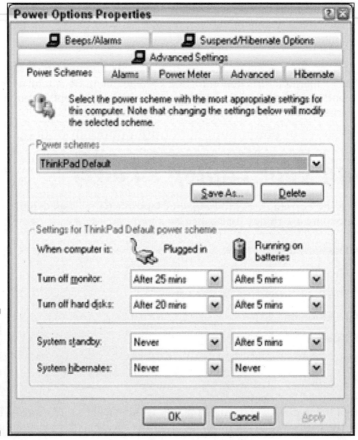

Figure 8-5:
Scheming
with
Windows
XP to
conserve
power.

Note the two major items in Figure 8-5: Turn Off Monitor and Turn Off Hard Disks. You can direct Windows to turn off those power-sucking hardware leeches after a given period of inactivity, greatly saving battery life.

When you find device custom settings that work for you, save them permanently. In Windows Vista, click the Create a Power Plan link on the left side of the Power Options window. In Windows XP, click the Save As button on the Power Schemes tab in the Power Options dialog box, and type something like My Scheme.

- ✔ Note the separate settings for when the laptop is plugged in and when it's running on battery power.

- ✔ No, you won't be seeing the screen saver if the monitor is suspended before the screen saver kicks in.

- ✔ It's a good idea to snooze the hard drive, especially if you don't plan on needing much hard drive access while using your laptop — for example, when you're writing something.

- ✔ Note that any disk access whatsoever wakes up the hard drive, which requires an extra squirt of energy. If you set the hard drive to sleep after one minute and it's constantly being revived, you're actually wasting power. Try another setting.

- ✔ You can tell when the hard drive has been sleeping because it takes a wee bit longer for disk access to complete (such as file saving, opening programs, and browsing folders).

- ✔ When a computer is plugged in, there's no reason to suspend the hard drive operation. That will just annoy you.

- ✔ Another power-saving option is to run the laptop's microprocessor at a slower rate. This option is automatically controlled in modern laptops, though older laptops may have some manual control over the CPU or bus speeds.

- ✔ Read Chapter 4 for more information about Stand By and Hibernation modes.

- ✔ Refer to Chapter 6 for more information on the Power Options icon in the Control Panel.

Part III
Yesterday Your Lap, Today the World

The 5th Wave   By Rich Tennant

"He saw your laptop and wants to know if he can check his Hotmail."

In this part . . .

The laptop computer presents an interesting paradox. On one hand, it must be utterly portable, lacking wires, tethers, anchors, and mooring lines. Yet, it must also be able to communicate. This need was evident early in the laptop's history (refer to Chapter 1); way back when laptops came with modems yet few desktops did. The laptop may lead a nomadic life, but it need not be a lonely one.

Laptops must communicate. Today, most laptops are equipped with multiple communications devices, many more than come with typical desktop PCs. And this communication doesn't necessarily involve wires; indeed, laptops came with wireless abilities for years before wireless networking became all the rage.

Communicating beyond your lap is such a vital part of the portable computing experience that I've dedicated this entire part of the book to the topic.

Chapter 9

All That Networking Nonsense

*Y*our laptop is a portable PC — the P stands for *personal*. A quarter-century ago, the notion of a *personal* computer was unique and went against the grain. Computers back in the 1970s and 1980s were impersonal. They were large behemoths, a central monster computer to which multiple users were shackled. The personal computer was quite the opposite.

My, how things don't change! Since the dawn of the Internet, it has been the goal of all computerdom to once again shackle computers together. The once wild and free PCs are now fated to become part of the One Computer, the Internet. This is actually a good thing because of how useful and helpful the Internet can be. So, obviously, although your laptop remains a PC and is therefore personal, it's also an impersonal networking device.

The chapter talks about sharing your personal laptop with others as well as sharing other's personal computers with your laptop. The whole big deal is called networking, and networking is all about sharing information and resources, whether it's between your laptop and your desktop computer, your laptop and other computers in the office, or your laptop and all the computers in the world.

✔ You can also use a network to connect to the Internet. This subject is covered in Chapter 10.

✔ In an office setting, please make sure that your networking administrator, or one of his minions, assists in setting up your laptop for networking.

✔ This book doesn't cover setting up a wireless network or managing a wireless hub, switch, or router. I assume that such a device is already up and running for your wireless laptop to use.

Adding Your Laptop to an Existing Network

When it comes to computer networking, the most delightful words to enter your ear are *existing network*. That term means that someone else has gone through the trouble and labored pain to bear the network into existence. You must further assume that the network is up and running and waits in eager anticipation for the addition of your laptop to its host of nodes.

Note that this section deals with traditional, wire-based networks. For wireless networking information, see the section "Look, Ma — No Wires!" later in this chapter.

Making the hardware connection

Networking is a combination of software and hardware, both working against each other to ensure that the experience is one of the most horrible of your life.

No, wait.

It's true that networking involves hardware and software. I admit to that. The software side is more difficult, so I put that off until the next section. The hardware side is rather simple: You need a NIC, or network interface card, inside your laptop to make networking happen.

Most laptops sold today come with a NIC standard. You can tell that it's there by looking for the RJ-45 hole or thing on the sides or back of your laptop's case. (Refer to Chapter 5.) If you see that hole, your laptop is ready for networking. You just need to use a network cable to connect your laptop to the network jack in the wall, to another PC, or directly to a network hub, switch, or router. That's it for the hardware side.

✔ Your laptop may also be ready for wireless networking. Refer to the section "Wireless networking hardware," later in this chapter, for the grimy details.

✔ The cable you use to plug your laptop into the network is commonly called *Ethernet* cable. It's also known as *CAT-5*. You can buy it in assorted lengths, colors, and flavors. It's available at any computer- or office-supply store.

✔ *Ethernet* is the name of the computer networking hardware standard.

✔ RJ-45 holes look like phone jack holes, but they're slightly larger. Do not confuse them! If the Ethernet cable doesn't fit into the hole, that particular hole is a phone or modem jack, not an RJ-45.

✔ A hub, switch, or router is a hardware device designed as a central locus for all computers on the network. Everything plugs into the hub, switch, or router.

✔ A *hub* is simply a place where Ethernet cables from various computers (or printers or modems) plug in.

✔ A *switch* is a faster version of a hub.

✔ A *router* is a faster, smarter version of a switch.

✔ No, you don't really need a hub-switch-router thing. If you're just connecting two computers, plug an Ethernet, or CAT-5, cable into each computer's NIC and then you can do what's called peer-to-peer networking. This is the fastest, most efficient way to connect two computers for exchanging information.

✔ If your laptop lacks a NIC or the RJ-45 hole, you can add one easily, by using either a PC Card or using a USB-Ethernet adapter. See Chapter 7.

Looking at the software side of networking on a laptop

Networking with your laptop isn't *that* difficult. Yeah, it's not exactly as easy as ordering a hamburger, a shake, and fries at a drive-through, but it's getting close.

The software side of networking begins by plugging your laptop into an existing network. Quite simply, that's all you really need to do. At that point, your computer is connected to a network, up and running.

To join a specific network or workgroup, more steps are involved, and they're not that complex. The following sections cover the details, with one set of instructions for Windows Vista and the other for Windows XP.

Viewing network stuff in Windows Vista

The first stop on your Windows Vista network tour is the Control Panel's Network and Sharing Center icon. Opening that icon displays a list of any current network connections, wireless and wired, as shown in Figure 9-1.

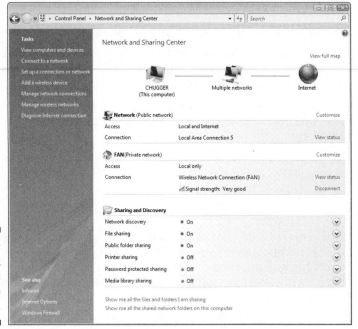

Figure 9-1: Network connections available to your laptop.

In Figure 9-2, you can see that two networks available, one is a wired network and the other a home-based wireless network. Everything is up and running.

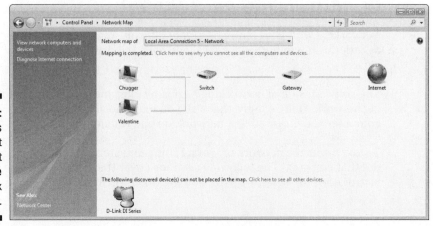

Figure 9-2: Windows Vista's best guess about what the network looks like.

Checking your networking connections in Windows XP

The first stop in your Windows XP networking adventure is the Network Connections window. There you see any and all network adapters attached to your laptop. Figure 9-3 shows two network connections: Local Area Connection is the standard Ethernet or wired connection, and Wireless Network Connection is a wireless NIC (duh).

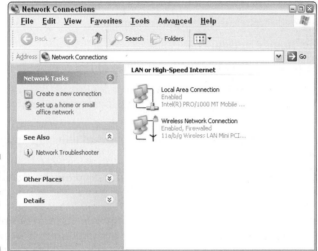

Figure 9-3: Network connections available to your laptop.

Connecting to a peer-to-peer workgroup

As far as this book is concerned, there are two types of wire-based networks you will use with your laptop. The first is a large network — so large that someone is employed to manage the network. In that case, you either follow a set of instructions or a person sets up the laptop for you. If so, that's great.

For smaller operations, you most likely connect your laptop to a peer-to-peer network. This includes everything from a home office that has only one other computer to a smaller company that doesn't need a large network setup. In that case, it helps to add your laptop to a specific workgroup. This stuff is cinchy.

The key to joining a specific workgroup is to supply your laptop with the workgroup's name. That way, your laptop appears on a list with other computers in the workgroup, and it makes workgroup resources (printers and hard drives) easier to locate.

The secret? Nope, don't bother looking in any of the networking icons in the Control Panel. For this task, you need to use the Control Panel's System icon, like so:

1. **Open the System icon in the Control Panel.**

2a. **In Windows Vista, click the Change settings link in the Computer Name, Domain and Workgroup Settings area.**

   If you're asked for permission here, click the Continue button.

2b. **In Windows XP, click the Computer Name tab.**

3. **Click the Change button.**

4. **In the Workgroup text box, type the name of the computer workgroup.**

   Unless you messed with things, the name is WORKGROUP, and that's okay. If you chose something else for your local workgroup, put that name into the box.

5. **Click OK to close the various dialog boxes, and close up any windows you opened as well.**

   At this point, you may have to restart your laptop for the changes to take effect. Do so when prompted.

Your computer is now a part of the named workgroup and can more easily access other computers and system resources attached to that workgroup. See the section "Finding other computers on the network," later in this chapter, to find out what else you can do on the workgroup.

Adding and removing your laptop to and from the network

After the network connection has been made and everything is set up, you can connect your laptop to the network by simply plugging in the network cable. There's no need to turn off the laptop or restart Windows. Plugging in the cable causes the network to be recognized instantly. You're in!

Similarly, when you need to disconnect from the network, simply unplug the network cable. The networking hardware and software recognize that the cable is no longer there and that the network is no longer accessible. No problem.

LAN party!

Thanks to the popularity of the film *Animal House,* toga parties were the rage on college campuses throughout the 1980s. Today's version of the toga party is just as popular, but far more geeky: It's the LAN party!

LAN parties can be planned, but they're mostly spontaneous. A group of laptop computer users suddenly find themselves together and create a small network, or LAN (local area network). After working out the protocols and other network nonsense (covered in the main part of this chapter's text), the LAN partiers go at it. No,

they don't sit around singing "Kumbaya" and sharing resources. They play games! Violent, network games!

Normally, you need access to the Internet or contact with some remote game server to play online games. But, with a LAN party, you can have anywhere from half a dozen to hundreds of computer users networked together and playing games. The next time you're in a coffee shop or high-tech bistro and someone looking like John Belushi shouts out "LAN party!," you'll know exactly what to do.

Finding other computers on the network

After the hardware and software connections are made, the next thing to do is browse to find out which other computers are connected to the network. You can view not only which computers share the same network, but also which resources those other computers offer up for your pleasure: They can share folders on disk drives, printers, and even modems. The only way to find out what's available is to look. The following sections show you how.

✔ Seeing computers displayed in the workgroup window is a sure sign of success that the network is up, connected, and ready for action.

✔ When you don't see any computers in the workgroup window, you have a problem. Either the network cable isn't connected, or it's bad. The network interface is bad. Or, the computers don't share the same workgroup name.

Seeing workgroup computers in Windows Vista

Choosing the Network item from the Windows Vista Start menu displays a list of networking devices available to your computer, such as what's shown in Figure 9-4. Each icon represents another computer elsewhere on the network, specifically in your network's workgroup.

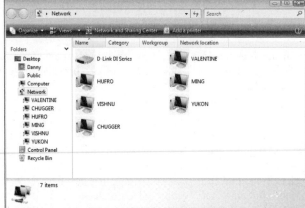

Figure 9-4:
Computers
sharing the
same local
network in
Windows
Vista.

To see which resources each computer offers, click to open its icon. If that computer is sharing a folder from one of its disk drives or a printer, you see the appropriate icon listed in the window.

My Networking Places in Windows XP

To view other computers on the network in Windows XP, open the My Network Places icon, either on the desktop or from the Start menu. Figure 9-5 shows a cozy, two-computer network I created by simply attaching an Ethernet cable to my desktop and laptop computers. (*Directly* means no hub or switch.) Both computers show up as icons, labeled with their computer names. The Workgroup name, Cat, appears on the Address bar and atop the window.

Figure 9-5:
Computers
in a
workgroup,
as seen by
Windows
XP.

Getting into another computer's disk drives

Accessing another computer's disk drives over the network is cinchy. To be more specific, however, you don't really access the entire disk drive. No, only specific folders on the drive are up for sharing. Even then, your access may be restricted by password, or you can only read, and not write or modify, any files in that folder.

No matter what, if a computer user is foolish, er, smart enough to share a folder on the network, that folder shows up as available for your computer to use.

In Windows Vista, open a computer icon in the Network window (refer to Figure 9-4) to see whether any folders or disk drives are available.

In Windows XP, shared resources are listed directly in the My Network Places window, as shown in Figure 9-5.

 To access a specific folder, double-click to open it, just as you would open any folder on your own hard drive. The contents of that folder are displayed on the screen, just as though it were a folder on your laptop's hard drive. Remember that the folder isn't on your hard drive; it's a folder elsewhere on the network.

If the folder is password-protected, you're asked to provide a password for access to the folder.

After the folder is open, you can access files in the network folder just as though they were on your own computer. Note that some folders can be shared as read-only, in which case the files and folders cannot be renamed or deleted or their contents modified.

 Practice polite network etiquette and close a network folder when you're done using it. If you forget and don't close the folder, a connection still exists between your computer and the one sharing that folder. If so, an error message may appear if the network connection goes down or the other computer disconnects from the network.

Accessing network printers

Printers can be connected to other computers on the network, or they can dwell on the network directly. Either way, after your laptop is on the network, it can access those other computers.

Windows XP directly displays any printers that are up and available on the network. They appear in the list of available printers, either in the Printers and Faxes window or from any Print dialog box.

Windows Vista, which is more security conscious, may not display all available printers. To access those printers, you must directly connect to them and then install the printer on your computer. For example, if you know that a printer is connected to the computer named XOG on the network, these are the steps you take in Windows Vista to add that network printer:

1. **Open the Network window by choosing Network from the Start menu.**

2. **Open the icon representing the printer-blessed computer, such as XOG, in this example.**

   The Network window displays the resources that XOG is sharing. You might see available folders, plus an icon representing the printer.

3. **Right-click the printer's icon.**

4. **Choose Connect from the pop-up menu.**

   A warning dialog box appears, primarily because Windows Vista is security conscious. Though the warning is legit, as long as you're practicing safe-computing habits, installing the printer drive software is okay.

5. **Click the Yes button if the warning appears.**

   Windows Vista connects to the printer and installs the software.

The printer now appears in the list of printers available in the Control Panel's Printers icon's window, as well as in the drop-down list of any Print dialog box.

- ✔ Using a printer directly connected to the network involves more setup than using or adding a printer connected to a network computer. Refer to the directions that came with the network printer for the details, including the printer's network name or IP address. Don't lose that stuff!

- ✔ To use the network printer, simply select it from the list of printers shown as available in the Print dialog box.

- ✔ The network printer is named using the form "Printer on Computer," where Printer is the printer's name or model number, and Computer is the network name of the computer to which the printer is connected (for example, `Lexmark X6150 on XOG`).

Sharing a folder from your laptop

Just like any stolid, unmovable desktop computer, various folders on your laptop's hard drive can be shared for others to use on the network. Although it's not necessary, it makes the file-swapping process easier between laptop and desktop. Alas, there are some details involved.

✔ You can only share folders, not individual files. They must be real folders, not compressed folders.

✔ It's a bad idea to share an entire disk drive. To do so is an incredible security risk. I would also recommend against sharing the entire My Documents folder.

✔ Don't share programs. Actually, I don't think that you can share programs and run them across the network (unless, of course, they're designed to do that in the first place).

✔ Other computers cannot access folders on your laptop when your laptop is turned off or in Stand By or Hibernation mode.

✔ You can continue to share folders, even when your laptop is on the road. That is, you don't need to "unshare" a folder just because the computer is disconnected from the network, but I would recommend it: The folders become available to others when a network is reconnected. Scary. See Chapter 16 for more information on laptop security.

Sharing the Public folder in Windows Vista

The best folder to share in Windows Vista is the Public folder, which was designed for that purpose. You copy into the Public folder the items you want to share or exchange with another computer. Likewise, others on the network can copy files into the laptop's Public folder. Here's how to share that folder:

1. **Open the Control Panel's Network and Sharing Center icon.**

2. **In the Sharing and Discover area, click on the down-arrow to the right of the item labeled Public Folder Sharing.**

3. **Choose the middle item, which is labeled Turn on sharing so anyone with network access can open, change and create files.**

    This selection allows full access. If you'd rather just have people get files from the Public folder rather than be able to put items there (or delete stuff), choose the middle option, the one that ends with "(Reader)."

4. **Click the Continue button if you're prompted by a User Account Control warning dialog box.**

    The Public folder is now "up for grabs" on the network.

You may also need to turn on Network Discover and File Sharing to provide complete access to the Public folder, especially by non-Windows Vista PCs. The method is similar to what's outlined above: in the Network discovery area, select the option labeled Turn on network discover; in the File Sharing area turn on the option labeled Turn on file sharing.

You can also share a specific folder from your laptop on the network. Refer to a good Windows Vista reference for details, although I believe that, for your laptop sharing, the Public folder is good enough.

 Folders shared from your laptop sport icons with little *people* beneath them. It's your visual clue that a folder has been shared.

Sharing a folder in Windows XP

You can easily share any folder on your hard drive with Windows XP, but I recommend sharing only the folder named Shared Documents. You can use that folder as a way station to store stuff between other computers on the network and your laptop. Here's how:

1. **Open the My Computer icon.**

2. **Locate the Shared Documents folder in the My Computer window.**

3. **Right-click the Shared Documents folder's icon and choose Sharing and Security from the shortcut menu.**

   A Properties dialog box for the folder appears.

   If you haven't yet set up your laptop for sharing folders, you have two options, as presented in the dialog box:

   Network Setup Wizard: Choosing this option runs the wizard, which is probably unnecessary, especially if you follow my advice in this chapter.

   If you understand the security risk . . . blah blah blah: Scary, huh? But if your network is already set up (you made a connection to other computers in the workgroup, as I describe in early sections of this chapter), choosing this option — despite the warning — is the fastest choice.

   a. **Choose the second option!**

   b. **In the next dialog box, select the Just Enable File Sharing option.**

   c. **Click OK.**

4. **Click the Share This Folder on the Network check box.**

5. **The folder's name appears in the Share Name text box. Enter a new name if the name that's shown is vague.**

6. **Ponder over the Allow Network Users to Change My Files check box.**

   By selecting this check box, you're allowing others on the network to delete, rename, move, or modify the contents of the files (and the folders and those files) in the folder you're about to share. Is this what you want? If so, check the box.

7. Click OK.

After some grumbling, the folder is put up for grabs on the network.

 Folders shared from your laptop sport icons with a little *serving hand* beneath them. It's your visual clue that a folder has been shared.

Look, Ma — No Wires!

The latest craze in computers is wireless *everything*. At the heart of the wireless mania lies wireless networking, which has been heralded as the biggest boon to communications technology since Morse code.

Then again, wireless networking can also be a real pain. It's not that easy to set up. It's a bear to maintain. And, wireless security is questionable. Despite that, wireless networking remains a craze, so I thought I should devote a few lucid moments to jotting down some worthwhile tidbits to share.

The ABGs of 802.11

Computers are chock-full of standards. You may have heard about a few: ANSI, ISO, IEEE, and other famous acronyms. The standard for wireless networking doesn't have a celebrated acronym. Instead, it has an illustrious number: 802.11, which is properly pronounced "Eight oh two dot eleven" or, to save time, you can omit the *dot*: "Eight oh two eleven."

As time marches on, newer and better wireless standards based on 802.11 come about. The first was 802.11a. Then came 802.11b, which is still around, although the most popular standard is 802.11g. Currently, the 802.11n standard exists, though laptop manufacturers are only now slowly adopting it.

The point to all this alphabetical soup is that in order to put the "work" into wireless networking, all the network devices must communicate with each other, which means that they need to share the same standard. For example, if the wireless adapter in your laptop, desktop, and wireless hub are all based on 802.11g, communications shouldn't be a problem. That's the whole point of the thing.

When your laptop uses 802.11b and the desktop uses 802.11g, you're not totally out of it. The 802.11g standard recognizes the older 802.11b standard, but the speed isn't as good as it would be if both were 802.11g. And, if either system is a *dual standard* (it supports more than one protocol), you're doing even better. Truly, for everything to work best, all the wireless networking devices must have the same-flavor letter as the 802.11 standard.

- I haven't seen any 802.11a devices in a while, so I think it's safe to say that they've all gone bye-bye.

- 802.11b is still quite popular, although most laptops sold today are of the 802.11g variety.

- Some wireless adapters span the alphabetic spectrum. I paid a little extra for my laptop's 802.11a/b/g adapter. It can scan and use all three standards, which gives me a broader range of connectivity options out there in the real world.

- I think I should be shot for writing "a broader range of connectivity options." It means that I've been reading too much computer sales literature lately.

Wireless networking hardware

To do the wireless thing, you need wireless networking hardware. An existing Ethernet port on (or NIC inside) your laptop just doesn't cut it. You need a specific wireless networking gizmo. Furthermore, you need a gizmo that supports whatever standard any existing wireless network uses: 802.11a, 802.11b, or 802.11.g.

If your laptop didn't come with the wireless network adapter, it's a snap to add one. Either by using the USB port or a PC Card, you can attach wireless hardware to your laptop in a jiffy. Plug it in, install the software (if it has any or if it's even necessary), and you're ready to go.

I recommend getting a wireless adapter with an external antenna. For some reason, the antenna makes picking up the wireless signal easier — especially if the antenna is directional (that is, it can be moved).

If your laptop doesn't have a directional antenna, don't sweat it.

As with the wirebound universe, setting up a wireless adapter in Windows is similar to setting up a wire-based Ethernet connection. Basically, Windows does all the work. All that's left to do is connect to the wireless network. That topic is covered in the next two sections.

Connecting to a wireless network

A laptop equipped with a wireless networking card can connect to any compatible wireless network. The first step is to find any available networks. The second step is to connect. The final step is to use the network and the goodies it provides. The following sections pound out the details for your version of Windows.

That Bluetooth thing

Bluetooth refers to a wireless standard for connecting computer peripherals, as well as other noncomputer devices. As long as your laptop is equipped with Bluetooth technology you can use various Bluetooth devices and gizmos with your laptop, including printers, keyboards, speakers, input devices, and so on. As the theory goes, as long as the device is flagged as Bluetooth compatible, you can use it right away with your laptop. In practice, however, it may require a bit of setup and configuring to get things working — a process you should be used to by now if you've been using computers for any time.

✔ The wireless network must use the same 802.11 protocol as your laptop's wireless networking hardware.

✔ There's a distance and interference issue with wireless networking, and the picture isn't as rosy as the brochures claim. Basically, the best way to connect with a wireless network is to be in the same room with the hub, switch, router, or other computer that's broadcasting the signal. Common things, such as walls, greatly reduce the potency of a wireless connection.

✔ A few wireless Internet locations offer their password and setup information on a USB flash drive. Simply insert the flash drive to connect to the network, or use the drive as indicated by the directions or when you're prompted to insert the drive when you connect to the network. Needless to say, this is a very handy thing to have — much better than retyping those long password keys!

✔ Refer to Chapter 6 for more information on finding the various networking goodies in your version of Windows.

Finding an available wireless network in Windows Vista

To hunt down a wireless network when Windows Vista is in charge, heed these steps:

1. **Choose the Connect To item from the Start menu.**

   The Connect to a Network window appears, as shown in Figure 9-6. The window lists various things you can connect to. The wireless networks broadcasting within range of your laptop's wireless networking gizmo are shown in the Wireless Network Connection area, as shown in Figure 9-6.

Figure 9-6:
Available
wireless
networks.

2. **Choose a network from the list to highlight it.**

3. **Click the Connect button.**

   Windows attempts to "make friendly" with the network.

   You may see a warning telling you that the network is unsecured. This message is common for certain free wireless networks that don't require a password for connection. Click the Connect Anyway option to proceed.

4. **Enter the network's password, if you're prompted to do so.**

5. **Choose whether the network is public or private.**

   This is a vital question. A public network is one that's out in public, one that others (strangers!) can also use. In that situation, you want to ensure that your laptop is locked down and not open to snooping.

   A private network is one in your home or office, available only to safe computers or folks you know. Such a network is more open than the public network.

6. **Choose whether to save the network's connection information.**

   I recommend that you save the information if you plan on using that wireless connection again. That way, you don't have to reenter the password every time you connect (in theory anyway).

7. **Click the Close button.**

8. **Click the Continue button if you're prompted by a User Account Control dialog box.**

You're now connected and ready to use the network. A wireless networking icon appears in the notification area on the taskbar, showing that you're connected; point the mouse at that icon for more information.

✔ You may be prompted by various User Account Control warnings. These are okay here because you're modifying the system in order to connect with the wireless network; freely click the Allow button.

✔ The password you enter may not be accepted. If so, you need to manually connect to the network. Refer to the section "'What if I don't know the SSID?'" later in this chapter.

✔ Sometimes, it pays to wait a few moments for the wireless connection to sync up (or something). Don't take the lack of an immediate "Connection made, yee-ha!" message as a sign of failure.

✔ The best way to hunt down wireless networks is to use a third-party wireless network browser. Such a program may have come with your laptop's wireless adapter, or it can also be found on the Internet; be sure that your wireless network browser is compatible with Windows Vista.

Finding an available wireless network in Windows XP

Tracking down a wireless network in Windows XP is done like this:

1. **Open the Network Connections window.**

2. **Right-click the wireless network connection's icon.**

3. **Choose View Available Wireless Connections from the pop-up menu.**

   The Wireless Network Connection dialog box shows up, as depicted in Figure 9-7. This dialog box lists any and all wireless networks that are within range of your laptop and compatible with your wireless networking protocol.

Figure 9-7: Desperately scanning for available wireless networks.

If your wireless networking gear supports more than one protocol, you see every matching protocol appear in the window.

In Figure 9-7, one network shows up as available. Its name is KITTY. The name is officially known as the SSID, or *service set identifier*. That's the mumbo jumbo term for the wireless network's name.

4. **Select the wireless network's name (if there's more than one).**

5. **Enter the password, if required, not once but twice.**

   Note that some passwords can be rather lengthy, so pay attention as you type them. Yeah, typing one of those 128-character passwords twice isn't the most thrilling thing to do.

6. **Click the Connect button.**

   If everything goes well, you see the little networking buddies appear in the notification area, plus a bubble alerting you to the wireless networking connection, as shown in Figure 9-8. You made it!

Figure 9-8:
A wireless network connection has been made.

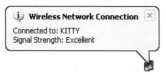

Well, maybe you didn't make it. The network may require further authentication or configuration to allow your laptop to connect. Continue reading through the next few sections for some solutions to potential problems.

"What if I don't know the SSID?"

For security reasons, some wireless networks don't broadcast their SSIDs. Obviously, you cannot connect to a network if you don't know its SSID, just as you cannot call out to a friend across the street when you don't know his name.

To get the SSID, you need to ask. The network manager or whatever human is in charge of the wireless network at your location should be able to divulge that information. After you know the SSID, follow the steps in the appropriate section to connect to that network.

Connecting to an unknown SSID in Windows Vista

A wireless network not broadcasting its SSID doesn't show up in the list of networks, as shown earlier, in Figure 9-6. What's a lonely laptop user to do? Why, you must manually connect in that case. Here's the secret:

1. **Choose Connect To from the Start menu.**

   Yes, it's the same list of networks with the one you want missing (refer to Figure 9-6). Give up not yet!

2. **Choose the Set Up a Connection or Network link at the bottom of the window.**

   The Select a Connection Option window appears.

3. **Choose the item Manually Connect to a Wireless Network.**

4. **Click the Next button.**

   The next window that's displayed allows you to set up a manual connection, as shown in Figure 9-9.

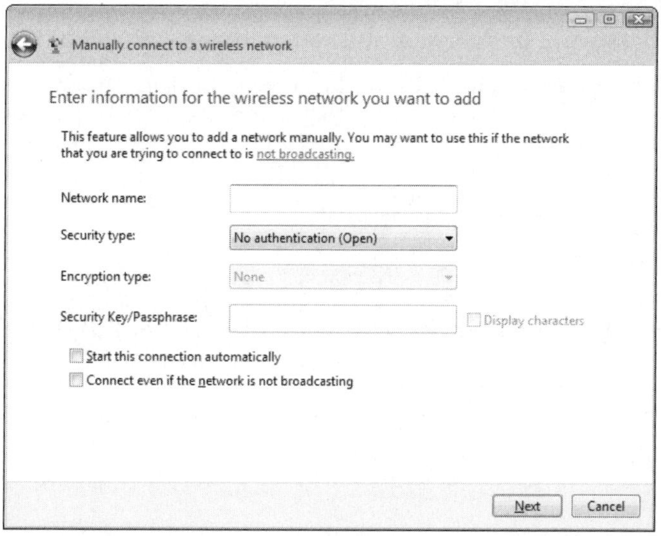

Figure 9-9: Configuring a manual connection in Windows Vista.

5. **Type the SSID in the Network name box.**

6. **Fill in the rest of the information as needed.**

   You need to check with the network administrator to see what other tidbits of information are required in order to complete the connection: security and encryption types and a password.

7. **My best advice: Put a check mark in the box labeled Start This Connection Automatically.**

This saves some time by not having to repeat these steps later.

8. Click the Next button.

Hopefully, Windows goes out and finds the mystery wireless network. If not, you probably goofed something up; check with the network administrator or the settings on your wireless hub. Otherwise, you're ready to connect.

9. Choose the Connect To option.

Surprise! You thought you were connecting to the network, but you were merely setting things up. Go to the section "Finding an available wireless network in Windows Vista," earlier in this chapter, to complete the connection.

Connecting to an unknown SSID in Windows XP

1. Open the Network Connections window.

2. Right-click the wireless network connection's icon and choose Properties from the pop-up menu.

3. Click the Wireless Networks tab.

4. Click the Add button, near the bottom of the dialog box.

In the Wireless Network Properties dialog box that appears (as shown in Figure 9-10), you can manually configure the connection to the unknown wireless network.

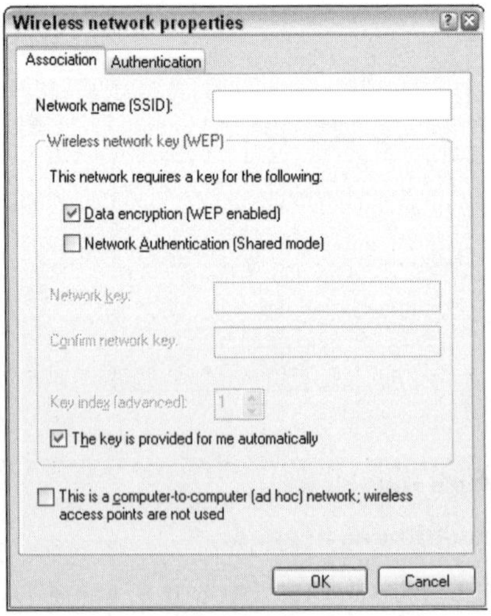

Figure 9-10:
Fill in this dialog box to connect to a wireless network.

5. Type the SSID.

6. Optionally, enter the network key or password.

If the network key box is disabled, as shown in Figure 9-10, another dialog box may appear and prompt you to enter the password.

7. Click OK.

At this point, the network should show up as available in the list. You can then connect to it by clicking its name, as described earlier in this chapter.

"What's my computer's MAC Address?"

Some wireless networks restrict access to only those computers they know. Not having eyeballs, a network needs some other piece of identification to distinguish between computers it knows and utter strangers. That piece of ID is the wireless networking hardware's MAC Address.

A *MAC Address* is a unique number assigned to every networking adapter on planet Earth. No two numbers are identical, and the MAC Address is very difficult to fake. By using the MAC Address, a wireless network can restrict access to only those computers that are known and registered.

- ✔ Know that MAC stands for Media Access Control — like that will make your day any brighter.

- ✔ The MAC Address is 12 digits long, broken up into pairs, like this:

    ```
    12:34:56:78:9A:BC
    ```

    It's a base-16 value (also called *hexadecimal*), so the letters A through F are also considered to be numbers.

- ✔ If the MAC Address is necessary to connect to a specific network, hand it over to the network manager or human in charge. That person will happily add your laptop's address to the list of allowed computers so that you can use the network.

Finding your laptop's MAC address in Windows Vista

1. Open the Control Panel's Network and Sharing Center.

2. Click the link labeled View Status by the connection you want to examine.

A Network Connection Status dialog box appears. At this point, you can continue with Step 4 in the next section.

Finding your laptop's MAC address in Windows XP

1. Open the Network Connections window.

2. Open your Wireless Network Connection icon.

This step displays a Status window.

3. **Click the Support tab.**

4. **Click the Details button.**

   A Network Connection Details dialog box appears. Locate the item labeled Physical Address, which is the MAC Address number.

5. **Copy down that number.**

6. **Close the various dialog boxes, windows, and whatnot.**

Renewing your lease

To keep goofballs out, some networks let you use their services for only a given amount of time. The time allotted is referred to as a *lease*.

What may happen, especially if you use a wireless network for a great length of time, is that your lease may expire. To renew it, you need to disconnect from the network and then reconnect.

The instructions for disconnecting from a wireless network are offered later in this chapter; for now, the simplest way to renew a lease is simply to restart Windows. Refer to Chapter 4.

Accessing a pay service wireless network

Not everything is free. Some people out there have the gall to actually charge you for using their wireless services. Imagine! Darn those capitalists!

I've seen pay wireless access work two ways:

- You pay a cashier, and then he or she hands you a slip of paper with the SSID and a password to use. Then follow the steps in the earlier section "'What if I don't know the SSID?'" for instructions on connecting to the network.

- In the more devious way, the signal appears to be strong and available, and connection isn't a problem. But, when you go to the Internet, the only Web page you see is a sign-up page. Until you fork over your credit card number, you can't go anywhere else on the Internet or access any other service (such as e-mail).

Yep. If it's a pay service, you gotta pony up!

Disconnecting the wireless connection

The main way I disconnect from a wireless connection is to close my laptop's lid. By putting the laptop into Stand By mode, the network connection is broken automatically. Opening the laptop's lid (assuming that I'm within range of the wireless hub) reestablishes the connection.

Likewise, you can also turn off the laptop to disconnect from the wireless network. When you turn on the laptop again, it might mention that it misses being connected to the network. Yeah, life has its letdowns.

- Some laptops have a handy on-off button associated with their wireless networking connections. You can press the button to instantly disconnect from the network by turning off the wireless networking card.

- This technique was just suggested to me: You can start running in any direction. By the time you feel tired, you're probably far enough from the wireless hub that the connection is broken, although breaking a connection in this manner seems extraordinarily silly.

Dropping the wireless connection in Windows Vista

Here's how you can drop a wireless connection in Windows Vista:

1. **Open the Control Panel's Network and Sharing Center.**

   You see the wireless connection displayed in the window, along with all sorts of information and handy links to click, as shown in Figure 9-11.

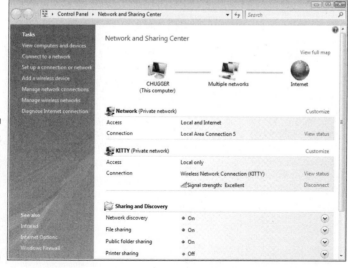

Figure 9-11: Information about the wireless connection in the Network Center.

2. **Click the Disconnect link.**

    It's on the right side of the wireless connection information, at the bottom, as shown in Figure 9-11.

Lo, the connection is gone. Poof!

Dropping the wireless connection in Windows XP

If you must manually disconnect, you need to follow these steps:

1. **Open the Network Connections window.**

2. **Right-click the wireless network connection icon.**

3. **Choose Disable from the pop-up menu.**

    The connection is gone.

Chapter 10

Laptop to Internet, Hello?

. . . .

In This Chapter

▶ Arming yourself for Internet access

▶ Using the network to get on the Internet

▶ Connecting to a DSL or cable modem or to a router

▶ Accessing the Internet through a dialup connection

▶ Configuring the dialup connection

▶ Dialing in to the Internet

▶ Disconnecting a modem connection

▶ Sharing a wireless Internet connection

. . . .

More than the desktop computer, it was the laptop PC that drove the need for online communications. The old Tandy 100 didn't have PC compatibility or even a disk drive, but it did have a modem, and that was enough to sell millions of those units. So, right away, any computer pundit worth his salt could easily predict that the future of laptop computing involved not only portability but communications as well.

Whether by modem or network connection, the most popular way to communicate with today's laptops is by using the Internet. This chapter covers the many ways to connect your laptop to the Internet.

What You Need to Get on the Internet

The Internet is not a computer program. Nor is the Internet a single large computer somewhere. And, no, the Internet is not owned by Bill Gates, though that's one of his most secret desires.

The Internet isn't one computer; it's thousands upon thousands of computers, all connected. Information is stored on many of those computers, and the protocols and methods of the Internet allow your computer, or any other computer connected to the Internet, to access and use that information. Indeed, any computer connected to the Internet is "on" the Internet.

You need five things in order to access the Internet:

- A computer
- A communications device
- Software
- An Internet service provider (ISP)
- Money

The computer, you already have. That's easy.

The communications device that you use to connect to the Internet is either a modem or an Ethernet connection (wired or wireless), both of which are common to modern laptops. Two down!

The software you need in order to access the Internet comes with Windows. The actual connection is carried out by Windows, and then you can use specific programs that come with Windows to access information on the Internet, read e-mail, and so on. Three down!

You connect to the Internet through an ISP. Or, to put it another way, to connect your laptop to the Internet, you must find a computer already connected to the Internet and then connect to the Internet through that computer.

The Internet isn't a single computer; rather, it's a multitude of computers all connected and sharing information and resources.

The ISP can be your office, where your company provides Internet service. Or, you may work for the government or a major crime syndicate, which also provides Internet access. Access can be had through the university you're attending or by a third-party service, as described in the next section.

Finally, you need moolah to get the Internet from an ISP. Like phone service or cable TV, the ISP extracts a given monthly offering in exchange for Internet access. You have to find this money on your own.

- Free Internet access is available in most community libraries, though you must use their computers.
- With wireless networking, it's possible to access the Internet for free by finding an open wireless connection. My local coffeehouse offers free

> wireless Internet access for the price of a cup of joe. (Well, I suppose I'm paying for the joe, but I view the Internet access as free anyway.)
>
> ✔ If you connect to the Internet at work, that connection is also considered more-or-less free. Be aware, though, that many businesses heavily filter their Internet access.

Finding a Good ISP

ISP stands for *Internet service provider*. It's a company that provides you with Internet access, plus maybe other goodies, including telephone support. Obviously, finding a good ISP means having a good Internet experience.

Unless you specifically selected your ISP with portable computing in mind, you probably missed some of the handy and often necessary features that laptop computers need when they're accessing the Internet. Here's my list for some bonus laptop goodies an ISP can offer.

Getting ISP access from all over the country

Internet access is available all over. If you need to specifically access your own ISP, it's preferable to have either a local access number or a toll-free number.

These suggestions are for dialup Internet only:

> ✔ Many national ISPs — such as AOL, EarthLink, and NetZero — have access points all over the country. Before you leave, check to see whether yours has any local access numbers for your destination. That way, you can use your laptop's modem to connect with your ISP just as you do at home.
>
> ✔ In addition to local access, your ISP might also offer a toll-free phone number to connect. Note that you may have to pay a surcharge for accessing this feature.

When you're lucky enough to find an Ethernet Internet connection while you're away, there's no need to use the modem or dial in to your local ISP. As long as your computer is connected to the Internet, you can access your e-mail or browse the Web just as you would normally do.

Checking for Web-based e-mail access

Some ISPs know that you may not always be at one location, so they offer a form of Web-based e-mail. This system allows you to access your e-mail through any computer connected to the Internet. Just navigate to your ISP's Web e-mail page and log in as you normally would. You can then read your e-mail on the Web rather than use an e-mail program.

See Chapter 13 for more e-mail tips and such.

Connecting Your Laptop to the Internet the Ethernet Way

Any laptop configured to access a local area network is also primed and ready to access the Internet. All you need to do is connect to a network that already has an Internet connection. When your laptop is on such a network, it too can access the Internet directly from that network.

For example, if you add your laptop to an existing network, as described in Chapter 9, and that network is connected to the Internet via a DSL or cable modem, your laptop is suddenly on the Internet. Nothing is easier. At that point, you can use your Internet software to browse the Web, pick up e-mail, launch nuclear missiles — or whatever your pleasure.

The same deal holds true for connecting to a public network, such as in a hotel with high-speed Internet access in the room or connecting to a wireless network in a public place or anywhere else Internet access is offered.

Getting on the Internet

You don't need to do anything special to connect to the Internet. As long as your computer is connected directly to the Internet or to a network on the Internet, you're done. Just open any Internet application — Web browser, e-mail, and so on — and you're ready to go.

Furthermore, you don't need to officially log off or disconnect from the Internet, though you will be disconnected from it when your laptop falls asleep (is in Stand By mode) or is turned off or when you yank out the Ethernet plug.

✔ Being "on" the Internet merely means that your laptop is connected to another computer that's already on the Internet. The Internet is just a bunch of computers all connected with each other.

 ✔ Internet software commonly includes a Web browser, such as Internet Explorer, and an e-mail program. There are other Internet programs as well — dozens, in fact — ranging from things you've heard of to things only nerds know and love.

Connecting your laptop directly to a DSL or cable modem

When it's just you, your laptop, and a DSL or cable modem, the laptop connects directly to the modem by using an Ethernet cable and your laptop's Ethernet connection.

The specific configuration is done either directly by your DSL or cable provider or the information for making the connection is provided in a pamphlet.

If you're on your own, refer to the information that came with the DSL or cable modem for the specifics. Usually, an illustration tells you exactly what you need, plugging what into what.

Connecting to a router

Very often, a device called a *router* sits between the DSL or cable modem and your computer or the rest of the network. The router is designed to provide an interface between the Internet and your local network. The router takes care of most of the more confusing networking options for you; plus, it provides *firewall* protection between the computers on your network and the rest of the wild, nasty Internet.

Physically, the router is situated between your computer and the Internet connection or broadband modem, as shown in Figure 10-1. In this setup, your laptop would connect directly to the router, not to the modem. (In fact, all computers on the local network connect to the router, not directly to the modem.)

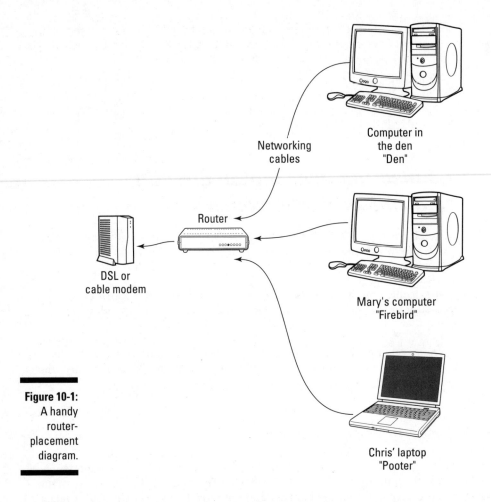

**Computer in
the den
"Den"**

**Networking
cables**

Router

**DSL or
cable modem**

**Mary's computer
"Firebird"**

Figure 10-1:
A handy
router-
placement
diagram.

**Chris' laptop
"Pooter"**

Yea, verily, even in a wireless setting, the connection is the same. In fact, a wireless router connects by wire to the high-speed modem. Then the rest of the computers on the wireless network connect wirelessly to the router. Figure 10-2 illustrates the shocking, wireless difference.

- ✔ Router rhymes with *chowder*. Do not pronounce it "ROO-ter."

- ✔ Broadband means *high speed*.

- ✔ A firewall is a form of protection, guarding your computer from unwanted access by other computers on the Internet. See Chapter 12 for more information.

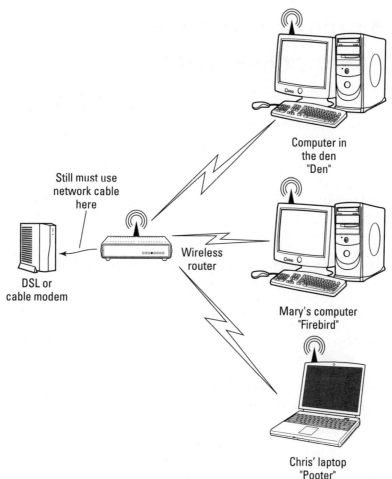

Computer in
the den
"Den"

Still must use
network cable
here

Mary's computer
"Firebird"

Wireless
router

DSL or
cable modem

Figure 10-2:
A handy
wireless
router
placement
diagram.

Chris' laptop
"Pooter"

✔ I highly recommend setting up your computer network for sharing an Internet connection as shown in this section. Use a router. Get a good one that offers firewall protection. Connect the router to the modem, and then connect all the computers on the network to the router.

✔ Routers are configured by logging in to them. The router has an IP address, and you use your Web browser software, such as Internet Explorer, to connect to the router, log in, and set the configurations. Instructions for doing this come with the router.

✔ See Chapter 12 for more information on Internet security.

Dialing Into the Internet the Old-Fashioned Way

Even if you've gotten used to the warm, comfy waters of high-speed Internet access, there might be a time when you need to pull out that old modem and use a 19th century technology to access the 20th century Internet on your 21st century laptop. It happens.

Yes, the modem needs to be connected to a phone jack to make dialup networking work! Get a phone cable and connect it to the phone jacks on the wall and your laptop. For more information on using your laptop's modem, see Chapter 11.

Configuring a dialup connection

Setting up your laptop for a dialup, or modem, Internet connection is something you have to do manually. Unlike with the Ethernet thing, you cannot just plug and go. As you're probably getting used to, the methods for configuring dialup access differ between Windows Vista and Windows XP. But, overall, you're configuring the same basic things:

- ✔ Your ISP's name (used to identify the dialup connection)
- ✔ The connection's phone number
- ✔ The username for your ISP account
- ✔ The password for your ISP account

Your ISP, or whichever outfit is giving you Internet access, provides this information for you. You then use the tidbits to configure the Internet connection per whichever convoluted way the operating system demands.

- ✔ Connect the laptop's modem to a phone jack before you dial the Internet!

- ✔ There are more options for dialing a phone number with a modem than most people would dare to dream of. Don't fuss over the options now; wait to read about the details in Chapter 11.

- ✔ When you're using more than one ISP, you need one dialup connection icon for each.

- ✔ AOL uses its own system to connect to the Internet. Refer to the AOL documentation for information on setting it up; I don't cover AOL in this book.

Setting up a dialup connection in Windows Vista

1. **Choose Connect To from the Start button menu.**

2. **Choose the item Set Up a Connection or Network.**

   A list of various things you can set up appears.

3. **Select the item in the list labeled Set Up a Dial-Up Connection.**

4. **Click the Next button.**

5. **Fill in the information as given to you by your ISP: the phone number, your account name, and your password.**

   The username and password here are those used to get into your ISP's account. They may be different from the username and password used to access your e-mail inbox, and definitely not the same as the logon and password you use for Windows.

6. **Place a check mark by the option Remember This Password.**

7. **Type a name for the connection.**

   My ISP is named CompuSoft, so I type CompuSoft in the box.

8. **Click the Connect button.**

   Windows uses your modem to test-dial the phone number that's listed.

If all goes well, you should be connected to the Internet. To dial up the Internet by using the modem in the future, see the section "Making the dialup connection," later in this chapter.

Setting up a dialup connection in Windows XP

Windows XP uses the New Connection Wizard to complete the setup process for a dialup Internet connection. Here's how that goes:

1. **Choose Start⇨All Programs⇨Accessories⇨Communications⇨New Connection Wizard.**

2. **Quickly ignore all printed text on the screen and click the Next button.**

3. **Select the Connect to the Internet option and click the Next button.**

4. **Select the Set Up My Connection Manually option and click the Next button.**

5. **Select the Connect Using a Dial-up Modem option and click the Next button.**

6. **Enter your ISP's name, and then click the Next button.**

   It doesn't have to be your ISP's name. This name is used to identify the connection's icon. You can use any name you like, proper or profane.

7. **Enter the phone number to connect to your ISP.**

   This is the phone number for the connection, not for its office or help line.

8. **Enter your account's username.**

   This name is supplied by your ISP. This isn't the logon ID you use for Windows XP (though they could be the same).

9. **Enter your account's password, first in the Password text box and then in the Confirm Password text box.**

   I have no idea why they do this.

10. **Click the Next button.**

11. **Click the Finish button.**

    Windows churns. Windows chugs. And the wizard goes away.

What? You were expecting more? Be thankful. I've known wizards that go on for weeks. In any event, the dialup connection has been set. The next step is to use it.

Making the dialup connection

A broadband connection — DSL, cable, or satellite — is also known as an *always-on* connection. As long as your laptop is connected to the broadband modem, or is connected to a network sharing the modem, you can access the Internet any time you want. 'Taint so for a dialup connection.

Before you do anything, ensure that your laptop is properly wired to the phone jack. The cord must plug in to the modem hole on your laptop and into a phone jack on the wall or else piggy-back on some other telephonic device.

The easiest way to connect to the Internet is to simply open or use an Internet program. For example, start up Internet Explorer to browse the Web, or tell your e-mail program to fetch new mail. Either action forces the laptop to look for an Internet connection, by either connecting automatically or presenting a list of connections for you to choose.

You can also manually make the dialup connection, as described in the sections that follow.

After the connection has been made, the little modem buddies appear in the notification area, as shown in Figure 10-3. They're your clue that you're connected to the Internet. You can now use any Internet software.

Figure 10-3:
The modem
buddies
happily
report that a
connection
has been
made.

> ✔ Yes, the connection speed you see may be much lower than what your modem is capable of. The speed depends on the quality of the connection and the phone lines connecting your laptop to the ISP.

> ✔ Rarely, if ever, have I connected at any speed higher than 49 Kbps.

> ✔ Rumor has it that the phone company guarantees connection speeds of only 14.4 Kbps. In some areas, that's as good as it gets.

> ✔ Do not plug your modem into a digital phone system! It will fry your modem's gizzard! Digital phone systems are common in hotels and medium- to large-size businesses. When in doubt, ask!

Dialing up the Internet in Windows Vista

1. **From the Start menu, choose the Connect To item.**

   The Connect to a Network window appears, listing the various and potential ways for your laptop to find the Internet or any other network. In the list are Dial-up and VPN options, which is what you're looking for.

2. **Choose the dialup connection.**

   Its name was chosen when you set things up.

3. **Click the Connect button.**

   Windows dials the modem and attempts to make the connection.

Dialing up the Internet in Windows XP

1. **Open the Network Connections window.**

   Refer to Chapter 6 for directions.

2. **Double-click the dialup Internet connection icon that you want to use.**

   In some instances, you see the Connect dialog box here as you attempt to dial out to the Internet.

3. **Click the Dial button to make the connection.**

Don't forget to disconnect the dialup connection!

Unlike the always-on broadband connections, a dialup connection must officially be disconnected when you're done using the Internet. Just as you said "Hello," you must always say "Goodbye." This is something you may forget, especially when you use dialup on the road and have broadband at home.

The simplest way to disconnect the modem from the Internet is to right-click the little modem guys in the notification area. Choose the Disconnect command from the context menu that pops up.

You can also just double-click the modem guys, which displays a Status dialog box, similar to the one shown in Figure 10-4. From there, you can click the Disconnect button to end your Internet session.

Figure 10-4: Connection status, trivia, and stuff like that.

Connecting to Another PC That Has Internet Access

This has happened a few times to me, so I'm guessing that it may happen to others: You're at some trendy wireless location, working on your laptop and sipping an overpriced cup of legal stimulant. You're okay because you bought this book and a laptop with wireless networking built in. But your companion has a mere mortal laptop with only an Ethernet connection. Can you help your poor friend?

Well, obviously, the answer depends on how much you like your friend! If he's buying the coffee, you can help out by sharing your wireless Internet connection. This involves two steps.

First, connect your laptop with the nonwireless laptop by using a standard Ethernet cable. You have one of those in your laptop bag because you read Chapter 22.

Second, you need to share your Internet connection. Yes, this is different for each version of Windows, as described in this section.

After everything is connected, your buddy should instantly be on the Internet. He can test it by opening his Web browser and navigating to some Web site. After profusely thanking you, simply recommend that he get this book — not *borrow* your copy, but buy his own! He'll be ever thankful.

Here's how you can help your nonwireless friend get on the Internet. First, ensure that he buys a fresh round of beverages. Then follow these steps:

1a. In Windows Vista, open the Control Panel's Network Center icon.

1b. In Windows XP, open the Control Panel's Network Connections icon; skip to Step 3.

2. In Windows Vista (only), on the left side of the window, click the link that says Manage Network Connections.

3. Right-click your laptop's Wireless Network Connection icon, the one you're using presently to get on the Internet.

4. Choose Properties from the pop-up menu.

If you see a User Account Control warning in Windows Vista, click the Allow button.

5. **In the network connection's Properties dialog box, click the Sharing tab.**

6. **Put a check mark by the box that says Allow Other Network Users to Connect through This Computer's Internet Connection.**

7. **Click OK, and close the Control Panel window.**

At this point, your buddy should be able to get on the Internet by using the direct Ethernet connection to your laptop.

Chapter 11

A Very Merry Modem

*Y*ears ago, modems were an expensive and technical peripheral, truly one of the most optional components of the desktop computer. Modems were for true nerds or communications freaks. But the laptop was another story. Laptops need communications. They need to speak with the desktop, by making contact while on the road every so often with the mothership. On a laptop, the modem was always a necessity. Only with the dawn of the Internet did the modem find a permanent place in the desktop computer.

As the era of broadband Internet access enters its peak, once again desktop computers are being sold without modems; as long as the desktop has Ethernet networking, modems are no longer necessary. That's not true for a laptop, where the modem remains able and ready if you once again need to phone home. You may never use it. You may use it all the time. Either way, this chapter covers all the merry modem nonsense you need to know.

The Modem Hardware

Modems come in many types. There are broadband modems, which help bridge the gap between your laptop and the Internet, either via cable, DSL, or satellite. But those aren't true modems in the traditional sense. No, you need a dial-up modem, one of the old types that once connected digital computers to the analog phone system.

Modems come standard as part of your laptop, integrated right into the main circuitry board, the *motherboard.* To connect the modem to the phone system, you use a standard telephone cord, by plugging one end into a phone jack and the other into your laptop.

The gauge of a modem is its speed; however, since the mid-1990s, nearly all dial-up modems are of the 56 Kbps variety. That means that the modem can send or receive information at about 56,000 bps, or bits per second. That's about seven pages of text a second, which is relatively slow.

✔ The only part of the modem you're likely to see is the hole, or *jack,* into which the phone cord plugs. Refer to Chapter 5 for information on locating the thing.

✔ Some laptops may have two modem holes or jacks. One is used to connect the laptop to the phone jack on the wall. That's the *line* jack. The second hole can be used to connect a phone. That's the *phone* jack. That way, you can still use the phone without having to unplug the modem.

✔ No, you cannot use the phone while the computer is online.

✔ The computer makes phone calls just like a human does: It dials a number, and then it screeches its unmelodic tones at the other computer, which also screeches back.

✔ Long-distance charges apply to modem calls just as they do to regular phone calls. Hotel surcharges apply as well.

✔ Some countries charge extra for modem-made phone calls. When you're traveling overseas, be sure to inquire about any extra fees before you use the phone.

✔ On the rare chance that your laptop lacks a modem, you can readily find a modem PC Card.

✔ *Modem* is a contraction of *mo*dulator-*dem*odulator. The electronic (digital) signal from the modem is modulated into an audio (analog) signal for the phone line. Likewise, a modulated analog signal is demodulated by the modem back into digital information for the computer. Or something like that.

Where the Modem Dwells in Windows

You probably cannot locate the modem's hardware inside the laptop, beyond the phone jack. That's not an issue. To control the modem, you must locate the spot in Windows where you can use software to set up the modem's hardware.

Here's how to find the modem in Windows:

1. **Open the Control Panel's Phone and Modem Options icon.**

   You see one of two dialog boxes. If you haven't yet set up your laptop's location, you see what's shown in Figure 11-1. If so, continue with Step 2.

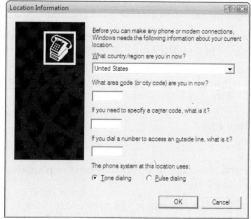

Figure 11-1: Windows demands to know where your laptop dwells most of the time.

   When you see a Phone and Modems Options dialog box that does not look the one shown in Figure 11-1, you're all set. Skip to Step 3.

2. **Fill in your initial location information.**

   You have to answer five questions. These help Windows configure the modem for dialing out. The questions must be answered according to where you'll keep the laptop most often, such as in your home or maybe at the office.

   a. **What country/region are you in now?** Choose your country from the list.

   b. **What area code (or city code) are you in now?** Enter the proper numbers.

   c. **If you need to specify a carrier code, what is it?** If you understand this question, type the proper numbers; otherwise, leave the box empty.

   d. **If you dial a number to access an outside line, what it is?** For example, if you need to dial an 8 or a 9 to escape the local PBX, enter that number; otherwise, leave the box empty.

   To insert a pause in dialing, use the comma. For example, if you have to dial 9 and then pause, type **9,** in the box.

   e. **The phone system at this location uses:** Check Tone Dialing or Pulse Dialing.

   Click OK to continue.

3. **Click the Modems tab.**

   A list of any modem (or modems) installed in your computer is shown.

4. **Select your laptop's modem from the list.**

   Yeah, it's probably the only one in the list.

5. **Click the Properties button.**

   A Properties dialog box appears for your modem. Adjustments to the modem are made according to the sections that follow.

On the odd chance that Windows Vista doesn't let you display the modem's Properties dialog box directly, use this workaround:

1. **Open the Device Manager.**

   Refer to Chapter 6 for the details.

2. **Double-click the word Modems to open that hardware category and display the laptop's modem.**

   The modem name is given by manufacturer make and model.

3. **Double-click the modem's name.**

   The modem's Properties dialog box is displayed.

The advice throughout this section uses the modem's Properties dialog box.

Setting the modem's volume

Most people like to hear the modem make its noise as an online connection is being made. Some folks dislike the noise. Others can't even hear the noise. All three of these issues are addressed in the same location: the Modems tab in your laptop's Modem Properties dialog box.

Use the slider, shown in Figure 11-2, to set the modem's volume. Loud is on the right. Soft is toward the left. Off is all the way over on the left. The new volume setting takes effect the next time you use the modem to dial out. Click the OK button to make the setting permanent.

Adding special modem-command settings

Some ISPs require you to give the modem special commands. This is done to improve the connection or, often, to troubleshoot a bad connection. The settings are entered into a text box labeled Enter Initialization Commands, on the Advanced tab of the modem's Properties dialog box.

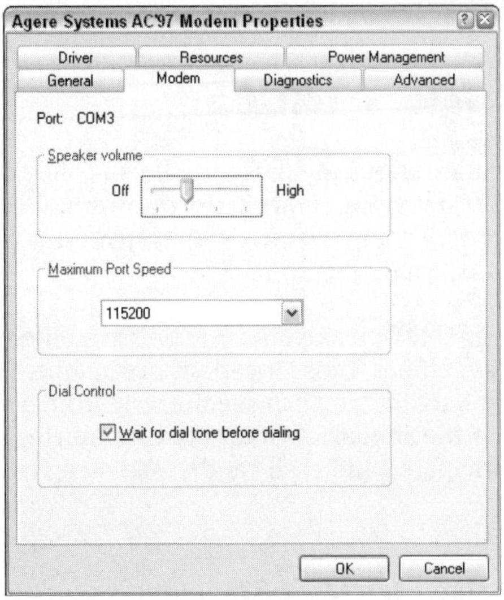

Figure 11-2:
Putting a
sock in it.

Suppose that you're told to use the modem command ATS58=33 to help set up the laptop's modem. If so, type that text into the box *exactly* as written. Click the OK button to close the dialog box and make this change permanent.

Disabling the modem

Because I don't often use my laptop's modem, I like to turn it off or disable it. That way, the computer isn't supplying power to a device that I don't use. The easiest way to do this is to click the Power Management tab in the modem's Properties dialog box. Choose the option labeled Allow the Computer to Turn Off This Device to Save Power.

On my laptop, the Allow the Computer to Turn Off This Device to Save Power option is dimmed and I cannot check it. My laptop's hardware is too dumb, therefore, to manage the modem's power. All hope isn't lost: You can still disable the modem's hardware permanently. Just click the General tab in the modem's Properties dialog box.

At the bottom of the modem's Properties dialog box, on the General tab, is the Device Usage option. From the drop-down list, choose Do Not Use This Device

(Disable). That tells Windows to ignore the modem, which means that you save power and that you cannot use the modem to connect to another computer or to the Internet or to send a fax (unless, of course, you enable the modem).

Dialing Outof Strange Places

Offbeat hotel rooms. Dank coffee shops at 4:00 a.m. The so-called business lounge in the Kinshasa airport. Even the Hyatt in downtown Indianapolis. No, these aren't places frequented by some dashing young spy. They're places you may find yourself with a laptop trying to make a phone call.

The laptop's portability implies that you may find yourself in a different environment every time you use it. Sometimes, those locations are unique. Sometimes, they're the same, such as that bargain "you can see the strip from here" Vegas hotel you keep returning to for the annual footwear convention. Regardless, Windows has these needs anticipated and easily addressed. Keep reading.

Location, location, location

Your laptop is mobile. It can be anywhere. There is no guarantee that your laptop will be at the same hotel in the same city every time you take it on the road. Now, maybe you will come back. If so, you can take advantage of that repeat visit by creating a dialing location in Windows. Or, even if you don't plan on coming back, creating a dialing location saves time every time you need to use the laptop's dialup modem.

Follow these steps:

1. **Open the Phone and Modem Options icon in the Control Panel.**

   The first question you're asked the first time you open this icon is to enter the main location. (Refer to the section "Where the Modem Dwells in Windows," earlier in this chapter.) After you fill in that information, the Phone and Modem Options dialog box appears, as shown in Figure 11-3. It has three tabs: Dialing Rules, Modems, and Advanced.

   The Dialing Rules tab is used to list the locations where you use your laptop. My Location is your home base, so why not edit its name to something more appropriate?

2. **Highlight the My Location item on the Dialing Rules tab.**

   If you're just starting out, My Location is the only location. Later on, as you create locations, you can use these steps to modify them in case you ever visit that spot with your laptop again.

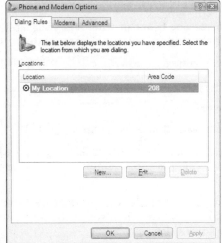

Figure 11-3:
The Phone
and Modem
Options
dialog box.

3. Click the Edit button.

The Edit Location dialog box appears, as shown in Figure 11-4. It allows you to customize the way the modem dials the phone, depending on your location.

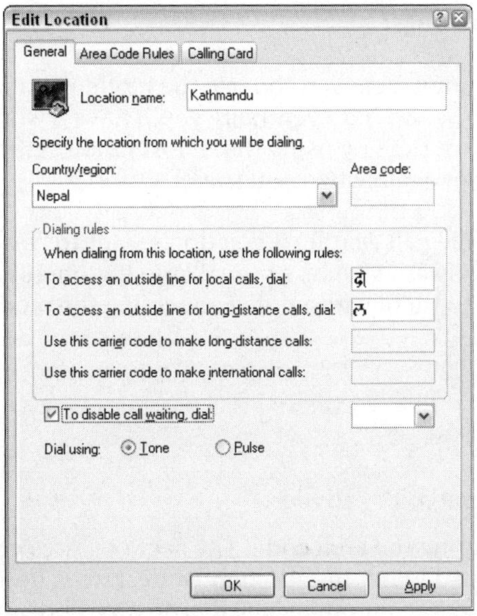

Figure 11-4:
Interesting
phone stuff
about your
location.

4. **Enter a name for your current location.**

   For example, enter Home or The Office or wherever your laptop is right now. If you're at the San Jose Hilton, enter that name instead.

5. **Select whichever country you're in now.**

6. **Enter the area code.**

7. **Fill in the Dialing Rules area.**

   You can leave these items blank if none is required.

   If your hotel requires you to dial an 8 before making a local call, and a 9 for making a long-distance call, put those numbers into the appropriate boxes.

8. **To disable call waiting while the modem is online, select the To Disable Call Waiting Dial check box. Then select the proper code sequence from the drop-down list.**

   The call waiting signal disconnects an active modem connection. You select this box to disable call waiting on a per-phone-call basis.

9. **Finally, select whether your connection requires tone or (the antique) pulse dialing.**

   You need to select the Pulse option only if your area is limited to pulse dialing. You'll be painfully aware of this annoyance; otherwise, you can choose Tone.

10. **Click OK to save the settings.**

Windows uses this information whenever you use the modem. It may seem silly to enter this information now, but eventually you'll have a whole collection of locations. You can save time by using that information rather than have to enter it over and over again when you travel.

✔ You don't need to disable call waiting if you don't want to. Various software programs and hardware gizmos are available that monitor incoming calls and alert you to them without disconnecting the modem. Check out the following sites:

```
www.catchacall.com
www.buzme.com
www.callwave.com
```

✔ If you use AOL, check out AOL Call Alert.

✔ Don't worry about entering the area code. The section "Area code madness! To dial or not to dial," later in this chapter, describes how and when you can direct the modem to automatically dial an area code for you.

Creating a new location

Come fly with me! Let's fly, let's fly away. . . .

Say you're off again in that cheesy Vegas hotel for a convention. Or, you're at your summer place, two houses away from the ocean, but if you stand on a stool and crane your neck, you can see the water. Or, you're away at college. Any time you set up shop in a new location, you need to tell the laptop's modem about it.

You have to enter this location and dialing information only if you're using the modem. If you're using an Ethernet connection to access the Internet, don't bother! Otherwise, create a new location.

To set up a new location, use the Phone and Modem Options dialog box as I describe in the previous section: Start with Step 3 and click the New button rather than the Edit button. Then continue with the steps, and enter the information as necessary for your new location.

Click the OK button when you're done. Then, in the Phone and Modem Options dialog box, be sure to select the location you just created so that Windows uses that location's dialing rules.

Area code madness! To dial or not to dial

For each location you set up, there will be various dialing rules. There will also be various headache-inducing area code rules.

Don't sweat it! You need to enter area code rules only if you need to use area codes when you dial your modem. When you're calling only one number and it's local to wherever you are, you can forget about the area code rules. When you call several numbers, however, and some require you to dial the area code and others do not, you can let Windows manage the hassle of when to dial the area code or when to dial the number the way you entered it.

To make area code modifications, obey these steps:

1. **Choose your current location in the Phone and Modem Options dialog box.**

2. **Click the Edit button.**

3. **In the Edit Location dialog box, click the Area Code Rules tab.**

4. **Click the New button to create a new rule.**

The New Area Code Rule dialog box appears, as shown in Figure 11-5. Here's how this works:

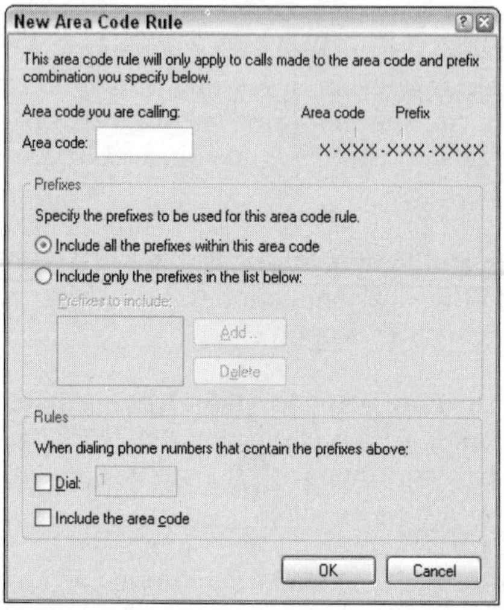

Figure 11-5:
Making up a
new area
code rule.

If you're calling into another area code and you must always dial 1 plus that area code, fill in the dialog box like this:

a. Enter the alien area code.

b. Click the Include All the Prefixes within This Area Code radio button.

c. Select the Dial check box and enter **1** into the box.

This step assumes that you dial 1 before dialing into another area code.

d. Select the Include the Area Code check box.

If you're calling locally and you need to enter the area code for only certain prefixes — the so-called local long-distance prefixes, or when you live in a large area covered by one area code and certain prefixes are long distance, fill in the dialog box like this:

a. Enter your own area code.

b. Click the Include Only the Prefixes in the List Below radio button.

Don't open the phone book and enter all the prefixes! Enter only those you have to dial. For example, in my area code, prefix 334 is local long distance, and I have to dial the area code.

c. Click the Add button.

   d. Type one or more prefixes into the box and click OK.

      You have to enter only those prefixes that the modem will be dialing.

   e. Select the Dial check box and enter **1** into the text box.

   f. Select the Include the Area Code check box.

Finally, if you have to always dial the area code, do this:

   a. Enter your own area code.

   b. Click the Include All the Prefixes within This Area Code radio button.

   c. Select the Dial check box and enter **1** into the text box.

   d. Select the Include the Area Code check box.

Every time you dial any local number, the modem automatically prefixes 1 and your area code to the number.

5. Click OK to add the new rule.

6. Repeat Steps 4 and 5 to create as many rules as necessary.

To put these dialing rules into effect, you need to select the Use Dialing Rules check box whenever you enter a new phone number for the modem to dial.

Yes, you can ignore and forget about all these things! You merely have to type the full number to dial every time you set up a new modem connection. But, if you're dialing a lot of numbers in different locations, setting up the rules can make things far easier.

Automatically using a calling card

The last tab in the Edit Location dialog box is for entering calling card information. This tab allows Windows to automatically blast out the calling card information as the modem connects, allowing you to charge, for example, a specific call at a business center to your company's credit card.

To enter calling card information, edit the Location information as described in the previous sections. Click the Calling Card tab, and you see a bunch of options. Fill them in with the information you need in order to use the calling card, and leave irrelevant items blank.

✔ If your card isn't listed in the Card Types list, click the New button. Then you can use the quite detailed dialog box that appears to enter information about your credit or calling card.

✔ Yes, this information is obviously sensitive. See Chapter 16 for information on laptop security.

Finding the Various Disconnect Timeouts

One of the sorrows of using a modem is that it occasionally decides to hang up on you. This can happen for a multitude of reasons: noise on the line, call waiting, or a timeout value setting in Windows.

Windows uses timeout values to ensure that people who fall asleep when they're online don't continue to tie up the phone lines. Ditto for people who wander away from their computers or, more often, die online. The timeout senses that no activity has taken place for a spell, and then it simply up and disconnects the modem.

You have two places to check modem timeout settings. The first is on the modem itself. The second is for the connection you've made. Having two settings means that you can set different timeouts for each connection and also have a general timeout.

The general timeout

The general modem timeout value is set in the modem's Properties dialog box. Refer to the directions earlier in this chapter for displaying that dialog box. Once you're there, heed these directions:

1. **Click the Advanced tab.**

2. **Click the Change Default Preferences button.**

3. **Select the Disconnect a Call If Idle for More Than check box and enter a timeout value into the text box.**

    Yes, if you leave this item unchecked, no general timeout takes place.

4. **Click OK and close the various open dialog boxes.**

Timeouts for each session

Timeouts are also set for each connection you make with the modem. These connections are discussed in Chapter 10; refer to that chapter for details beyond what's mentioned here. Follow these steps:

1a. In Windows Vista, choose Connect To from the Start menu.

1b. In Windows XP, open the Network Connections window.

2. Right-click the dial-up connection you want to modify.

3. Choose Properties from the pop-up menu.

4. Click the Options tab in the Properties dialog box.

5. Set the timeout value by the item titled Idle Time before Hanging Up.

6. Click OK and close the various open dialog boxes and windows.

Putting the Fax in Fax/Modem

Your modem may be called a mere *modem,* but its secret identity is *fax/modem.* In the early 1990s, modem manufacturers discovered that it was devilishly easy to put standard fax technology into a computer modem. The result is a device that not only lets computers chitty-chat, but also lets them chitty-chat with fax machines.

✔ There's no need to confirm anything! Trust me, your laptop's modem can send and receive faxes.

✔ The following sections describe how to use the faxing facility inside Windows. Other faxing programs are available that you might find easier to use and manage than what Windows offers. Visit your local Software-O-Rama to see the variety.

✔ Not every version of Windows Vista comes with faxing software.

✔ The faxing facility described in this chapter might be available only if the Microsoft Office suite of programs has been installed on your laptop. I'm not really sure about this, seeing as how I can't find a laptop without Office installed to verify it.

✔ Faxes are a bit antique when you think about it. The e-mail attachment has supplanted the fax as the standard way documents are sent these days. Even so, I recognize that the legal and medical communities continue to use faxes. So, it's obvious that I just can't wiggle out of writing about this stuff.

✔ See Chapter 13 for more information on e-mail.

Setting up the fax modem

A fax machine is really nothing more than a remote printer. Although it's the modem's hardware that carries out the faxing, you need to look for your computer's fax machine in the list of Printers: Open the Control Panel's Printers or Printers and Faxes icon.

- ✔ If you see a fax machine or anything named Fax in the list of printers, you're all ready to go.

- ✔ Note that although the fax machine appears as an icon in the list of printers, you don't use that icon to send a fax. That subject is covered in the next section.

- ✔ If you don't see a fax machine in Windows Vista, your copy of Windows Vista may not come with faxing abilities; get a third-party fax program for your modem.

- ✔ To add the fax printer to Windows XP, click the link, on the left side of the Printers and Faxes window, that says Install a Local Fax Printer. Heed the directions to complete the task.

To send a fax

Faxing works just like printing does, although the printer is a fax machine you connect to by using your laptop's modem. So, sending a fax starts with the standard printing operation. Do this:

1. **Prepare the document you want to fax.**

   You can fax from any application that has a Print command on the File menu.

2. **Choose File➪Print, or use whichever command prints a document in your application.**

   Do not click the Print button on the toolbar! That often just prints the document on whatever "default" printer you selected. If the default printer is the fax machine, fine. Otherwise, beware!

3. **Choose the fax modem as your printer.**

   If you don't see the fax machine sitting there, it hasn't yet been set up. Refer to the previous section.

4. **Make any other selections as needed in the Print dialog box.**

   For example, set which pages to print, the number of copies, and other options as they're available in the dialog box.

5. Click the Print button.

> If this is your first time to send a fax, you're asked to set up the fax connection. Be sure to use your laptop's modem, not a remote fax server. Work through the steps to set up the fax modem thing, which should be painless and quick.

What happens next depends on your version of Windows. In Windows Vista, faxing works more like sending an e-mail message. In Windows XP, various steps are required in order to create address book entries and other nonsense. Sadly, you must wade through this junk to send your fax.

In many instances, finding and clicking a Send button sends your fax immediately. Simply enter the destination phone number and click the Send button, and the fax should be on its way.

Fax Central

To observe all the fast-paced, thrilling fax action as it happens (or even after the fact), visit Fax Central in Windows. To get there, open the Printers or Printers and Faxes icon in the Control Panel. Then double-click to open the Fax icon.

In Windows Vista, you see the Windows Fax and Scan window.

In Windows XP, the Fax Console is displayed.

For both versions of Windows, Fax Central resembles an e-mail program of sorts, with an inbox for incoming faxes and an outbox for faxes you sent. You can even go hog wild and create subfolders and organize your faxes and just have a merry time of it.

Fax Central is also where you can cancel a fax, if you have a modem or connection problem. Simply locate the fax by opening the Outbox folder. Click to select the fax, and press the Delete key on your laptop's keyboard. This is necessary because simply unplugging the phone cord from the fax modem merely delays sending the fax.

Receiving a fax

When you're aware of a thundering fax speeding your way, summon the Fax Central window, as described in the previous section. Ensure that the modem is connected. Wait for the ring (if you have another phone attached to the incoming line). Then choose Tools⇨Receive a Fax Now (in Windows Vista) or File⇨Receive a Fax Now (in Windows XP).

Sit and wait. *Doh-dee-doh-do.*

After the fax has been received, a pop-up bubble may appear, or you may notice the little Pending Fax Guy in the notification area. That's your clue that a fax has come in.

Any fax that's received appears in the Inbox — just like e-mail. To view the fax, double-click its icon or select the fax and then click the View button on the toolbar. The fax is displayed in a special window, from which you can print, save, or mess with the fax.

Faxes are received as *image* files. Specifically, they're TIFF images. You cannot edit the files as text documents. Faxes are *images*.

Chapter 12

Internet Security

*W*hen those few dignified scientists (and Al Gore) sat down years ago to design the Internet, they didn't say, "Hey! What can we do to be lax about security so that our invention can induce terror, frustration, and heartache into its millions of users?" No, they probably said, "Hey! This is cool!" You see, unlike on television, scientists in the real world are not evil, and rarely do they go "Bwaa-ha-ha!"

The Internet was designed to work and to survive a nuclear attack. Thanks to those well-intentioned, ethical, and honest scientists, though, they didn't anticipate the full impact that humanity and its rabble would inflict upon their innocent invention. The Internet can survive a nuclear attack, most certainly; but when a 14-year old antisocial hacker cops an attitude, the Internet is definitely in peril.

Today, the words *Internet* and *security* go together like ants and picnics, 40-year-old fat guys and cats, and Texas and big hair. If you're using your laptop as a doorway to the Internet, be prepared to get a nice, heavy door and some solid, reliable locks. This chapter covers the ins and outs of online security.

General laptop security is the domain of Chapter 16.

The Four Horsemen of Internet Protection

Many disastrous things can happen to your computer on the Internet. Like in real life, however, most disaster can be avoided by cautiousness. In fact, most of the truly nasty things that come from the Internet happen because people are plain gullible. So, it helps to stay vigilant, as well as to have some protection.

The best protection you can afford are four warriors to help you stem the tide of Internet nastiness. These come in the form of special programs, also called *tools* or *utilities*, to arm you and your laptop against an attack:

✔ A firewall

✔ Antivirus software

✔ Anti-spyware software

✔ Anti-hijacking software

A *firewall* is used to filter Internet traffic both coming into and going out of your computer. The firewall protects you against nasty programs that can take over your computer and carry out evil or flood your laptop with unwanted junk.

Antivirus software protects your laptop against special programs called *viruses* or *worms*. These programs take over your computer, often destroying data and erasing files. Some worms scour the hard drive for passwords and credit card numbers, and then send off that information to be used by the bad guys. Some viruses use your e-mail list to mail copies of themselves to all your friends. O! It's nastiness in the worst form!

Anti-spyware software helps protect your computer against programs that quite literally spy on your Internet activity. The Web sites you visit are monitored, and as a result, specific advertising is flooded into your computer.

Hijacking software is used to take control over your Web browsing adventures. What happens is that you may want to visit one Web page, but instead are hijacked and taken to another Web page. Often, you cannot visit anywhere you want to go and are always taken back to some advertising-infested Web page. It can be very frustrating.

The sections in this chapter tell you more about these nasty things on the Internet, and specifically what you can do on your laptop to fight them.

Between the two versions of Windows covered in this book, Windows Vista is far more Internet-safe than its predecessor, Windows XP. If your laptop can stand the upgrade, I highly recommend going with Windows Vista simply for security's sake.

Behind the Firewall

In my opinion, the most important tool you can use on your laptop is a firewall.

In the real world, a firewall is a specially constructed part of a building designed to impede the progress of a fire. The firewall is constructed so that a raging blaze takes a given amount of time to burn through the wall, thereby saving the entire building from combustion. The firewall acts as protection for whatever lies on the other side.

In your computer, a *firewall* provides similar protection, keeping nasty things from the Internet from either coming into your laptop or escaping from the laptop. This item is necessary because your computer is connected to the Internet in dozens of ways. Each connection is referred to as a *port.* Each of those ports is designed to communicate information in a specific way or for a specific type of program.

The problem with a standard Internet connection is that all the ports are left hanging open. And, just like leaving all the windows open in your house, eventually a bad guy will come waltzing into the unprotected environment.

Just like a real firewall, a computer firewall either closes off specific ports completely or allows only the stuff you specify to access and use the ports. That's the good news. What's better is that Windows comes with firewall software to help protect you. What's better than that is that you can easily find software from other sources that works even better than Windows own firewall.

✔ Without a firewall in place, your computer is wide open to attack from any number of nasties on the Internet.

✔ No, it isn't up to your ISP to protect you from such things.

✔ The best firewall is a hardware firewall. Most decent routers come with such a feature and are more than capable of defending your Internet connection, as well as all computers on the router's network, from incoming attacks.

✔ When you have a hardware firewall on a router, there's no need to run a redundant software firewall in Windows.

✔ The survival time of an unprotected, non-firewalled Windows computer on the Internet averages just 13 minutes. After that time, your laptop *will be* infected and overrun by nasty programs sent from the Internet.

Behold Windows Firewall

Windows comes with firewall software. The best firewall software comes with Windows Vista. Windows XP Service Pack 2 comes with a fine firewall, but still one that's limited in its ability to detect and filter *outgoing* Internet traffic. (A good firewall should filter both incoming and outgoing traffic.) Windows XP, the original version, has a firewall that is next to useless.

The Windows Firewall is accessed from the Control Panel, by using an icon curiously named Windows Firewall.

In Windows Vista, opening the Control Panel's Windows Firewall displays a Windows Firewall window, which summarizes how the firewall is working. In that window, click on the Change Settings link to see the Windows Firewall dialog box, shown in Figure 12-1.

In Windows Vista, opening the Windows Firewall icon in the Control Panel displays the Windows Firewall dialog box, as shown in Figure 12-1.

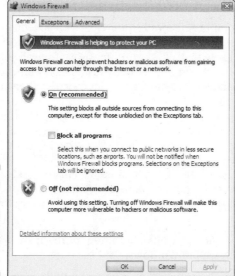

Figure 12-1:
The
Windows
Vista
firewall
dialog box.

In Figure 12-1, the firewall is shown as being turned on. That's good. In fact, that's about all you need to do with the Windows Firewall. You're set. Keep reading the next few sections anyway.

Before Windows XP Service Pack 2, the firewall settings were accessed from the Internet Connection icon located in the Network Connections window. If you're still using that older version of Windows, I recommend instead that you get third-party firewall software to protect you (assuming that you cannot update your version of Windows).

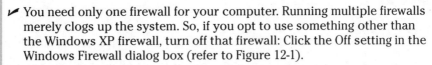

- ✔ Firewalls specifically became a necessity with the advent of high-speed, or broadband, Internet connections. Even so, dialup computers are also at risk and should also use a firewall.

- ✔ Good third-party firewall software is available from the Norton or McAfee Internet security suites. Also check out Zone Alarm from `www.zonelabs.com`.

- ✔ You need only one firewall for your computer. Running multiple firewalls merely clogs up the system. So, if you opt to use something other than the Windows XP firewall, turn off that firewall: Click the Off setting in the Windows Firewall dialog box (refer to Figure 12-1).

- ✔ When the Windows Firewall is turned off, an annoying warning is displayed each time you start Windows, to alert you to the missing firewall.

Monitoring the firewall

An ideal firewall lets you know when suspicious Internet access is taking place. You should see a pop-up message alerting you to some program that's attempting to access the Internet, a program that may be okay but is unknown to the firewall software.

In Figure 12-2, you see a warning about a program on your computer trying to access the Internet. The name of the program is provided in the dialog box, in this case it's Microsoft Windows Fax and Scan. Yes, at the time the message appeared, I was trying to send a fax. Therefore, the access is okay: click the Unblock button. (Furthermore, click the Allow button in the User Access Control that modifies the Windows Firewall.)

Take those firewall warnings seriously! Do not get in the habit of automatically clicking the Unblock button.

When you're in doubt about a program, you can click the Ask Me Later button. Doing so blocks access, but not permanently. To permanently forbid the program from accessing the Internet (or your laptop), click the Keep Blocking button.

- ✔ Generally speaking, when you're trying to use the Internet, expect the firewall to alert you. Only after you've trained it should the firewall stop alerting you as much.

Figure 12-2:
Is it okay
for this
program to
access the
Internet?

- You train the firewall by clicking the Keep Blocking and Unblock buttons.
- Some firewall programs use the terms Allow and Deny rather than Unblock and Keep Blocking, respectively.

Checking the list of blocked programs

Windows keeps track of those programs you block and which are allowed. To see the list, open the Windows Firewall dialog box by following the directions listed earlier in this chapter. Click the Exceptions tab to see the list of specifically blocked programs, as shown in Figure 12-3.

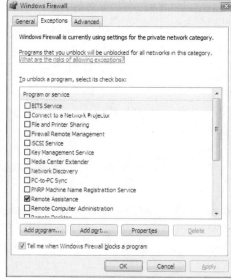

Figure 12-3:
Programs
specifically
blocked
from
Internet
access.

> # Which programs are okay to allow, and which should be blocked?
>
> The best rule about blocking programs with the firewall is "When in doubt, keep blocking." Honestly, you really need to be a computer nerd to know which programs are worthy of blocking and which deserve access. Even so, a good way to tell is whether you're using a program at the time that needs Internet access. If so, such as when you're uploading an image to a Web page, allow access. But, when you're surprised to see a firewall warning (seemingly out of the blue), *block, block, block.*

The programs that are listed have been specifically blocked. Don't think that's the limit, though; Windows Firewall blocks any program you haven't specifically given permission to use the Internet. In other words, the firewall basically blocks *everything*.

Putting a check mark by an item in the list allows that item to access the Internet again through the firewall. Remove the check mark to reblock the program.

Setting Up Antivirus Software

The oldest Internet threat is the computer virus, which existed long before the Internet. Early computer viruses were exchanged via floppy disks, usually disks containing pirated programs or pornography. The computer user would start, or boot, the computer by using the infected floppy disk, and then the computer was infected.

Today, viruses and other nasty programs arrive from the Internet mostly through e-mail. Say that you get an e-mail from your old pal Joe. The message says "This file is hilarious! Please open the attachment!" So, you open the attached file, which is a program that runs and may in fact do something cute. But the program has also infected your computer.

The infection can do a number of nasty things, including

✔ Destroy files on your hard drive.

✔ Store pornography on your hard drive and use your computer to distribute those images.

- Scan your hard drive for valuable information, such as passwords, bank account numbers, or credit card numbers.

- Take over your computer to launch attacks on other computers on the Internet.

- Take over your computer, to be used by spammers to spew out bulk e-mail.

- Do other nasty, horrible things!

To protect yourself against this scourge, you need to run antivirus software. You need to run it all the time. You need to use this software to protect your computer.

- Don't blame your e-mail buddy! That virus you got by e-mail may or may not have come from the person indicated. Most nasty viruses try to cover their tracks, so although you see Joe's or Aunt Mildred's name listed in the message, they most likely didn't send you a virus.

- Viruses have many names. The term *worm* is also used to describe a computer virus, and some nerds weave tales of how a worm is different from a virus. Many white papers have been written. Yadda-yadda-yadda. Worm. Virus. Same thing.

- A *Trojan horse* is a type of virus where the nasty program masquerades as something else. The program may really do the advertised task, but secretly, inside, the Trojan horse program does something malevolent.

- A general catch-all term for all bad computer programs — viruses, worms, Trojan horses, and even spyware and hijacking programs — is *malware* (*mal* comes from *malevolent*, and *ware* comes from *software*).

- A firewall cannot protect your computer from a virus. It may prevent the virus from replicating itself on other computers, but it doesn't stop the virus from coming in. You should use *both* antivirus and firewall software.

Scanning for viruses

You should have and use antivirus software on your computer. There is a problem, however: Windows XP doesn't come with its own virus scanner. For that version of Windows, you have to get a third-party virus scanner. See the list at the end of this section for my suggestions.

Windows Vista comes with antivirus protection in the form of Windows Defender. You can access this program by opening the Windows Defender icon in the Control Panel. Figure 12-4 shows the thrilling Windows Defender window.

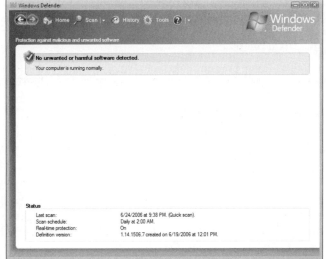

Figure 12-4:
The thrilling
Windows
Defender
window.

No matter which antivirus program you have, there are two ways you can use it: actively and passively.

To actively scan for viruses, the antivirus program does a complete scan of memory, and then the hard drive, and then files on the hard drive. Everything is checked against a database of known viruses. In Windows Defender, choose the Full Scan command from the Scan menu to completely scan your system for viruses.

The passive virus scan is done as files are received into your computer. Each file coming in is individually scanned and then checked against the virus database. Most virus programs are configured to do this automatically. For example, when you receive an e-mail message with a virus attachment, your antivirus software alerts you to the fact and immediately destroys or "quar-antines" the bad program.

✔ Alternative antivirus programs include the popular Norton AntiVirus and McAfee VirusScan. Other antivirus programs to consider as well are listed here:

  • Avast! Antivirus; www.avast.com

  • AVG Anti-Virus; www.grisoft.com

  • Kaspersky antivirus protection; www.kaspersky.com

- ✔ Obviously, each antivirus program does things differently. You have to refer to the documentation that came with your antivirus software program to see how things work. For Windows Defender, refer to a good Windows Vista reference.

- ✔ Generally speaking, I recommend turning off the active virus scan after it finishes scanning once. Try to configure your antivirus software so that it scans incoming e-mail, e-mail file attachments, and any downloads you collect from the Internet. That should keep you safe.

- ✔ Another tip: Sometimes it helps to have and run *two* antivirus programs — not at the same time, but perhaps run one first, and then shut it down and run a second antivirus program. The second one may catch some things that the first one misses.

- ✔ Yes, some antivirus programs require a paid subscription. You don't pay for the program, but rather for accessing and updating the antivirus database. Believe me, the cost of the subscription is *worth it!* Don't delay in updating your antivirus database!

- ✔ Another term for the information in the virus database is a *signature* file. Each virus has its own, unique signature, by which various strains and families of viruses are identified.

- ✔ Although I'm certain that most of the Web-based virus-scanning utilities are legitimate, I would avoid using them. Only if you're darn certain that the software is okay would I tell you to trust it; otherwise, who knows what kind of program you're letting into your computer?

Shutting down your antivirus program

Sometimes, you're asked to turn off your antivirus software. For example, when you install a new program, the directions may suggest turning off any antivirus software. Doing so helps the installation go smoothly and doesn't distress the antivirus program, by making it believe that a new virus, and not a new program, is being installed.

To temporarily disable your antivirus software, locate its icon in the notification area. Right-click the icon and choose a Disable, Exit, or Quit option. That temporarily shuts down the antivirus software, allowing your new software to be installed.

Windows Defender doesn't need to be disabled when you install new programs in Windows Vista. But, remember that when you install a new program, Windows Vista displays a User Account Control (UAC) dialog box, where you must allow permission for the software to be installed. That's safe enough. (It's when you see a UAC that you're not expecting that trouble may be brewing.)

After the software installation is done, restart your computer. That also restarts the antivirus software.

Good advice to help protect you from the viral scourge

Viruses happen to good people, but they also happen to fools who don't heed good advice, such as what's in this list:

- ✔ Don't open unexpected e-mail file attachments, even if they appear to be from someone you know and trust. If you weren't expecting anything, don't open it! (When I send something to someone, I always send them a preview e-mail, letting them know that the following e-mail is legitimate and which file attachments it contains.)

- ✔ Especially avoid any file attachment that is a program. These include files ending in the following letters: BAT, COM, EXE, HTM, HTML, PIF, SCR, or VBS.

- ✔ Avoid opening compressed zip files, or Compressed Folder attachments, specifically when they require a password to open them.

- ✔ A plain-text e-mail message cannot contain a virus. But a virus may be in an e-mail signature or attachment!

- ✔ Odds are good that if you don't open the attachment and just delete the message, your computer will not be infected.

- ✔ If your e-mail program automatically saves e-mail file attachments, delete them from the folder they're saved in.

- ✔ Microsoft Outlook Express is particularly vulnerable to e-mail viruses. Consider getting an alternative e-mail program, such as Web-based e-mail (see Chapter 13) or another program, such as Eudora (www.eudora.com).

- ✔ The best protection against nasty programs in e-mail is to use antivirus software.

Concealing Yourself from Spyware

Spyware is a relatively new category of evil computer software, or *malware*. It sounds innocent: The software monitors your activities on the Internet in order to target you with better, more appropriate advertising. In fact, many people willingly sign up for such services.

The problem is that spyware is often installed without your permission or knowledge. Often, the spyware is disguised as some other program, computer utility, or cute little game. It purports to do one thing, but it's secretly monitoring your Internet activity.

The worse case of spyware consists of programs I can't mention here because the program developers are very litigious. These programs just cannot be uninstalled or removed from your computer. You try, and they come back — again and again and again. Only by using effective anti-spyware software can you get rid of such nasty pests.

✔ Your antivirus software may not check for nor remove spyware programs. You may need specific, anti-spyware software.

✔ As a bonus, try to find and use anti-spyware software that also provides protection against hijacking and phishing. See the section "Foiling a Hijacker and Fooling a Phish," later in this chapter.

✔ Your firewall cannot protect against spyware. That's because you typically invite spyware into your computer (whether you're aware of it or not). The firewall does, however, detect when the spyware uploads its vital information back to its mothership; a good firewall stops such activity from taking place.

Protecting yourself from spyware

The best way to protect yourself from spyware is to be very, very cautious about which files you download (get) from the Internet and which Web pages you visit. Sites that claim to be for children; sites that offer free items, pirated music or video; and pornography sites are full of means and devices for delivering spyware directly into your computer. If you can avoid such sites, do so.

In your Web browser, it helps to eliminate third-party cookies from being deposited on your computer. Third-party cookies come from advertisements on Web pages. This type of cookie is often totally unnecessary to using the Web page you're viewing, so it's perfectly acceptable to turn it off.

Follow these steps to disable third-party cookies for Internet Explorer:

1. **Open the Internet Options icon in the Control Panel.**

2. **Click the Privacy tab.**

3. **Click the Advanced button.**

4. **In the Advanced Privacy Settings dialog box, select the Override Automatic Cookie Handling check box.**

5. **Under First-Party Cookies, select the Accept option button.**

6. **Under Third-Party Cookies, select the Block option button.**

   See Figure 12-5.

7. **Select the Always Allow Session Cookies check box.**

8. **Click OK and close the various other dialog boxes and windows.**

Blocking third-party cookies helps, but to really fight the spyware plague, you need software help. Keep reading in the next section.

Finding some anti-spyware software

You can find many good anti-spyware programs out there. Heck, you May even have one included with your Internet firewall or antivirus program suite. Be sure to check!

Some free and nearly free programs are available on the Internet to help fight spyware and clean the spyware crud from your laptop. Here are my favorites:

- ✔ Ad-Aware, from `www.lavasoft.de`
- ✔ Spybot Search & Destroy, from `www.safer-networking.org`
- ✔ SpywareBlaster, from `www.javacoolsoftware.com`

Any of these programs does the job. They're easy to install and figure out. Download and run one just to see what evil lurks on your laptop's hard drive!

Windows Vista also helps in preventing the nastiest of spyware from occupying your computer. That's because any program that attempts to install itself inside your computer triggers a User Account Control (UAC) dialog box. Whenever you see a UAC dialog box that you weren't expecting, click the Cancel button. *Whew!* You're safe.

Foiling a Hijack and Fooling a Phish

Two relatively new Internet scourges are known as hijacking and phishing. They both prey upon the innocent by redirecting your Web browsing from the site you think you're going to, directly to another Web site, usually someplace obnoxious or offensive.

A *hijack* happens inside your computer by resetting your Web browser's home page. So, instead of MSN or Google, for example, you go to some advertising or porn page.

Phishing (say "fishing") happens in both a Web browser and in e-mail. You believe that you're clicking a link to take you to your bank or some other official Web site, but the Web site is really run by the bad guys. Often, you're asked sensitive questions; requested to submit credit card numbers, PINs, or your Social Security number; or give other information you should never tell anyone. Because the fake Web page looks official, many people fall prey to this scam.

Antivirus and anti-spyware software can help avoid a hijack. For Windows Vista, hijacks are thwarted by the User Account Control (UAC) dialog boxes, which can appear unexpectedly when a hijack is occurring; click the Cancel button.

For Windows XP, specific anti-hijacking utilities are available, although some can be quite technical to use. My advice is to ensure that your antivirus or anti-spyware software also prevents hijacking.

The best solution to avoid a phishing scam is to use a Web browser that informs you of a bogus Web page. Internet Explorer 7 can do this, so I highly recommend that upgrade. To ensure that the phishing filter is active in Internet Explorer 7, heed these directions:

1. **Open the Internet Options icon in the Control Panel.**

2. **In the Internet Properties dialog box, click the Advanced tab.**

3. **Scroll through the list to the Security heading, and then look for the Phishing Filter subheading.**

4. **Choose the item labeled Turn on Automatic Website Checking.**

5. **Click OK.**

This option is available only for Internet Explorer version 7.

Chapter 13

Portable Web Browsing and E-Mail Tips

*I*t took years, but our society is finally aware that computers can and will be portable. O, I remember the bad old days: In 1992 I published a laptop book, and one of the required chapters described how to disassemble — using spare wires, clamps, and a pair of tweezers — a hotel's telephone system so that you could connect a modem. It had to be done! Today, places are far more receptive to the traveling computer user.

Although the environment may have changed, a laptop computer user still needs to do quite a few basic things to get the most out of the portable computing experience. I'm talking about the Internet and battery power. It's vital that you know a few tricks when you're picking up e-mail or working on the Internet, tricks designed to extend your laptop's battery life and, well, just make you a more efficient computer user. That's what this chapter is all about.

Web Browsing When You're Out and About

I have only one suggestion for Web browsing on the road, especially if you're away from an Internet connection for some time (such as on an airplane): *Save your Web pages!*

For example, before you go, leaving behind your beloved high-speed Internet connection, go to a few of your favorite Web pages and quickly browse around. As you do, save those Web pages to your hard drive for offline reading while you're away.

The only thorny thing you get into when saving a Web page is to properly choose which format to save.

In older versions of Internet Explorer, choose File⇨Save As. In Internet Explorer 7, choose the Save As command from the Page button's menu.

Four options are on the Save As Type drop-down list, which appears at the bottom of the Save As dialog box:

✔ **Web Page, Complete (*.htm, *.html):** This option saves everything on the Web page, including graphics, sounds, and fun stuff like that. It takes up quite a bit of hard drive space, creating a special folder to hold all the graphics and nontext items referenced by the Web page.

✔ **Web Archive, Single File (*.mht):** This option saves the Web page itself, but uses the Internet storage cache to supply the images. This method takes up the least amount of hard drive space, and I recommend it, especially for reading.

✔ **Web Page, HTML Only (*.htm, *.html):** This option saves only the bare Web page; that is, just the text — no graphics or multimedia. It's okay for offline reading, but not the best option.

✔ **Text File (*.txt):** This option saves the Web page for editing purposes that don't apply here.

Choose the Web Archive, Single File option for reading. Only if the Web page has graphics that you want to peruse later should you choose Web Page, Complete.

✔ Go through your regular Web-page-perusing schedule. Don't stop to read! Just collect and save those Web pages on your hard drive for offline reading.

- ✔ You can open any saved Web page just as you open any other file on your hard drive. The Web page opens in your Web browser, and you can read it just as you would on the Web.

- ✔ None of the links on the Web page you save will be active. Only when you reconnect to the Internet does clicking the links actually lead somewhere.

- ✔ If you use the Web Page, Complete option, some of the images may not appear on the Web page.

E-Mail Away from Home

Picking up e-mail on a laptop isn't a problem, even when you're on the road. As long as you have a connection to the Internet, you have really only a few things to think about. In fact, the most drastic change happens when you have to use a dialup account on battery power. In that case, you not only have to think about the phone charges but also the act that the modem drains the battery faster than Ethernet or wireless networking.

- ✔ If you have a broadband connection at home, using the Internet on the road with a broadband connection works exactly the same. This is why it's so easy for folks to pick up their laptops from the office and take them out to some wireless locations. Enjoy that laptop freedom!

- ✔ *Broadband* means a fast Internet connection, either directly through the laptop's Ethernet port or by wireless networking.

- ✔ Don't despair if your primary connection to the Internet is dialup. You can still use broadband on the road (if broadband is available). But you can also use dialup if a phone jack is handy. If so, note that long-distance and other types of phone charges apply.

- ✔ Refer to Chapter 11 for information on using a modem in strange and wonderful places away from home.

- ✔ If you need to dial into your ISP directly, check to see whether it has a toll-free number.

Reading your e-mail on the Web

Normally, you pick up your e-mail by using an e-mail program. That program, such as Microsoft Mail or Outlook Express, connects to your ISP's mail server, which then divvies up any pending e-mail. But there's another way to do e-mail: the Web.

Before you leave, check to see whether your ISP has a Web-based e-mail system. This isn't the same as getting a Web-based e-mail account, such as a Yahoo! or Hotmail account (covered in the next section). Instead, it's merely an alternative way to check your e-mail when accessing the ISP's e-mail server directly isn't possible (or incurs an extra expense).

In Figure 13-1, you see my own ISP's preview and pickup page. After logging in to this Web page, I can see all e-mail pending for me. (It's all spam in Figure 13-1.) I can click a message to read it, click a link to view an attachment, or just delete the messages.

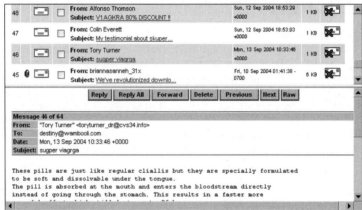

Figure 13-1:
An ISP's
Web-based
e-mail
preview
and pickup
page.

Note that any mail you don't delete remains on the ISP's server for later pickup. That can be handy if you would rather wait until you're back at the desktop computer to pick up some e-mail.

✔ Be sure to check with your ISP to see whether this type of service is available.

✔ Some national ISPs, such as AOL, offer a Web-page system for picking up and previewing e-mail.

Getting a Web-based e-mail account

You can find many free Web-based e-mail services that you can subscribe to, which makes e-mail available to you anywhere you can find Internet access. The good news is that using most Web-based e-mail systems is easy. The better news is that nearly all of them are free!

For example, you can get a free account on Yahoo! Mail and either tell everyone to send your mail to that account when you're on the road or have your regular mail forwarded to that account. (Forwarding e-mail is covered later in this chapter.)

Some people even use their Web-based e-mail accounts as their main accounts and keep their main accounts secret or reserved for private e-mail. That way, the main account remains relatively spam-free. And, when the public Web-based e-mail account becomes overwhelmed with spam, it can be discarded and a new free Web-based e-mail service used.

✔ You can access Web-based e-mail from any computer that has Internet access. You have nothing further to set up.

✔ Unlike e-mail software you must run on your computer, Web-based e-mail stays on the Web until you delete it. That way, you can keep messages in your Web e-mail inbox and have them still waiting there when you return home and use your desktop computer.

✔ Web-based e-mail is available from the following providers. This is by no means a complete list:

    http://mail.yahoo.com

    www.hotmail.com

    http://mail.myway.com

    http://gmail.google.com

✔ Most of those free, Web-based e-mail accounts have a size limit. You have to occasionally delete your old e-mail to keep the account from filling up.

Accessing your e-mail from a friend's computer

I don't think that Miss Manners covers this topic: What do you do when you're visiting friends or relatives and the urge to check your e-mail hits you?

If you have a laptop, and your friends or relatives have their own network, it's easy to hook into their network and use your laptop that way (assuming that they're open to the idea).

They may offer to set up a personal account for you on their computer. That's nice, and it's a good thing to do for security reasons. But all you really need in order to pick up your e-mail is a computer with Internet access. Then you can use your ISP's Web-based e-mail system to peruse your mail or visit any mail waiting for you on a Web-based e-mail system (Hotmail or Yahoo!, for example).

- ✔ I do not recommend setting up your own e-mail account on a friend's or relative's computer. It's just too much of a security risk.

- ✔ The best option is to pray that your friends or relatives have a wireless connection, and then use your laptop's wireless network adapter to hook into their network for full Internet access.

- ✔ If Internet access is disallowed, keep in mind that you still have the library as an option. Cybercafés and wireless hotspots also have Internet access that you can consider.

Forwarding your e-mail

E-mail servers have the option of forwarding all incoming e-mail if you know that you're going to be away for a while and want to pick up your e-mail at another address. This is known as *e-mail forwarding,* and your ISP may offer it as a free service, or your company or business may have it available as a feature.

For example, if you know that you're going to be out for three weeks, you can have your e-mail forwarded to your Web-based e-mail account for that time. Any e-mail coming into your regular account is immediately redirected to that other account. That way, you don't miss a thing.

There is, sadly, a problem with forwarding your e-mail, which is why you may not find it available as an option. Occasionally, e-mail gets stuck in the space-time continuum, in what's scientifically referred to as an *endlessly forwarding loop.* Your mail gets forwarded to you, which then reforwards the mail back to you, which then repeats the process. Eventually the system becomes clogged with e-mail, and when the IT guys figure things out, they just delete your e-mail account to fix things. That's a bad thing.

So, if e-mail forwarding is an option, look into it. But be careful to ensure that your e-mail is being forwarded to a real account and isn't just lost in a loop. In, fact, test things by forwarding all your e-mail a day or so before you're set to leave so that you can ensure that everything works.

- ✔ Refer to your ISP for more information on e-mail forwarding. Sometimes it's something you can set up for yourself, such as an option to choose on the ISP's e-mail Web site. Sometimes it's something that someone there may have to configure for you. Sometimes it's just not available.

- ✔ Although it's possible to configure your e-mail program to forward your e-mail, it's difficult to pull off: You must direct a computer — at home or at the office, for example — to automatically fetch and forward e-mail. So, although it's possible, it's something that is generally beyond the abilities of most computer users.

✔ Don't forget to stop forwarding your e-mail when you return.

E-Mail Options Worthy of Consideration

Deep within the bosom of your e-mail program dwell many complex and puzzling options. The reasons for these options may seem obscure or unnecessary — until you understand how they can be used, and specifically how those options can be an advantage to the laptop user away from home or desperately low on battery juice.

This section covers some of those strange e-mail options that have a rightful purpose and place for the laptop on the road. Note that this information is specific to Microsoft Mail and the older Outlook Express. Other e-mail programs have similar features.

Omit your password

Having Windows remember your Internet and e-mail passwords is handy for a desktop — a desktop in a secure location or one with adequate password protection. But even with password protection on your laptop, do you really want your e-mail password to be kept inside the computer? If not, here's how to suppress it:

1. **In Microsoft Mail or Outlook Express, choose Tools⇨Accounts.**

   The Accounts dialog box reports for duty.

2a. **In Microsoft Mail, click to select your e-mail account from the list; skip to Step 4.**

2b. **In Outlook Express, click the Mail tab.**

3. **In Outlook Express, click to select your ISP's mail server in the list.**

4. **Click the Properties button.**

   Your ISP's e-mail connection Properties dialog box appears.

5. **Click the Servers tab.**

6. **Erase your password from the Password text box and deselect the Remember Password check box.**

   See Figure 13-2.

Figure 13-2:
Removing
your
password
from the
Internet
e-mail
account.

7. **Click OK to make the change.**

8. **Click the Close button to dismiss the various windows you've opened.**

You have to repeat these steps when you have more than one e-mail account listed; remove the password for each of them.

Because you've removed your e-mail password, you're prompted for it each time you go to pick up e-mail. A dialog box appears. Just enter your password, and then you can pick up your mail.

Also refer to Chapter 16, which covers laptop security in more detail.

Disconnect after picking up e-mail

When you're using a dial-up account, keep in mind that you don't need to be connected to the Internet while you read your e-mail. Especially given how much power the modem draws, I recommend having your e-mail program immediately hang up (or disconnect) after sending or receiving e-mail. Here's where to check those settings in Microsoft Mail and Outlook Express:

1. **Choose Tools⇨Options.**

   The Options dialog box duly appears.

2. **Click the Connection tab in the Options dialog box.**

3. **Select the Hang Up After Sending and Receiving check box.**

4. **Click OK.**

You may also want to disable automatic checking, as covered in the next section.

This setting isn't needed for broadband access.

Disable automatic checking

When you're connected to the Internet all the time, especially at the office, you probably have your e-mail program configured to check for new messages every so often. On a laptop with a dial-up connection, however, that may mean that you're faced with a sudden panic as you realize that your computer is once again dialing out of the hotel during peak hours to pick up new e-mail.

Rather than have to worry about skillfully removing the phone card, just disable the automatic mail-checking feature. Here's how it goes:

1. **Choose Tools➪Options.**

2. **In the Options dialog box, click the General tab (if needed).**

3. **Uncheck the Check for New Messages Every [blank] Minutes check box.**

4. **(Optionally) From the If My Computer Is Not Connected at This Time drop-down list, choose Do Not Connect.**

   Setting this option ensures that merely starting your e-mail program doesn't cause it to try to dial in to the Internet.

5. **Deselect the check box by the option Send and Receive Messages at Startup.**

   This step is optional but recommended. The setting prevents Outlook Express from immediately contacting the Internet when you first start the program. That way, you can read pending messages and then connect with the Internet when you're ready.

6. **Click OK.**

To connect with the Internet and send or receive messages, click the Send/Recv button, or use the keyboard shortcut Ctrl+M.

Making these settings only saves you time and battery power when you use the dial-up modem to retrieve your e-mail.

Send everything in one batch

As you peruse your e-mail, you read messages, reply to messages, and then click the Send button to send those messages. But rather than cause your e-mail program to dial in, connect, send, and then disconnect over and over, I recommend sending all your e-mail messages at one time, in a single batch. To do this, you tell your e-mail program to queue the messages rather than send them individually. Here's the lowdown for Microsoft Mail and Outlook Express:

1. **Choose Tools⇨Options.**
2. **In the Options dialog box, click the Send tab.**
3. **Deselect the Send Messages Immediately check box.**
4. **Click OK.**

The messages now sit in the Outbox and wait until you connect again.

This option can help both dialup and broadband users. Obviously, for dialup, it allows you to save time by sending all your outgoing messages at one time. Beyond that, I enjoy the opportunity to review and occasionally edit (or delete) messages waiting to be sent; they sit waiting in the Outbox.

To pick up or leave on server

When I leave for a conference or on vacation, I typically lie and tell people that I will not be checking e-mail. That sort of keeps away most of the trivial messages, but occasionally something important floats in. So, I want to check my e-mail, and I still want to keep it all available for the desktop computer when I get home.

Rather than try to coordinate incoming e-mail between my laptop and desktop, I use a different solution: I keep all my e-mail on the ISP's e-mail server. That way, I can read my e-mail, respond if necessary, and then trust that the same e-mail will be waiting for me when I return.

Here's how to set up the "leave on server" e-mail option:

1. **Choose Tools⇨Accounts.**
2a. **In Windows Mail, select your e-mail account from the list; skip to Step 4.**
2b. **In Outlook Express, click the Mail tab in the Internet Accounts dialog box.**
3. **In Outlook Express, choose your ISP's mail server from the list.**

4. **Click the Properties button.**

5. **In the Properties dialog box, click the Advanced tab.**

6. **Put a check mark in the box labeled Leave a Copy of Message on Server.**

   That way, even after you pick up your e-mail on the road, it's still available for pickup from the server later.

7. **Optionally select the check box by Remove from Server when Deleted from 'Deleted Items.'**

   That way, if I answer and delete a message, it's also deleted and doesn't appear again later when I pick up my mail back at the office.

8. **Click OK, and then close any open windows or dialog boxes.**

For me, this solution solves the problem of wanting to receive important e-mail on two different computers — and without the bother of trying to coordinate Inbox files at a later date.

✔ As an alternative to this approach, consider using Web-based e-mail instead. That way, you can continue to read all your e-mail at home or away without worrying about coordinating e-mail between a desktop and laptop system.

✔ Be aware that your ISP may have a size limit on what can be stored in your inbox. I used this exact technique on a protracted vacation once, only to discover that after 14 days, my e-mail account was full and all new incoming mail was being rejected. The solution there is just to pick up and deal with your e-mail when you're away and not bother leaving it on the server.

✔ You just can't escape technology!

Skip messages over a given size

If your remote e-mail connection must be made over a dialup modem, you probably don't want to waste time downloading huge files. For example, a 500K e-mail attachment may take a blink of an eye to receive at your office, where high-speed Internet is the norm. But, on the road with a lousy 28.8K connection at the Dubuque Motel 5-point-9, it just doesn't cut it.

Some e-mail programs have a settings option that lets you skip over e-mail of a given size. For example, in Eudora, the message text is downloaded and the attachment isn't; you're alerted to the presence of the large attachment and given the option to download it now or later.

In Microsoft Mail or Outlook Express, you must create a mail rule to specifically skip over messages of a certain size. Here are the steps to take:

1. **Choose Tools➪Message Rules➪Mail.**

   A New Message Rule window appears.

2. **In Area 1, scroll through the list to find the option labeled Where the Message Size Is More Than Size; put a check mark in that box.**

3. **In Area 3, click the word *Size*.**

4. **Enter a size in kilobytes (K).**

   Short files seem to be okay, and I often expect files in the 70K to 120K range, so I set the value at 200KB.

5. **Click OK.**

6. **In Area 2, choose the option labeled Do Not Download It from the Server.**

7. **In Area 4, name the rule something descriptive, such as** Skip 200K messages.

8. **Click OK to create the rule.**

9. **Click OK to close the other dialog box.**

The sad part about this approach is that you never know that any huge messages are pending for you. When you return to the desktop, or any e-mail system that lacks the "Skip 200KB messages" (or similar) rule, you discover and download the big messages. (Unlike Eudora, Outlook Express doesn't let you know that the big message is pending and give you the option of downloading it.)

Chapter 14

The Desktop-Laptop Connection

*I*ntroductions can be so awkward. There's the anxiety about acceptance, bashfulness at presenting oneself, and fear over having something green stuck to your teeth. When things go well, the angst quickly dissolves into a warm and, hopefully, lasting friendship. Of course, enough about your laptop and desktop computers! Now let me talk about human relationships. . . .

Seriously, there's a need for folks with both laptop and desktop systems to get those computers to hold hands, share, and love. When you use a desktop computer as your main system, you doubtless want to copy over files to take on the road. Likewise, when you're back from the road, you want to copy the files back. It's that desktop-laptop connection that's covered in this chapter.

Connecting Desktop and Laptop

Exchanging information between two computers has been an issue ever since the second computer was developed. Back then, computers were stubborn beasts, rude to humans — let alone disgusted at the idea of communication with another computer. Yet, just like the notion of a portable computer, the need to share information between two different computers proved a lasting one, and one that would be solved no matter what the computers thought about it.

The hard way: Sneaker net

Computers are designed around information input and output, which you might have heard of in terms of I/O (Input/Output). Computers are also all about the storage of information. Back in the early days, one of the ways to share information between computers was simply to yank the storage device out of one computer system and place it in another. That still happens today by using removable disks: floppy, CD, DVD, flash drives, and so on.

Over time, exchanging computer files by using disks was referred to as using a *sneaker net*. That's because the actual transfer of information was done by humans on foot (wearing sneakers) as opposed to the computers themselves working out some sort of solution.

Yes, even today, you can exchange information between your laptop and desktop computers by using disks, but not necessarily floppy disks. I've used a USB flash drive many times to copy a batch of files between my desktop and laptop computers. I've also used a CD-R for an older laptop that lacked USB ports. But there are better and easier ways to do things, solutions that involve wires and not disks.

The easy way: Over the network

The simplest way to send files between laptop and desktop is to place them both on the same network. Configured and connected properly, you can share and access either the desktop or laptop's hard drive to easily exchange files and whatnot.

When computers are connected over the network, moving files back and forth is done as easily, and almost as quickly, as moving files around inside a single computer. Plus, various programs help you coordinate files between your laptop and desktop. Refer to the section "Synchronizing Files between the Desktop and the Laptop," later in this chapter.

  ✔ Networking is the preferred way to connect two computers. Even if all you have is a desktop and a laptop, I highly recommend getting networking hardware to make connecting the two a snap.

  ✔ Refer to Chapter 9 for more information on networking your desktop and laptop, both with and without wires.

Connecting Desktop and Laptop the Primitive Way

Before networking, there were two ways you could connect a laptop and desktop computer: directly, by using a special octopus cable, or "null modem," or by using the neglected infrared port. I don't recommend either method, especially given how simple it is to connect today's computers by using a simple Ethernet cable.

This section discusses the infrared port and direct cable connection, as well as the old Windows XP Direct Connection software. Windows Vista lacks this ability, and rightly so: this is just an awkward way to connect two computers. It might still be available, so the information is included here, but this will be the last edition of this book to include such information.

Using the infrared port

When both desktop and laptop have an infrared (IR) port (which is doubtful, but I have to write about it anyway), you can use that port to beam information between the two systems.

The best thing to do is to orient the laptop and desktop so that the IR ports are doing a Mexican standoff with each other — eye-to-eye, as it were. That way, nothing comes between them to break the connection. With the computers looking like the hero and the bad guy from a John Woo film, you're ready to make the transfer. See the later section "Toiling with the Windows XP direct connection" for more information.

- ✔ I know of hardly any desktops with IR connections, although it's not unheard of. I think a few IBM models sport that feature.

- ✔ Ensure that the IR port is enabled before you proceed. Check with Chapter 16 for more information. (Chapter 16 covers laptop security, and an enabled IR port is considered a security risk. Enabling the IR port for this type of file transfer is okay, though.)

That ugly wire thing

Before a networking standard appeared, computer users could connect their desktop and laptop computers by using both systems' serial or parallel ports. To accomplish this, an ugly cable octopus was used, similar to what's shown in Figure 14-1.

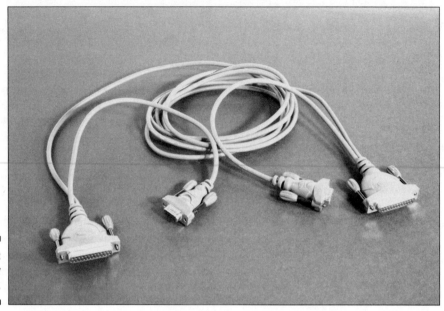

The ugly wire cable has both serial and parallel (printer) port connections on both ends, providing a variety of ways to connect a desktop system and laptop system. Strangely enough, this contraption is still being sold, even though "networking" both computers by connecting them with an Ethernet cable is a better, faster, and more efficient option.

Merely connecting the two computers isn't enough, however: You also need software to help make the connection happen. The software comes in two parts, one for the laptop and another for the desktop. Both parts must be running simultaneously for the dang thing to work. See the next section for more information.

- ✔ Printer port = parallel port. It might also be called the LPT port or PRN port.

- ✔ Serial port = RS-232C port. (Although it's not really the RS-232C port any more, the old term lingers.)

- ✔ Between the serial and parallel connections, the parallel one is faster.

Toiling with the Windows XP direct connection

When you're stuck in the past and can connect your desktop and laptop computers only by using the antique serial or parallel ports or the infrared port, you need to configure Windows XP for a direct connection. That sounds well and good, but in practice it's not that easy to set up, and it's even harder to get going. So, if you have the stamina for it, here are the steps to take. First comes the desktop computer:

1. **Open the Control Panel's Networking Connections icon.**

   This displays various Network Connection icons.

2. **Click the Create a New Connection task over in the Network Tasks part of the window (on the left).**

   Or, you can choose File⇨New Connection.

   The New Connection Wizard rears its boring head.

3. **Click the Next button.**

4. **Choose the Set Up an Advanced Connection option.**

   Why this is considered advanced is beyond me.

5. **Click the Next button.**

6. **Choose Connect Directly to Another Computer.**

7. **Click the Next button.**

8. **On the desktop computer, choose Host. On the laptop computer, choose Guest.**

   It doesn't matter which is which, but one computer must be the host and the other the guest.

9. **Click the Next button.**

   The remainder of the rules in these steps apply to the host computer. The steps for the guest computer appear later in this section.

10. **From the drop-down list, choose the port you're using to connect.**

    This choice depends on the cable, but also on which ports are available. Be sure to choose the right one! Most desktop systems have two serial ports, labeled COM1 and COM2.

    Note that this is also how you set up the infrared connection, by choosing that port from the drop-down list.

11. **Click the Next button.**

12. **Choose the users who are allowed access to your computer.**

    Select the login name from the list.

13. **Click the Next button.**

14. **Click the Finish button.**

    A new icon appears in the Network Connections window. For the host computer, the icon is named Incoming Connections.

After completing these steps for the host computer, you must do the same on the guest computer. Here goes:

1. **Complete Steps 1 through 9 in the preceding list, and then continue to Step 2 in this list.**

2. **Type a name for this connection, such as** Desktop.

    This is merely the name applied to the icon that appears in the Network Connections window. For example, you can give the icon the same name as the desktop computer.

3. **Click the Next button.**

4. **Choose the port you're using to connect to the desktop computer.**

    Serial ports are labeled COM1 and COM1, and the parallel (printer) port is LPT1. The infrared connection, if available, can also be chosen from the list. Choose the port that you'll be using based on the way you're connecting the two systems.

5. **Click the Next button.**

6. **Click the Finish button.**

    Well . . . you really aren't finished yet.

7. **Click the Cancel button to close the Connect Desktop dialog box.**

    Windows is eagerly jumping the gun here. Anyway, the connection icon appears in the Network Connections window. Now you're ready to run through a direct connection.

When both computers are configured, you can then connect them. Plug in the connecting cable to the proper ports. Then, to make the connection from the laptop, double-click the desktop computer's connection icon in the Network Connections window. (The *guest* connects to the *host*.)

Fill in the Connect dialog box with your account name and password for the desktop computer. Click the Connect button. The desktop computer should answer and create the connection. After it's set, the two computers are "networked," and you can use standard networking methods to access each system's resources. (Refer to Chapter 9.)

To disconnect the guest machine, you can revisit the Network Connections window, right-click the connection icon, and choose Disconnect. Or, you can just rip out the cord, though I think the computer enjoys itself more when you disconnect properly.

And now, the bad news: This method doesn't work as well as it could. The chances of making a successful connection are iffy at best. A few third-party programs are available, such as PC Anywhere, and they can do a better job. (Some programs even come with their own cables.) So many variables and adjustments are necessary to make the Windows XP direct connection workable that it can be a nightmare.

- ✔ When the direct connection has been established, the host computer displays an icon indicating the guest's connection, as shown in the margin.

- ✔ Any other network connections that the host computer has are also shared with the guest computer.

- ✔ Note that regular Ethernet networking is about a jillion times faster than direct connection. Don't be surprised when you discover that this is a slow way to keep your laptop updated.

- ✔ If you've tried and this really doesn't work, I highly recommend that you avoid the frustration of troubleshooting the connection and instead get the Ethernet cable and network your desktop and laptop PCs the "real" way.

- ✔ Chapter 9 discusses setting up an Ethernet connection as well as how to share resources, such as folders and printers, between two networked computers.

Synchronizing Files between the Desktop and the Laptop

After the desktop-to-laptop connection is made, the next step is most likely some type of file transfer. Specifically, what you want to do is *synchronize* the files between your laptop and desktop systems.

For example, you might want to carry with your laptop some files to work on while you're away. When you return to the desktop, you want to ensure that only those files you worked on are updated on both computers. How can you tell?

Never mind! Let the computer do the work, thanks to the handy Briefcase. This section covers the details.

Creating a Briefcase

The Windows Briefcase has been around for quite some time. It's a sadly neglected feature, one that's avoided by most users. That's probably because the name is just really stupid. Despite that, making a Briefcase in Windows is the starting point for sharing files between two computers. It's cinchy:

1. **Open any folder window on your desktop computer.**

   For example, open the My Documents window. Or, you can use the desktop.

2. **Right-click a blank spot in the window (or on the desktop) to display a shortcut menu.**

3. **Choose New⇨Briefcase from the menu.**

   The Briefcase icon appears, named New Briefcase.

4. **Optionally, rename the Briefcase icon.**

   The icon is ready to be renamed in Windows Vista; in Windows XP, press the F2 key to give the thing a new name. Otherwise, the name New Briefcase is fine.

Yes, you're done. All you need to do is create a single Briefcase folder on your desktop computer. The laptop doesn't need a Briefcase folder.

The sections that follow discuss how the Briefcase folder is used to synchronize files between the desktop and the laptop.

✔ The Briefcase works kind of like a folder, but it's not really a folder. It's a storage unit you can use to shuttle files between two computers.

✔ I lied about needing only one Briefcase on a desktop computer. When you happen to have more than one laptop, you need more than one Briefcase to help keep files synchronized between those laptops. In that case, create a Briefcase for each laptop and name each Briefcase appropriately.

✔ Refer to Chapter 6 for information on finding the My Documents window.

✔ In older versions of Windows, the Briefcase was one of the standard desktop icons. Starting with Windows XP, it's no longer standard, and you can place it in any location you want (not always the desktop).

Populating the Briefcase

After you have created a Briefcase, the next step is to copy over to it those files and folders and documents you want to take with you on the laptop, just like you would pack a suitcase before a vacation, though without the suntan lotion.

Put files into the Briefcase just as you would copy those files in Windows: You can drag the icons to the Briefcase icon. You can copy the files and then open the Briefcase icon and paste things there. Or, you can use any of the other 4,999 ways to copy files in Windows; refer to a good Windows reference for the boring details.

The Briefcase folder itself holds duplicates of the files you copy into it, listing the file's original location and its status, as shown in Figure 14-2.

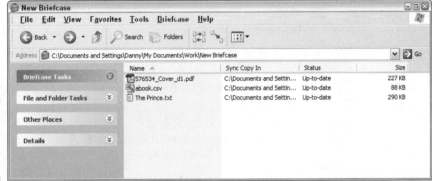

Figure 14-2:
The New
Briefcase
window.

Close the Briefcase window when you're done with it.

After filling the Briefcase with files and stuff you want on your laptop, the next step is to copy the Briefcase to your laptop. That's covered in the next section.

✔ Only *copies* of files are kept in the Briefcase.

✔ I recommend using the Details view when you're perusing files in the Briefcase window. In Windows Vista, choose Details from the Views button; in Windows XP, choose View⇨Details.

✔ When you open the Briefcase folder, you might see a Welcome to Windows Briefcase window displayed. I have no idea how to stop that, but clicking the Close or Finish button makes it go away.

Moving the Briefcase over to your laptop

To take files in the Briefcase from your desktop to your laptop, you need to move the Briefcase icon from one computer to the other. This is no big deal; it works just like copying any file between two computers. Here are the steps to take:

1. **Close any documents you're working on that you plan on taking with you.**

   Obviously, if you want to edit your Great American Novel, you need to save those chapters to disk and close them in your word processor.

2. **Open the Briefcase icon.**

3. **Update all the files by clicking either the Update All Items button or the Update All button.**

   When you update the files, you're confirming that the Briefcase contains the most recent versions of the files you want to take with you.

4. **Connect the laptop and desktop.**

   Various methods for this step are covered in the earlier sections in this chapter. Again, the best way to make the connection is over a network.

5. **Open your laptop's shared folder, one that allows you both read and write access.**

   In Chapter 9, I recommend sharing the Public folder in Windows Vista and the Shared Documents folder in Windows XP. That works fine. Use the Network or Network Neighborhood icon to open that folder from your laptop's computer.

6. **Move the Briefcase icon to the shared folder on your laptop.**

   Windows always moves the Briefcase; it isn't copied. That way, you cannot be confused by multiple Briefcases for the same laptop.

   If you already have a Briefcase on your laptop (which means that you're not following my directions in this book, but that's beside the point), it's erased when you finish Step 6. There should be *only one* Briefcase shared between the laptop and desktop computers.

7. **Free the laptop!**

   After the Briefcase has been moved to the laptop, you're done. You're free to take the laptop and its desktop files, nestled in the Briefcase, with you to some remote locale.

Tips for using Briefcase files on your laptop

After the Briefcase icon, and all its contents, are moved over to the laptop, you're ready to go on the road and continue working on your files. Here's what I recommend you do:

- ✔ Keep the files from your desktop computer in your Briefcase icon.

- ✔ If you copy the files out of the Briefcase, you lose the ability to synchronize the files and keep things up-to-date.

- ✔ Files in the Briefcase can be opened just like any other files. Just remember to save them back to the Briefcase icon.

- ✔ If you create any new files on the road that you also want to keep on the desktop, save them in the Briefcase folder as well.

Synchronizing your files when you return

When you return with your laptop and modified files, you need to synchronize things between your desktop and laptop systems. You want to ensure that those files you modified on your laptop are now modified on the desktop system as well. Everything needs to be up to date. Dance this jig:

1. **Connect the laptop and desktop.**

   Networking is the best way to do this; reattach your laptop to the desktop's network.

2. **Open the shared folder on your desktop from the laptop.**

   Or, actually, you can do this any way you want. The idea here is to be able to easily copy the Briefcase from the laptop to the desktop. Whether you carry out this operation on the desktop or laptop computer, it's the same.

3. **Move the Briefcase from the laptop to the desktop.**

   Yes, this is a move operation; the Briefcase is moved from one computer to the other, complete with its updated contents.

4. **On your desktop computer, open the Briefcase icon.**

5. **Click the Update All the Items or Update All button.**

   You can use the Update dialog box to preview the files that need to be updated or changed.

6. **Click the Update button to update the files.**

7. **Close the Briefcase window when you're done.**

Any new files added in the Briefcase must be manually copied from that folder to another folder on the desktop. Notice that these new files are flagged as Unchanged in Briefcase.

Deleting files in the Briefcase folder doesn't affect the originals elsewhere on your hard drive.

Is the Briefcase the best answer?

My opinion is no: The Briefcase isn't really the best solution to synchronize files between a desktop and a laptop computer. Instead, I offer these suggestions:

✔ Place any project you plan on sharing between desktop and laptop on a USB or flash drive. Keep the files on that drive, and simply move it between desktop and laptop, updating and saving files on the drive.

✔ Keep the files you plan on exchanging in a specific folder on the desktop. When it comes time to go on the road, copy that folder to the laptop. When you return, copy the folder from the laptop back to the desktop, replacing the original folder.

✔ Use an Internet disk drive, or online storage system for your files. The so-called *net drive* stores all your projects, which you can equally access from the desktop or laptop. Note that using a net drive involves some type of fee.

Accessing the Desktop from Elsewhere

This desktop-laptop trick is something amazing: Access your desktop computer from your laptop (or any other computer), and use it just as though you were sitting at the desktop computer in person.

This type of remote access is really something, and it's also really a security risk. Do you really want every creep on the Internet using your desktop? It can happen! Therefore, I strongly advise that you try the following tricks only with a well-established firewall in place — specifically, one designed to let in only your laptop and not any other computer system. (This may take the abilities of a computer security expert to set up, but that's good. This isn't something to try casually.)

The amazing Windows Vista Remote Desktop

Windows Vista finally got things right with its Remote Desktop feature. It's amazingly easy to set up and works well, especially compared to its ugly implementation in Windows XP (covered later in this chapter). I recommend using Remote Desktop only in a security environment — say, over a local net-work and not over the Internet. It's another amazing way to work between laptop and desktop computers.

Setting up a PC for remote desktop

You can configure either the desktop or laptop computer for remote access; either way works fine. Here's what you do:

1. **Open the Control Panel's System icon.**

2. **In the list of tasks on the left side of the window, choose Remote Settings.**

   If a User Account Control (UAC) dialog box appears, click the Continue button.

3. **In the System Properties dialog box, on the Remote tab in the Remote Desktop area, choose the item labeled Allow Connections from Computers Running Any Version of Remote Desktop.**

4. **Click OK, and close the Control Panel window.**

That's it. The computer is now open to sharing its desktop remotely with another computer on the network.

For the Remote Desktop to work you'll have to create an exception for the Windows Firewall. You might have noticed this warning in Step 3 above. Here's how to enable that exception:

1. **Open the Control Panel's Windows Firewall icon.**

2. **In the Windows Firewall window, click the link that says Change Settings.**

   Click the Continue button if prompted by a User Account Control warning.

3. **In the Windows Firewall Settings dialog box, click the Exceptions tab.**

4. **Scroll through the list to find the item called Remote Desktop, and place a check mark by that item.**

5. **Click the OK button, and then close the Windows Firewall and Control Panel windows.**

Accessing the remote desktop

After you make a computer open to the idea of a remote connection, the next step is to use another computer on the network — say, your laptop — to access that computer and use it remotely. Yes, this sounds like mind control, but I'm going to avoid the temptation to make references to any religion or the book *The Puppet Masters*.

To access the other computer's desktop, heed these directions:

1. **From the Start menu, choose All Programs⇨Accessories⇨Remote Desktop Connection.**

   The bold and mighty Remote Desktop Connection dialog box appears, as shown in Figure 14-3. Okay, maybe it's not so mighty.

Figure 14-3:
Remote
Desktop
Connection
is more
powerful
than it looks.

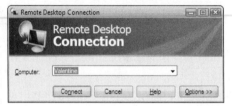

2. **Choose a computer from the drop-down list, or choose the Browse for More option in the list to find a computer on the network.**

   The computer must already have been configured to accept a remote desktop connection; refer to the previous section.

3. **Click the Connect button.**

   You must log in to the remote computer by using an account on that computer.

4. **In the security window, choose your account name from the list or select Use Another Account.**

5. **Enter your username (if necessary) and the password.**

6. **Click the Submit button.**

   Peruse the security warning that appears; chances are that all the settings are okay and, as long as you know that the computer is used fairly and not sloppily with regard to security, connecting to it is okay.

7. **Click the Yes button in the Security Warning dialog box.**

   Windows makes the connection with the remote computer, eventually displaying its desktop on your computer screen.

After the connection is made, the remote computer might log off any user and display the Welcome screen.

Using the remote desktop

When the remote desktop is set up and connected, what you see on your computer's screen is actually the display of another computer on the network. Moving the mouse on your computer moves the mouse on the other computer, and ditto for the keyboard. It's just as though you're sitting at that computer, when you're actually working things from a remote location.

The remote desktop can be displayed on a full screen or in a window. In Full Screen mode, a strip appears across the top of the screen and acts as a sort of window control. In Window mode, the remote desktop appears in a window on your computer's screen.

Sadly, you cannot copy files and folders between the remote system and your own computer by dragging things into and out of the remote desktop's window. The Remote Desktop Connection is more of a control and access feature than a file exchange utility.

Disconnecting from the remote desktop

To break the remote desktop connection, simply close the remote window, or click the X button on the strip across the top of the screen. Click the OK button in the confirmation dialog box. The connection is broken, and you're back to using only your own PC.

Note that any programs you've started or any activities you're run on the remote desktop continue to run after you disconnect. You must specifically stop them before you disconnect, if that's what you want.

The awkward Windows XP Remote Desktop

Windows XP comes with a Remote Desktop feature, one that allows you to connect to your computer from another computer on the network (or over a direct connection) or another computer system on the Internet. Sounds nifty, and when it works, it can be fun.

Golly by gosh, the Windows Remote Desktop feature is truly a royal pain to configure. I counted 50-odd steps when I did it, and, honestly, between Windows Remote Desktop and the VNC program (covered in the next section), it just isn't a contest. I don't want to waste your time: Use RealVNC, as covered next.

Real Virtual Network Computing

A fine company in the U.K., RealVNC, produces a free product that lets you access and use your computer from any other location on the Internet. Yes, again, the product is free. It's easy to install and use, beating the pants off Windows XP Remote Desktop. Here's the lowdown:

Go to the Web page at `www.realvnc.com`. Read a bit about virtual network computing (VNC), and then download the viewer for your laptop and both the viewer and server for your desktop.

The viewer doesn't require any installation; you simply run the program. The server requires a bit of installation, but it's cinchy to follow the instructions on the screen.

 To set things up on the server, right-click the VNC icon in the notification area. This displays the VNC Server Properties (Service-Mode) dialog box. On the Authentication tab, select the VNC 3.3 Authentication, No Encryption option. Then click the Set Password button to choose a system password.

If you know the IP address from which you'll connect to the desktop, enter it on the Connections tab, as shown in Figure 14-4. In the Access Control area, click the Add button, and then enter the IP address. That limits access to your desktop from only that IP address. (Furthermore, you need to modify the Internet firewall protecting the desktop computer to allow access through port 5900. Have an expert help you set it up.)

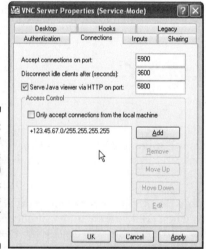

Figure 14-4: Only IP address 123.45.67.0 can access this computer remotely.

Click the OK button to close the dialog box when you're done.

To make the connection, run the viewer program on your laptop. In the dialog box that appears, enter the network name or IP address of your desktop computer, and then click the OK button. Enter the proper password, and the other computer's desktop appears in a window on your screen, similar to what's shown in Figure 14-5.

Figure 14-5: Another computer's desktop appears in a window.

When you move the mouse on the laptop, the mouse moves on the desktop. Open a window. Run a program. What you see on the laptop is happening over the network on the desktop.

When you're done, just close the other computer's window on your laptop. That breaks the connection.

Firewall advice

I do not recommend that you leave your computer wide open for full access over the Internet. Even without running a remote desktop, your Windows XP desktop computer is one of the most vulnerable computer systems on the Internet. You need protection! Get a firewall!

Firewalls don't just block all incoming traffic. They can, when configured properly, allow in specific types of traffic. For example, to use virtual network computing (VNC), you can tell your firewall to allow all traffic in through port 5900 (which is what VNC uses). If you're using a router or central firewall for a network, you can direct all traffic through port 5900 to a specific computer on the network. And, if you know the IP address of the remote system, you can even configure the firewall to allow traffic only from that IP address into port 5900 on the local computer.

Is this driving you nuts? That's why a network security expert can help you set up and configure a firewall, which is what I recommend. Never leave your computer open for attack. If you're in doubt about any of this, do not use remote access.

Part IV
Hit the Road, Jack

In this part . . .

I remember when I took a computer outside for the first time. It was a hot summer back in 1983. I rigged up all the wires, set out an ice chest, and dreamed of working outside on a lovely balcony overlooking an industrial parking lot. Everything was perfect until I turned on the monitor. Nope, I just couldn't see that old video screen outside, no matter how hard I tried.

Today's laptops are designed for outside. And I must say, one of my many joys is taking my work away from the dreary office and plopping down my laptop in some new, stimulating environment. I've used my laptop on airplanes; in coffeehouses, diners, midnight cafés, city parks, and in my car; at the library; and even when I was pulling technical duties in the community theater and we waited 90 minutes between light cues. Laptops can go anywhere.

If you haven't yet hit the road with your laptop, it's high time that you do! This chapter covers lots of on-the-road topics in several nifty little chapters. Read them. Enjoy them. And take your laptop on the road!

Chapter 15

On the Road Again . . .

My grandmother amazed me. She would be leaving for a trip in two weeks, yet she was already packed. My father (her son), on the other hand, traveled quite a bit. For him, packing was done in the morning, mere minutes before leaving. Both approaches worked. With more experience in traveling, however, my dad was able to make packing decisions quickly with less worry over making a mistake.

If you've never taken a laptop on the road, whether to your local Starbucks or overseas, you might spend some time wondering what to take with you. But, why bother? Rather than go through the agony, just read this chapter, where I offer suggestions on what to take with you and how to prepare for the trip before you go. The idea is to make your pending road-warrior laptopping experience fully enjoyable, without fussing for two weeks over what to pack and what not to pack.

Nancy Drew and the Case of the Laptop Case

Your laptop needs a laptop case, not because carrying a laptop computer by itself makes you look like a nerd, but more because the laptop is only one part of a larger collection of stuff you take on the road. Furthermore, the laptop needs a comfy storage place to protect it from damage and disguise it from thieves. Getting the proper laptop case is just a darn good idea.

✔ Your laptop needs a case.

✔ Suggestions about the stuff you should pack into your case are covered in Chapter 22.

Avoid the manufacturer's case

Many laptop manufacturers provide cases for their laptop systems as bonuses or extras — perks for being such wise customers as to purchase that particular brand of laptop. Generally speaking, such a case is probably the worst choice you can make.

Manufacturers generally give you a case in either of two extremes. First, they provide you with something that they call a "case," but it's really little more than a zippered pouch. That's just cheap and shameful.

Second, manufacturers provide you with too much case. They go overboard on size and give you something hulking and unwieldy. Figure 15-1 shows a manufacturer's case that's just too bulky to be useful — despite its "luxurious leather." The case shown in Figure 15-2 is also from a manufacturer, but it's too boxy. The case is mostly padding to keep the laptop from sliding around. Who wants to tote around padding in a laptop case?

The bottom line with manufacturer laptop cases is that they just don't give you any choice. Unless you've researched laptop cases and the manufacturer happens to offer one of the brand-name cases that agrees with you, just set aside any notion of getting a brand-name computer manufacturer's case.

Figure 15-1:
A computer manu-facturer's bulky yet luxurious leather case.

Figure 15-2:
This case is mostly unnecessary padding.

Things to look for in a case

I always look in a new case to see whether there's any money in it. That's one thing to look for in a case. But, seriously, the title of this section deals with features to look for when you're buying a laptop case. Here's a list:

✔ Does your laptop fit into the case? This question doesn't imply that the case needs a compartment designed to fit your specific laptop. Instead, you want to ensure that your laptop fits comfortably inside the case and that the case can zip up or close easily with the laptop inside.

✔ Actually, you *don't* want a case with a compartment designed to fit your specific laptop. You may not be using the same laptop years from now, but it's nice to keep using the same case.

✔ Get a soft case, not something hard, like the traditional briefcase. I think that a soft case holds the laptop more securely, whereas a laptop tends to jostle around inside a hard case.

✔ Does the case have plenty of pouches? You need pouches for storing accessories, office supplies, discs, manuals, Altoids, year-old receipts, and other things you plan on carrying around with you. The pouches can also be used for smuggling.

✔ I recommend a case that opens to display two large and separate areas. You can slide your laptop into one and put paper, notepads, or computer accessories into the other area.

✔ Zippers are preferred over snaps, buckles, or latches. Be sure, however, that the bag isn't so snug that the zipper can damage the laptop. In that case, look for those Velcro or "touchless" zippers.

✔ Having an easy-access pouch on the case's outside helps with storing important documents and other information that you need to grab quickly.

✔ A carrying handle is a must, but also consider a shoulder strap.

✔ A backpack can also make a great laptop carrying case. The bonus here is that shouldering the backpack keeps both your arms and hands free. That way, you can hold your boarding pass in one hand and coffee in the other and still carry the laptop with you.

✔ If you know that you have to carry lots of stuff (extra material for your job or perhaps something heavy, like a printer or video projector), consider getting a laptop case with wheels and a retractable handle.

✔ Keep in mind that the bag needs to fit beneath the seat in front of you on an airplane! Don't get something too big.

✔ The idea behind your laptop bag is to safely carry and protect the laptop while you're traveling; plus, it needs to carry all your laptop toys and other, related goodies. Go nuts on the extra features if you must. But, honestly, if you can find a solidly made case, bag, or backpack that does what you need, you're set.

Recommended brands

I used an Eddie Bauer soft briefcase as my laptop bag for 15 years. The same nylon bag is shown in Figure 15-3. It has plenty of pouches, zippers, and storage compartments, plus room left over for me to toss in magazines and books or even a box of chocolates to take home. That bag has been all over the world with me.

Figure 15-3: My trusty old Eddie Bauer soft case.

Recently I switched to using a backpack, primarily because it's roomier but also because thieves don't suspect backpacks to contain laptops as much as they do briefcases. If you choose a backpack, ensure that it's well put together, with reinforced seams on heavy-duty material.

The following is a list of brand-name bags that I can recommend or that have been recommended to me. If you have an outlet mall or retail location near you, pay the place a visit and peruse the stock. Don't forget to take your laptop with you for a test fitting!

- ✔ www.ebags.com
- ✔ www.eddiebauer.com
- ✔ www.targus.com
- ✔ www.thenorthface.com

✔ Perhaps the coolest laptop bag I've ever seen is the Oakley SI Vertical Computer Bag. The thing is *built*. Check it out at `http://oakley.com/`.

✔ Avoid a laptop case that's too tiny! Some trendy cases hug the laptop like a thong on a stripper. That's ineffective! (Well, for the laptop, not for the stripper.) You need a laptop case with some extra room in it. Think sweat pants, not hot pants.

I'm Leaving on a Jet Plane Checklist

You may not be jetting across the country. Perhaps you're just walking over to the neighborhood coffee bistro. Either way, consider this section your laptop checklist.

Things to do before you go

Here are some things you should consider doing before you toddle off with your laptop:

✔ Charge the battery! In fact, this is probably something you want to do well in advance before you leave. For example, I typically charge my laptop batteries the night before I leave on a trip.

✔ If you're lucky enough to have a spare battery, charge it as well.

✔ Synchronize your laptop with your desktop. Refer to Chapter 14 for more information.

✔ Back up your important files. The easy way to do this, if your laptop has a CD-R/RW drive, is to drag a copy of the My Documents folder from the laptop's hard drive to the CD-R/RW drive and then burn that disc. Keep the disc in a safe place (such as a fire safe).

✔ Remove any CDs or DVDs from the drive. This avoids having the drive spin into action when you start up on battery power. It also helps to put that disc with your other discs so that you don't forget about it or neglect it.

✔ Go online and save a few Web pages to your hard drive for offline reading while you're away. (Refer to Chapter 13.)

Things to pack in your laptop bag

A good laptop case is useful for holding more than just the laptop. Otherwise, it would be called a laptop *cozy* and not a case. When you're at a loss about what to put into your laptop case, consider this list for inspiration:

- ✔ Two words: office supplies. Pens. Paper. Sticky notes. Paper clips. Rubber bands. Highlighter. And so on.

- ✔ Pack the power cord and AC adapter!

- ✔ Bring any extra batteries you should have.

- ✔ Bring along your cell phone, although many people prefer to keep their phones clipped to their belts or stuffed in purses.

- ✔ When you're traveling overseas, remember to bring along a power conversion kit or overseas power adapter.

- ✔ Bring a phone cord if you plan on using a modem.

- ✔ Bring a 6-foot Ethernet cable — even if you don't plan on using a network.

- ✔ Bring headphones if you plan on listening to music or watching a DVD. It's more polite than sharing the noise with those sitting next to you.

- ✔ If you're making a presentation, don't forget the presentation! If you need your own video projector, pack it too!

- ✔ Pack any necessary peripherals: mouse, keyboard, PC cards, and external storage, for example.

- ✔ Ensure that you have some screen wipes.

- ✔ A deck of cards. (You need something to play with after the battery drains.)

- ✔ If you're taking along a digital camera, don't forget the camera's computer cable or a memory card reader. It's nice to be able to save those digital images right to the laptop when you're away.

Also take a look at Chapter 22 for more goodies you may want to take with you.

Looming Questions at the Airport

Taking a laptop onboard a commercial airliner today is about as normal as bringing onboard a newspaper and cup of coffee. That's good news. It means that bringing your laptop with you on a commercial airline flight isn't unusual and that the airlines are willing to accommodate your needs and not consider you as some oddball exception.

Is your laptop case one carry-on bag or half a carry-on bag?

Sadly, your laptop's case is often your only carry-on luggage. Some airlines let you carry the laptop case plus the typical overnight bag — the same kind of bag many folks try to jam into the overhead bins. Other airlines are less forgiving.

Do not check your laptop as luggage! You don't want to subject the laptop to the kind of torture that most checked bags suffer. You don't want your laptop to be in the subzero cargo hold, and you don't want to risk your laptop being stolen. Do not check your laptop!

When the plane is full and you've tried to sneak on too much carry-on luggage, check the luggage, not the laptop.

If you absolutely must check the laptop case, keep the laptop with you; just check the case.

Laptop inspection

Thanks to the takeover of airport inspections by the Transportation Security Administration, the security-screening procedures for laptop computers are pretty standard all over the United States. Here's what you need to do:

1. **Before you get into the inspection line, remove your laptop from its carrying case.**

   Yes, you'll be burdened with *stuff* for a few moments. You have to carry your boarding pass, picture ID, laptop case, coat, and carry-on bag — plus any small children, coffee cups, croissants, and whatnot. But it's only for a few moments.

2. **When you get to the X-ray machine, place your laptop in its own container and put the container on the conveyer belt.**

   You might want to alert the baggage screeners to the laptop's presence.

   Do not put your coat over the laptop. Don't toss your car keys into the same bin. In some places they may let you toss in your cell phone and PDA with the laptop, but don't stack things on top of each other.

3. **Mind your laptop through the X-ray machine.**

4. **Pick up your laptop on the other end of the X-ray machine.**

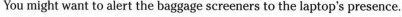

After the ordeal, you can put everything away, replacing the laptop into its case and storing all the other stuff that was disassembled or removed during the screening process. Then you're on your way to the gate.

✔ Watch your laptop! The X-ray machine is a popular spot for thieves! Refer to Chapter 16.

✔ The X-ray machine doesn't harm the laptop.

✔ You may be asked to turn the laptop on. That's a good reason to have the batteries fully charged. If they're not, be sure to pack the power cord; most X-ray stations have a wall socket you can use.

All aboard!

When you get into the plane, find your seat. Try to store the laptop under the seat in front of you. It's okay to put it in the overhead storage, but I recommend the underseat storage, which is easier to get to and avoids the peril of having latecomers jamming their steamer trunks and body bags into the overhead bins and crushing your laptop.

Keep the laptop in its carrying case! Wait until you hear the announcement that it's okay to turn on your electronic devices before you whip out your laptop.

✔ Obviously, it helps to avoid the bulkhead seats, which lack underseat storage.

✔ I prefer window seats for computing aloft. That way, I can control the window blind, to shield my laptop's screen from the sun. Plus, it's easier to angle the laptop toward me and away from prying eyes in other seats.

✔ 3M makes a special laptop display cover, the 3M Laptop Privacy Filter. It prevents peering eyes from seeing what's on your laptop screen, which is a problem on airplanes. The 3M Laptop Privacy Filter can be found at office-supply and computer stores all over.

Up, up in the air

After the announcement allowing you to use your electronic devices in the plane is made, you can whip out your laptop and . . . do whatever with it.

Of course, the real conundrum is trying to find a place for the thing. Some seats are so close together that it's nearly impossible to open the laptop while it's sitting on your tray table. And, when the guy in front of you lowers his seat, computer time is over!

When you can get the laptop open and running, the real choice becomes this: Do you get work done or play games, or perhaps watch a DVD movie? Hmmm.

How long you have to use the laptop depends primarily on the battery life, but also on the flight duration. When the announcement comes to shut down electronic devices, shut down Windows and turn off (or hibernate) your laptop.

Air power

The airlines have heard your cries for help, and many of them now offer AC power for use with your laptop on many flights. Three power plans are now available:

AC power: This is the power you're used to, provided with a standard U.S. or European power outlet. Sometimes it's a two-prong outlet, and sometimes there's a grounding plug.

Cigarette DC power: This kind of power is the same as what's offered in your car, with what is still curiously called the cigarette lighter. You need a cigarette power adapter to use this type of power with your laptop.

EmPower DC power: The most common type of laptop electricity available on airlines is EmPower. You need a special EmPower adapter to use this system, or you can use a cigarette power adapter / EmPower adapter — an adapter adapter.

Note that the power adapters aren't universal. You need to ask the airlines whether your flight has a power adapter you can use, and, furthermore, to ensure that your seat is near a power adapter. An extra fee may also be involved, although most of these adapters are in Business or First Class, so my guess is that you already paid the extra fee when you bought your ticket.

Remember that your laptop comes with batteries. Use them whenever power isn't available. Just because the airplane lacks something to plug into for power doesn't spell doom for your laptop computing abilities aloft.

- ✔ Cigarette and EmPower adapters are available wherever laptop goodies are sold. Also check the iGo Web site: www.igo.com.

- ✔ AC means *alternating current*. It's the same type of power that comes out of the wall in your home or office.

- ✔ DC means *direct current*, which is the type of power you get from a battery.

✔ Apparently, the 747 aircraft has a standard U.S. wall socket located near one of the exit doors. This is used to plug in the vacuum for cleaning the plain, but you can probably sneak your laptop into that socket during a flight. Don't tell anyone I told you this.

Café Computing

It used to be that you'd go into a coffeehouse, order a cappuccino, sit around with artsy folks dressed in black, and discuss Marxism. Today, you go to the coffeehouse, order your double-tall decaf machiatto, sit around with frustrated people dressed in "Friday casual," and discuss how to connect to the café's WiFi. The gal sitting next to you may still be a Marxist. But so what? If she knows the SSID and WEP, you can have a conversation.

This section mulls over a few of my observations while café computing:

✔ It doesn't have to be a café. In fact, a park in a major U.S. city soon became a hub of activity with all sorts of people using their laptop computers. The reason? The new business next to the park set up a wireless network *without security*. So, laptop users were "borrowing" the free Internet access.

✔ You see one other difference between the cafés of yesterday and today: Whereas a Marxist could sit in a café all day, laptop users eventually get up and leave when the battery juice runs dry.

Where to sit?

Before visiting the counter to order your beverage and hard-as-fiberboard bread snack, scout out the entire café for a good place to sit.

You want a table, unless you think that it's fun to balance a laptop on your knees while you sit on a sofa or an old sack of Columbian coffee beans.

Grab a table that's either away from the windows or facing the windows. You want to avoid having that bright light from the windows reflecting on your laptop screen and washing everything out. (You can tilt the screen to avoid the glare when there's nowhere else to sit.)

Another suggestion: Be mindful of high windows and skylights. As a sunny day grows long, the sun sweeps a slow swath of bright light across some tables. You don't want to be sitting at a table that's in the path of that moving shaft of light. (The voice of experience is speaking here.)

When you really want to get work done, find a spot away from the door and away from the sales counter. Do the opposite if you prefer to be social.

Be a socket sleuth

Another important factor in determining where to sit is the presence of wall sockets. Without trying to look like you're searching for bombs, duck down and look under some tables or up against walls for a helpful AC power source.

When you find a power source, great! Grab that table.

If you want to be honest about things, inquire at the counter whether it's okay to plug in. Otherwise, just sneak a cord over the socket as nonchalantly as possible.

Note that not all the power sockets will be on. My favorite coffeehouse in my hometown has a row of very obvious wall sockets next to some nice tables. Those wall sockets, sadly, are usually turned off. You can tell when you plug in: Your laptop doesn't alert you to the AC power presence and continues sucking down battery juice.

When you do manage to plug in, try to arrange the power cord so that no one trips over it. If someone does trip over your cord, expect expulsion.

Other tips 'n' stuff

It's always good to buy what they're selling when you're computing in a coffeehouse, diner, or café. Get a cup of coffee. Have a biscotti. Get a snack. The management at some places may enjoy having you there because it adds to the atmosphere, but these places are also in the business of making money. It has already been proven in court that they can throw you out for using their wireless networking without buying something, so buy something!

In my book *PCs For Dummies* (Wiley Publishing, Inc.), the rule is simple: No beverages near your computer! That goes double for the laptop, where the keyboard and computer are in the same box. But who am I to deny you a nice, delicious, warm cup of Joe? If you want to drink and compute, get your beverage in a heavy, hard-to-topple, ceramic mug. Also grab yourself a nice thick wad of napkins, Just In Case.

Never leave your laptop unattended! If you have to go potty, close down the laptop and put it away, or maybe even take it with you. *Never* leave your laptop unattended at the table. It will be stolen. (Also see Chapter 16.)

Don't forget to pack a mouse in your laptop bag! When I work on the road, especially in a spot where I'm setting up shop for a few hours, the external mouse is a blessing.

Sometimes you may be asked to leave or relocate, especially when you're taking up an entire booth all by yourself. Be knowledgeable about this situation in advance. If you see the place filling up, try to move to a smaller table or just pack up and leave.

Laptopping in Your Hotel Room

Most of this stuff about your hotel room is review information from other chapters in this book:

- If you're using a dialup modem, be sure to create a location and a set of dialing rules for the hotel. Especially if you plan on returning, creating the location and rule set now saves you time in future visits. See Chapter 11.

- Many hotels have broadband, or high-speed, Internet access. You pay for this, usually in 24-hour increments. An Ethernet cable is usually provided; look for it either in the desk drawer or (oddly) hanging in the closet. After connecting the network cable, open your Web browser and follow the instructions on the screen to set things up.

- I recommend staggering the 24-hour periods that the hotel grants for Internet access. Start your 24-hour session at 6:00 p.m. That way, you can use the connection that evening, and then the following morning, and all through the next day's afternoon.

- If you're planning on staying a week or more, see about negotiating a lower Internet connection rate. Also check to see whether any of your credit cards or the Auto Club offers free Internet access at that hotel.

- Beware of digital phone lines! Do not plug your modem into anything other than a hole properly labeled Modem.

- Use the inexpensive printer: Send a fax to the hotel's fax machine. Refer to Chapter 11.

- It's a security risk to leave your laptop set up in the hotel room. It's not that the housekeeping staff will steal it; they probably won't. It's more likely that an information thief will get hold of your laptop to cull out passwords and credit card numbers. See Chapter 16 about security issues while in a hotel.

✔ Another security risk is the hotel's wireless network. Be very careful when you're sending sensitive data — passwords, account numbers, credit card information, and so on — over the wireless (or even wired) network. Who knows how secure that network is or whether hackers are lying in wait nearby?

✔ Occasionally, I find the rare hotel room that lacks enough power sockets by the desk. Note that if you unplug a lamp or TV in some hotels, it activates the security system. So, if the hotel dick comes knocking at the door, be prepared to tell him that he can keep the lamp — you just want to use the wall socket. (And, consider a more trustworthy hotel for your next trip.)

Dealing with the Low-Battery Warning

Thanks to smart battery technology, your laptop can be programmed to tell you when the juice is about to go dry. In fact, you can set up two warnings on most laptops. (Refer to Chapter 8.) The idea is to act fast on those warnings when they appear — and to take them seriously! Dally at your own risk. It's your data that you could lose!

The real trick, of course, is to ration what battery power you do have. Here's a summary of tips, some of which are found elsewhere in this book:

✔ **Be mindful of the power-saving timeouts.** Setting a Stand By timeout for 15 minutes may be great in the office, but on the road you may want to adjust those times downward. Refer to Chapter 8.

✔ **Modify the display to use a lower resolution or fewer colors on the road.** In fact, for most computing, a resolution of 800 x 600 with 16-bit color is fine. Such a setting uses less video memory, which requires less power to operate and keep cool.

✔ **Mute the speakers!** Not only does this strategy save a modicum of power, but it also saves the ears of those next to you from hearing those silly noises that your laptop makes.

✔ **Disable unused devices.** If you're not using the modem, turn it off. If you don't need the CD/DVD drive, remove its disc. Speaking of which. . . .

✔ **If your laptop's CD/DVD drive is removable, consider removing it when you go on the road.** That saves a bit on weight as well as on power usage.

✔ **Save some stuff to do when you get back home or reconnect to a power source.** Face it: Some stuff can wait. If that 200K file upload isn't needed immediately, save it for when you're connected to the fast Internet line back at the office.

 ✔ **Hibernate!** When time is short and your laptop has the Hibernation smarts, just hibernate. Refer to Chapter 8.

Minding the Laptop's Temperature

One reason that your laptop doesn't have the latest, fastest microprocessor is heat. Even in a desktop PC, cutting-edge technology generates lots of heat. Managing that heat in a desktop is a huge chore, so you can imagine the things your laptop has to do to keep cool.

So much electronics is packed into the laptop's case that, when coupled with the battery, which heats as it discharges, there be a whole lot of heatin' goin' on. The laptop comes with a wee li'l cooling fan, one that may even have two speeds for when the temperature gets too hot. But that may not be enough! It's important not to let your laptop get too hot.

 ✔ Avoid putting your laptop anywhere that it will be in direct sunlight.

 ✔ Do not store the laptop in your car's trunk.

 ✔ Don't let the laptop run in a closet or any closed environment where air cannot circulate.

 ✔ Do not block the little vents on the laptop that help it inhale cool air and expel hot air.

 ✔ When the laptop continually runs too hot, especially when the battery compartment becomes too hot to touch, phone your laptop dealer for service.

 ✔ As a suggestion, consider buying your laptop a cooling pad. Chapter 21 covers this and other gizmos.

Beware of magnets

Should you be paralyzed by fear over the thought of exposing your laptop to a magnet? Perhaps.

Magnets aren't really the problem. No, the problem is with the *magnetic fields* the magnet generates. If you recall from when you slept through high school science class: magnets, electric motors, stereo speakers, and the planet Jupiter all generate magnetic fields.

In the olden days, computer users avoided magnets because even the slightest magnetic field would scramble the data on a floppy disk. Floppy disks are now part of the past, but those magnetic fields are still around and should be avoided. Something like a blender can generate a magnetic field that may interfere with a laptop right next to it.

It's a good idea to avoid leaving your laptop near appliances with electric motors or large stereo speakers, and definitely don't take the laptop to Jupiter. Or even Saturn.

Chapter 16

Laptop Security

· ·

· ·

*L*aptops are hot! I don't mean that they're hot as in the best new technology or that they're selling extremely well. And I don't mean that they're hot in that a Pentium laptop generates enough heat to turn bread into toast. No, I mean that laptops are one of the favorite things that crooks like to steal.

Thanks to their mobile nature, not to mention that most laptops cost at least a thousand dollars, your favorite portable computer ranks high on the lust list of the common thief. Laptops are easy to lift, easy to conceal, and easy to resell. For the typical thief, that's good news. For you, it's bad news.

This chapter covers the things you can do to help prevent your laptop from becoming yet another statistic. It covers things you can do beforehand, things you can do on the road, and even stuff that makes your laptop itself tell you when it has been the victim of a crime.

Laptops Are Easy for the Bad Guys to Steal

Unless you stole this book, you probably don't have the mind of a thief. This is good news for humanity. In fact, most of us aren't thieves and tend to be fairly trusting. Sadly, it's our trusting nature that the bad guys take advantage of.

First, the good news: Most laptops are forgotten and not stolen. As silly as that sounds, people leave their expensive laptops sitting around unattended more often than someone sneaks off with them. But don't let that trivial tidbit lull you into a false sense of security. Many laptops are stolen right out from under the eyes of their owners.

Think of the laptop as a sack of cash sitting around. To a crook, that's exactly what it is. Treat the laptop as a bag full o' money, and chances are that you'll never forget it or have it stolen.

The best way to protect your laptop is to label it. Specific instructions are offered later in this chapter. Keep in mind this statistic: 97 percent of unmarked computers are never recovered. Mark your laptops! (See the next section.)

Other interesting and potentially troublesome statistics:

- The chance of your laptop being stolen is 1 in 10.
- Most laptop theft occurs in the office. That includes both coworkers and Well-Dressed Intruders, or thieves in business suits.
- Laptop theft on college campuses (from dorm rooms) is up 37 percent.
- A thief who steals a $2,000 laptop typically gets about $50 for it on the street.
- According to law enforcement, 90 percent of laptop thefts are easily avoidable by using common sense.

What to Do Before It's Stolen

Any law enforcement official will tell you that a few extra steps of caution can avoid a disastrous theft. Thieves enjoy convenience just as all shoppers do; if your laptop is more difficult to pinch than the next guy's, it's the next guy who loses.

This section contains helpful hints and suggestions on things you can do ahead of time to help prevent theft or recover your laptop if it goes missing.

Mark your laptop

This advice is most important: It helps with the recovery of a stolen laptop if you've marked your laptop by either engraving it or using a tamper-resistant asset tag. After all, the best proof that something is yours is your name on the item in question.

✔ You can use an engraving tool to literally carve your name and contact information on your laptop.

✔ I know some folks who are clever and merely write their names inside their laptops, either on the back of some removable door, inside the battery compartment, or in other places a thief wouldn't check. Use a Sharpie or other indelible marker.

✔ Asset tags are available from most print shops. The tags peel and stick like any stickers do, but cannot be easily removed or damaged. For an investment of about $100, you can get a few hundred custom tags, for not only your computers but also other valuable items (cameras, bicycles, and TVs, for example).

✔ The STOP program offers bar code asset tags that leave a special tattoo if they're removed. The program also offers a recovery system that automatically returns stolen (or lost) property directly to your door. STOP stands for Security Tracking of Office Property, although home users and (especially) college students can take advantage of the service. Visit www.stoptheft.com for more information.

Avoid using an obvious laptop carrying case

That carrying case with the emblazoned Dell logo (or IBM logo or what-have-you) isn't just a proud buyer-appreciation and marketing gimmick. The custom laptop case is a sure clue to the casual thief that something valuable lurks inside. This is why I recommend, in Chapter 15, against getting a manufacturer's laptop case.

✔ A nondescript, soft laptop case works best.

✔ Backpacks are also good places to store laptops.

Register the laptop and its software

Be sure to send in your laptop's registration card, as well as the registration for any software you're using. If the laptop is then stolen, alert the manufacturer and software vendors. Hopefully, if someone using your stolen laptop ever tries to get the system fixed or upgraded, the company cares enough to help you locate the purloined laptop.

- ✔ This trick assumes that the person fencing the laptop doesn't fully erase the hard drive.

- ✔ Be sure to keep a copy of the laptop's serial number and other vital statistics with you — specifically, in a place other than in the laptop's carrying case. That way, you know which number to report to the police as well as the manufacturer.

Be mindful of your environment

They say that gambling casinos are a purse-snatcher's paradise. That's because most women are too wrapped up in the gambling to notice that their purses are being purloined. Purse can be on the floor, at their feet, or even in their laps. Thieves know the power of distraction.

When you're out and about with your laptop, you must always be mindful of where it is and who could have access to it. Watch your laptop!

For example, when you're dining out, put the laptop in its case beneath the table. If you need to leave the table, either take the laptop with you or ask your friends to keep an eye on it for you.

Take your laptop with you when you go to make a phone call.

Keep your laptop with you when you go to the restroom.

Secure your laptop in your hotel room's safe. If the hotel lacks a room safe, leave it in the hotel's main safe at the front desk.

Be especially mindful of distractions! A commotion in front of you means that the thief about to take your laptop is behind you. A commotion behind you means that the thief is in front of you. Thieves work in pairs or groups that way, using the commotion to distract you while your stuff is being stolen.

Here's one place to watch out for a group of thieves pulling the distraction ploy: At the airport screening station! Just one raised voice or "the woman in the red dress" can divert your attention long enough for your laptop to be gone. Also be aware of distractions on crowded escalators, where the movement of the crowd can knock you down and someone can easily grab the laptop bag and be gone.

The old ball and chain

In Chapter 5, this book takes you on a tour around your laptop's externals. One thing I point out over there is the place for the old ball and chain: a hole or slot into which you can connect a security cable. That hole has an official name: the Universal Security Slot, or USS.

The USS is designed to be part of the laptop's case. Any cable or security device threaded through the USS cannot be removed from the laptop; only the cable itself can be cut (or unlocked) to free the laptop.

Obviously, the USS works best when the laptop is in a stationary place. Like using a bicycle lock, you have to park the laptop by something big and stable and then thread the cable through that big thing and the USS for the lock to work.

- ✔ The best place to find a security cable for your laptop is in a computer- or office-supply store.

- ✔ Some cables come with alarms. You can find alarms that sound when the cable is cut, plus alarms that sound when the laptop is moved.

- ✔ Another way to anchor a laptop is to get a docking station where the laptop can be locked into place. A thief would rather steal a laptop than a full-size computer (or laptop in a docking station).

- ✔ It kind of tickles my fancy to read the title of this section and actually consider such a thing: Imagine a laptop chained to a 16-pound bowling ball. A thief would have to be desperate to try to flee with such a setup!

Protecting Your Data

Passwords protect only your laptop's data, not the laptop itself. Most thieves are looking to make a quick buck; generally, for drugs. They don't care about the contents of your laptop; they just want the quick cash it brings. But, a data thief wants *into* your laptop.

Data thieves want to find your passwords. They want to locate credit card numbers, which are valuable to sell. Furthermore, they can use your own computer to order stuff on the Internet or make transfers from your online bank account to their own.

The sad news is that password protection really doesn't stand in the way of most clever data thieves. They know all the tricks. They have all the tools. At best, you're merely going to slow them down.

This section offers various ways to protect the data on your laptop. These methods may not prevent a theft, but they help keep the information on your computer away from the weirdoes who want it.

Use the BIOS password

Your laptop's Setup program allows you to affix a password on the system, a password that's required well before the operating system loads. Although this is the first line in data defense, I cannot recommend it because of two things.

First, if you forget your password, you're screwed. Many people march forward with this BIOS password scheme and then end up leaving the laptop on 24 hours a day and, over time, forgetting the password. That's bad.

Second, it's possible to circumvent the BIOS password because so many people forget it. Just about every manufacturer has some method of overriding the password, which essentially nullifies the reason for having it in the first place.

✔ If your laptop manufacturer has assured you that the BIOS password cannot be circumvented, corrupted, erased, or overpowered, feel free to use it. But, do not forget the password!

✔ You're prompted for the password every dang doodle time you start your laptop.

✔ Some data crooks just yank the hard drive from the laptop so that they can steal the information from your hard drive by using their own special equipment. In this instance, the BIOS password doesn't protect you.

✔ Refer to Chapter 4 for more information on the BIOS setup program, which is how you can access and change the system's BIOS password.

Use the NTFS file system

Ensure that your laptop's hard drive is formatted using the NTFS formatting scheme. The NTFS format is more secure than older methods of formatting a hard drive. The how's and why's of a disk format are technical, but knowing whether your laptop uses the format is easy to confirm:

1. **Open the Computer or My Computer window.**

   Refer to Chapter 6.

2. **Click your laptop's hard drive icon to select it.**

   This is usually Drive C.

3. **Locate the Details panel.**

   In Windows Vista, it's at the bottom of the Computer window.

    In Windows XP, look on the left to see the Details information. You may need to click the downward-pointing chevrons to display the Details information.

4. **Check to see that it says File System: NTFS in the Details information.**

5. **Close the window.**

If your hard drive isn't using NTFS (it's using FAT32, for example, or some other format), you can update your hard drive to the NTFS format. This is done by running the CONVERT utility at the command prompt. I recommend that you have your dealer or computer guru do this for you.

Set a password on your account

Another method of reasonable protection is to ensure that your account on Windows has a password. When data security is important to you, definitely add a password to your account in Windows.

Computer security nabobs say that you should change your password every few months or so, and more often in a high-security area. Whatever. If you're duty-bound to change your password, open the Control Panel's User Accounts icon and, if necessary, click your account's image to bring it up. Then choose either Create a Password or Change Your/My Password to add or update a password on your account. Follow the directions on the screen for entering or deleting your password.

 ✔ The *strongest* passwords (that is, passwords that are the toughest to crack) use a combination of letters and numbers that's eight characters long or longer. Of course, such passwords are also easy to forget, so most people make the mistake of going with something short and simple.

✔ Never use the word *password* as your password. It's too easy to figure out.

 ✔ If you forget your password, you're screwed. It's possible to recover Windows, but all your account information may be utterly lost and not retrievable. Keep that in mind when you're choosing a password.

Use good, strong passwords

Too many passwords are easy to figure out. Do you know what the most common password is? It's *password* — believe it or not! People use as passwords their own first names, simple words, single letters — all sorts of utterly unsecure things.

If you're serious about protecting your computer's data, get a serious password. The computer jockeys like to call it a *strong* password. That usually involves two unique and often unrelated words plus some numbers — for example, something like `ibrake4cats`.

Two words are necessary because password-cracking programs simply skim through the dictionary and a list of common names.

Unrelated or nonsensical words work best together. Indeed `easterparade` is a poor password choice; `plumbercapacitor` is better.

Numbers are good because they add an element of unpredictability to the password. Avoid something like your address, though: `1600pennave` isn't as good as `nuts632poison`.

Try to avoid using symbols other than numbers in your passwords. They may not be accepted in some instances.

When you have trouble remembering your password, write it down! Just don't keep the password list near your computer. I know folks who write their passwords on their kitchen calendars or in their address books. Random words and numbers there may not mean anything to casual onlookers, but it's helpful if you forget the password.

Disable the Guest account

The Windows Guest account allows anyone to enter your computer. Even considering that the Guest account is highly limited, that's just enough for a data thief to get a foothold and start hacking away.

To remove the Guest account, follow these steps:

1a. **In Windows Vista, open the Control Panel's User Account Control Panel icon.**

1b. **In Windows XP, open the Control Panel's User Accounts icon.**

2a. **In Windows Vista, choose Manage Another Account.**

   Click the Continue button if you're visually assaulted by a User Account Control warning.

   If the screen says Guest account is off, then everything is fine and you're done.

2b. **In Windows XP, look to see whether the text Guest Account Is Off appears; if so, you're done.**

3. **Click the Guest account image to select it.**

4. **Choose Turn Off The Guest Account.**

5. **Close the User Account window.**

Lock Windows

Windows has a unique locking command. By pressing the Windows key (Win) and the L key, you can quickly lock the computer, temporarily logging yourself off Windows. Only by logging in again — which requires you to type your password — can you regain access.

If you plan on leaving your laptop for a moment, consider locking it: Just press Win+L. That way, even if you trust the other folks with you, they're prevented from doing even the most harmless mischief.

If your laptop lacks a Windows key, you can lock windows in two other ways:

 ✔ In Windows Vista, choose the padlock icon from the Start menu.

 ✔ In Windows XP, choose Log Off from the Start menu, and then click the Switch User button in the Log Off Windows dialog box.

Note that on some systems, pressing Ctrl+Alt+Delete automatically locks the computer.

Encrypt important files or folders

Windows can scramble or encrypt your files, if your hard drive is set up with the NTFS formatting thingy, covered in the section "Use the NTFS file system," earlier in this chapter.

The encryption is transparent: You can access the files just as you normally would. The files are decrypted as you open them and encrypted when you close them. So, they're saved on your hard drive in a scrambled state — which is good.

To encrypt files or folders, follow these steps:

1. **Right-click the file or folder to encrypt.**

2. **Choose Properties from the pop-up menu.**

3. **Click the Advanced button on the General tab.**

4. **In the Advanced Attributes box, select the Encrypt Contents to Secure Data check box.**

   See Figure 16-1.

5. **Click OK to close the Advanced Attributes box.**

6. **Click OK to close the file or folder's Properties dialog box.**

   An Encryption warning may appear. When you want only the file, and not the entire folder, encrypted, choose the Encrypt the File Only option and click OK.

The file shows up with green text in its name, which is your only real clue that it's encrypted.

You can repeat these steps to remove the encryption, but considering that encryption doesn't slow things down or otherwise hinder you, what's the point?

This feature may not be available in some versions of Windows.

Disable the infrared port

Apparently, some mysterious software out there can tunnel into your laptop via the infrared (IR) port. I was surprised by this, considering how obscure it is, but I defer to the greater wisdom of the computer security experts.

To disable your laptop's IR port, comply with these steps:

1. **Open the Device Manager.**

   Refer to Chapter 6 for specific directions.

2. **Click the Infrared Devices item (shown in Figure 16-2) to open it.**

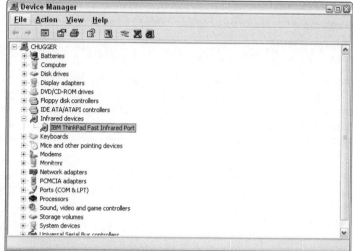

Figure 16-2:
Out, out,
infrared
spot!

3. **Double-click the Infrared Port item that appears beneath the Infrared Devices thingy.**

4. **In the bottom of the Properties dialog box, locate the Device Usage drop-down list and choose the Do Not Use This Device (Disable) option from the list.**

5. **Click OK to close the Properties window.**

6. **Close the Device Manager.**

If no infrared item is listed in the Device Manager, your laptop most likely lacks an infrared port. That's fine.

Back up your data!

When you lose a laptop, you lose two things. First you lose the laptop's hardware. Secondly, and more important, you lose the data on the laptop. If that data means something to you, I highly recommend that you keep a backup copy of that data.

You can back up data in many ways. The simplest is backing up over a network to a large-capacity hard drive. Just drag your My Documents folder to that network hard drive, and that's pretty much it (although this description is rather simple).

Why can't you just password-protect your files?

In 20 years of writing computer books, the most common question I've received is "Why can't individual files or folders have their own passwords?" It makes sense. And, it's a feature that I wish the operating system had. People apparently want it. Yet, it just isn't to be.

Of course, you're not stuck in the mud. Windows Vista lets you restrict access to certain files and folders by using *permissions*. That way, you can grant or restrict access to a folder or file to only certain people using your computer, or to no one but yourself.

In Windows XP you can password-protect Compressed Folder, or Zip file, archives. These archives are commonly used to send files and programs over the Internet. The compression allows larger files to be sent in less time. The archive also allows more than one file to be sent in a single batch.

You can choose File⇨New⇨Compressed (Zipped) Folder in Windows to create a compressed folder. Then copy into that folder the files you want to password-protect.

To set the password, open the Compressed Folder icon and choose File⇨Add Password. Enter the password twice, and then click OK. That's about as good as it gets.

The best way to back up data is to get real backup software, stuff that lets you back up your data to a network drive as well as to a CD-R or DVD-R drive, if your laptop has one.

In Windows XP, you can use a wide variety of third-party programs to back up your laptop's data. (The Windows Backup program that comes with Windows XP just isn't up to the task.) I can recommend Retrospect Backup, from Dantz, as well as the Norton Ghost program.

Windows Vista comes with a decent backup program: From the Start menu choose All Programs⇨Accessories⇨System Tools⇨Backup. Unlike older versions of Windows Backup, the Windows Vista version can back up to CD-R and DVD-R media.

Having the Laptop Phone Home

This feature is perhaps one of the most ingenious ways ever to protect your laptop. It involves having your laptop make a phone call and tell you where it is. Amazingly enough, it works.

This technique was supposedly discovered by accident. It went something like this: A laptop user programmed his system to phone his home computer every night at about 8:00. The two computers then exchanged data and updated each other.

One day, the laptop was stolen from work. But then a few days later, the phone suddenly rang at 8:00 p.m. The owner of the laptop picked up the phone and heard the sound of the laptop's modem making the call. He immediately grabbed the incoming Caller ID and used that information to help the police nab the laptop thief.

The laptop was recovered because it was programmed to phone home at a specific time every day. This program ran automatically, so when the thief (or whoever ended up with the stolen laptop) plugged in the system, the program continued to run.

You don't need to be a programmer to set up a similar system on your own computer. Many such programs do basically the same thing as I describe: They make the laptop phone home, or often they alert a tracking service over the Internet. The result is the same: The laptop's cry for help is heard, and the system is eventually recovered.

For more information, refer to the following Web sites of companies that offer such "phone home" services:

✔ www.ztrace.com

✔ www.computrace.com

✔ www.xtool.com

Your Thumbprint, Please

The latest trend in security devices is the thumbprint reader. It requires that you press your thumb on a special gizmo as a form of identification. If it's the correct thumb, the reader's software unlocks the laptop and lets you proceed. Or, depending on the reader, it may simply automatically "type" the proper password for you.

Obviously, a thumb reader is a far more secure method of identification than a password. I mean, who ever forgets a thumb?

Thumbprint readers are available as external (USB) devices or as part of a mouse, and some newer laptops include them as part of the laptop itself.

I've toyed with a USB thumb reader, but was underwhelmed. First, the thing was one more cord and gizmo to tote around with my laptop. Second, all it did was automatically type my password for me, so it really didn't save any time or trouble. Oh, well.

Chapter 17

Giving a Presentation

. . . .

In This Chapter

▶ Preparing for your presentation

▶ Using PowerPoint

▶ Connecting to the video projector

▶ Using handy PowerPoint keyboard shortcuts

. . . .

I suppose that, for the longest time, the main reason to lug around a laptop was to give one of those infamous video presentations. You've been there. You're in a darkened room. Warm. Too little sleep from the night before. A "presenter" talking in a droning monotone. Dull, lifeless information. Soon, you're starting to nod off. Try not to snore (or drool).

Because of the close relationship between laptops and presentations, I thought I'd throw in one more chapter just to brush up and review on the subject.

✔ These days, it's often not necessary to bring a laptop to a presentation. Merely having the presentation files on a CD-R is enough.

✔ Some handheld devices can be used to "drive" the video projectors that give presentations.

Setting Up PowerPoint

I suppose that the most nerve-wracking part about giving a presentation is ensuring that everything works. When you get everything working correctly, the speech itself should go smoothly, right? Even when they're well prepared, few folks enjoy speaking before large groups, especially groups of business folk who are used to — and often unimpressed by — computer presentations.

Oy. Another PowerPoint presentation. Yawn!

In most circumstances, you're allowed to set up your laptop and run through a test to ensure that everything works before giving your presentation to an audience. A technician might be available and even do everything to set it up for you. That's great. But it still doesn't make the situation any less nerve-wracking.

Creating the presentation

Before you leave and hit the road with your dog-and-pony show, you must first create your presentation. The program of choice for doing this is Microsoft PowerPoint, which can be purchased as an individual program or as part of the Office suite of applications.

PowerPoint creates documents generically referred to as *slide shows*. Each slide can contain text, graphics, pictures, or some combination of each one. You can add animations and sound effects, plus interesting fades and transitions between the slides.

All in all, PowerPoint is a fairly easy program to figure out and is fun to use with enjoyable results. That may not make the subject matter more enthralling, but just keep in mind that creating your presentation isn't the worst job in the world.

- ✔ PowerPoint must be installed on your laptop.

- ✔ Microsoft offers a PowerPoint viewer , which lets you play, but not edit, PowerPoint presentations. You can see a presentation even when you don't have PowerPoint (for example, if the laptop you're using doesn't have PowerPoint installed). This viewer program can be obtained from the Microsoft Web site (www.microsoft.com) in the Downloads area.

- ✔ One trick I've used to keep a presentation from getting too boring is to engage the audience during the show. Ask questions or have the audience fill in the blanks. That strategy not only makes the show more lively, but also helps keep people awake and on their toes.

- ✔ Another way to keep the audience awake is to provide hard copies of the slide show. You don't need to put one slide on each page. Instead, put six slides on a page to save paper. (This technique also avoids the crush of fans who want a copy after the presentation.)

- ✔ The first slide of any presentation I make is not the first slide shown. Instead, the first slide is used to help set up the laptop and video projector (covered in the next section). On that slide I have some text to test the focus as well as some sort of sound effect so that I can test the audio system.

✔ Indeed, you should complete the presentation before you leave. Even so, I'm one of many folks who work on presentations up until the minute that they're given!

✔ Yes, it's an *excellent* idea to create a backup copy of your presentation on a CD-R or USB flash drive. That way, if you lose the laptop or suddenly discover an incompatibility, you can use the CD-R or flash drive with someone else's computer to deliver the talk.

✔ You might also consider running the Microsoft Office Package for CD on your presentation, to move it into a portable format as a secondary backup. The Package for CD format can be easily read by other computers in case something happens to your laptop.

Hooking up to the video projector

For a small presentation, showing the PowerPoint slide show on your laptop screen and sitting at the end of a table is perfectly fine. Most of the time, however, you connect your laptop to a video projector. The video projector works like a giant monitor, displaying its image on a large screen at the end of a meeting room or convention hall.

The hook-up process is easier than it seems. In the best-case scenario, a helpful technician is there to assist you, and the connection is made and confirmed in advance. But even when no technician is available, you can generally figure things out:

1. **Connect your laptop's external video connector to the video projector.**

   You can use either the S-video or external monitor port. You can do this with the laptop on or off, though eventually you do need to turn it on. Oh, what the heck: Turn on the laptop now!

2. **Connect the laptop's audio-out port to the projector or to the location's sound system.**

   Chapter 5 helps you find that pesky audio-out jack.

3. **As long as you're connecting things, see whether you can plug the laptop into an AC socket.**

   No sense in wasting battery power for a presentation — or running out of battery juice in the middle of a presentation!

4a. **In Windows Vista, open the Personalization icon in the Control Panel, and then click Display Settings.**

4b. In Windows XP, open the Display icon in the Control Panel, and then click the Settings tab.

The job of View the Settings, shown in Figure 17-1, is to confirm that your laptop's hardware is working and that it recognizes the external "monitor" as the video projector. For most modern laptops, this happens automatically; the only time you really need to use the Settings dialog box is when things are hinkey.

Figure 17-1:
This laptop is ready to make presentations.

5. Check the image; preview the slide show.

At first, the projector may just show your laptop's Windows desktop. That's not why people are coming to the meeting, though. Take your presentation for a "pre-run." Load that main slide and ensure that it shows up on the screen. If so, you're ready to go.

If the slide show has sound effects, preview them as well to ensure that the sound system is working.

6. Close the laptop's lid, and go mingle or sit at the dais and wait to be introduced.

I leave my laptop at the podium, lid closed, ready to go. When I open the lid, the presentation is ready to run. Only when too many people are around and security is a concern do I take the laptop with me.

At other times, the video projector acts as the laptop's second monitor. The laptop shows the regular laptop screen, but the presentation appears on the video projector. (That's just PowerPoint being smart.)

✔ Be sure to pack an extra bulb when you're using your own video projector. You want to be able to replace a burned-out bulb quickly, and they usually don't sell those bulbs in the hotel's sundry store.

✔ Some laptops sport a special function (Fn) key on the keyboard, used to activate the external video port. You may need to press this key to switch the display over to the video projector.

✔ Some laptops may have dual video built in, allowing you to use the video projector as a second monitor. To confirm this, open the Display Properties dialog box and click the Settings tab. A second monitor should already be configured (refer to Figure 17-1). If so, you're set and ready to go.

PowerPoint Keyboard Shortcuts Worthy of Knowing

In this section, I describe a few keys you can use in PowerPoint to help save your rear in times of panic and dread.

Keys to display the next slide:

✔ Spacebar

✔ Enter

✔ N

✔ Down-arrow key

✔ Right-arrow key

Keys to redisplay the previous slide (or to back up through an animation sequence):

✔ Up-arrow key

✔ Left-arrow key

✔ P

✔ Backspace

Keys to display a blank screen in the middle of the presentation:

- ✔ B (black screen)
- ✔ . — the period (black screen)
- ✔ W (white screen)
- ✔ , — the comma (white screen)

Keys to start over, end, or go to a specific slide:

- ✔ n, Enter (go to slide number *n*).
- ✔ 1, Enter (go to the first slide).
- ✔ 99, Enter (go to the last slide or to slide 99).

Keys to cancel the show:

- ✔ Esc
- ✔ - (hyphen)

Keys to hide the pointer and navigation box:

- ✔ A
- ✔ = (equal sign)

Part V
Troubleshooting

The 5th Wave

By Rich Tennant

"I tell him many times — get lighter laptop. But him think he know better. Him have big ego. Him say 'Me Tarzan, you not!' That when vine break."

In this part . . .

Computers can be subject to all sorts of woe. Imagine!
And, you don't need a clever Captain Kirk to confuse
and thwart the computer with some logic sonnet, either.
Computers foul up because of things we do, things that
are accidentally done, and, most often, for that one unde-
niable reason: *just because*.

Troubles follow a computer around like a cat pursues a
little kid who sat down in a tuna fish sandwich. Trouble is
inevitable. Laptops are not immune. In fact, laptops can
be more troublesome than desktops. The two chapters in
this section cover the woes of computer troubleshooting
as well as the vital topic of upgrading and repairing your
laptop.

Chapter 18

Major Trouble and General Solutions

- -

- -

*C*onsider that not every computer is the same. Computers have different hardware configurations plus different software programs and different versions of those programs and, indeed, different versions of Windows. Multiply that by the potential for trouble, and there are perhaps a gazillion things that could go wrong with any computer. *Egads!*

Fortunately, trouble only occasionally visits upon the typical computer, so most of the time you can use your laptop to get something done as opposed to constantly fixing the thing. That's a good thing. When trouble does come to roost upon your laptop, this is the chapter to turn to for quick advice and some easy solutions.

For more information on PC troubleshooting, I highly recommend my book *Troubleshooting Your PC For Dummies*, from Wiley Publishing and available exclusively on Planet Earth.

Soothing Words of Support for the Computer Weary

Odds are really good that when your laptop is having problems, it's because *something has changed.* It might seem obvious — I mean, duh! The thing doesn't work any more! But, usually, some change took place *before* the trouble started and is to blame.

Computers are really a house of cards waiting to collapse at the slightest whiff of error. It's amazing that they run well at all. Adding new hardware or new software or changing an existing configuration can lead to trouble. So, the question you need to ask when trouble comes is simple:

What has changed recently?

Anything new? Think back a few days. Chances are good that whatever you added to the computer, whatever you changed or modified, is the cause of the error. Reversing the change often fixes things.

- ✔ Changing or modifying your data files (such as Word documents, MP3s, or JPEGs) isn't the type of change referred to in this section. No, changing or modifying *programs* or parts of the Windows operating system is what can lead to trouble.

- ✔ When you know that the trouble is related to a specific hardware or software change, contact the hardware or software developer on the Internet. Look up the Web page's support section and see whether any of your issues is mentioned or solutions offered.

- ✔ Removing or undoing the change often fixes things. Also refer to the section "The Miracle of System Restore," later in this chapter.

The Universal Quick-Fix

Sometimes computers just act weird. There might be nothing wrong, though I refer to this syndrome as "tired RAM." The solution, as well as the first thing you should try at the hint of trouble, is to restart Windows.

Often times, restarting Windows unclogs the drain and allows your computer to work properly once again. At the least, it's worth a try.

Refer to Chapter 4 for information on restarting Windows.

You don't need to reinstall Windows

Once upon a time, technical support was provided as a form of customer service. The developer felt that it owed after-sale support to its customers. But that was then. Now, tech support seems more like an obligation, and the support that's offered isn't often very helpful. In fact, because the bean counters measure tech support on a per-call basis, the real desire of the support personnel isn't to solve the problem, but rather to get you off the phone as quickly as possible.

Industry-wide, the average call for tech support must be less than 12 minutes. When the call reaches 10 minutes, tech-support people are advised to direct you to simply reinstall the Windows operating system to fix your problem. Does this fix your problem? That's not the issue. It fixes *their* problem, which is to get you off the phone.

I've been troubleshooting and fixing computers for years. Only a handful of times has reinstalling

Windows been necessary to fix a problem — and that's usually because the user deleted parts of the Windows operating system either accidentally or because of a virus or other computer disaster. Beyond that, with patience and knowledge, any computer problem can be solved.

Reinstalling Windows is drastic. In the entire history of computers, only now is reinstalling a computer operating system considered "routine." It shouldn't be. The operating system is the bedrock on which you build your computer house. Reinstalling Windows is like rebuilding your home's foundation when all you need to do is fix a leaky faucet.

When someone tells you to reinstall Windows, run. No, better: Scream, and then run. Try to find another source of help. ***Remember:*** Only in drastic situations is reinstalling Windows necessary. If you can find someone knowledgeable and helpful enough, he can assist you without having to reinstall Windows.

The Miracle of System Restore

As I mention earlier in this chapter, most of the problems you have with your laptop are because something was changed. You modified something in Windows. You installed a new piece of software. You upgraded or added hardware. After such a change is made is when the problem shows up. So, the solution — in a magical world — would be to go back in time *before* the problem. Ah, would it were so. . . .

Hey! It can be so! Thanks to the handy program System Restore, you can take Windows back in time. You can restore your computer system to the state it was in just before you installed the new hardware or software or made that fatal change. System Restore is the time-travel pod you take on your journey toward fixing your laptop.

Enabling System Restore

To use System Restore, you have to ensure that it's turned on. Some folks turn it off because System Restore uses mass quantities of hard drive space molecules. My advice is to leave System Restore on because it's a powerful and useful tool. Either way, check to confirm that System Restore is enabled according to the sections that follow.

✔ Enabling System Restore uses more disk space than when it's turned off. In fact, it might have been turned off to save disk space.

✔ System Restore in Windows XP can also be a security risk. Quite a few viruses and nasty programs take advantage of System Restore as a hiding place, and to ensure that using System Restore doesn't erase their evil presence.

Confirming System Restore Settings in Windows Vista

1. Open the Control Panel's System icon.

Refer to Chapter 6 for more information on both the Control Panel and the System icon.

2. Click the link on the left that reads Advanced System Settings.

Click the Continue button in the User Account Control dialog box.

3. In the System Properties dialog box, click the System Protection tab.

4. Ensure that there's a check mark by each disk drive you want protected with System Restore.

Removing the check mark disables System Restore for that drive.

5. Click OK to confirm your settings and (optionally) close the Control Panel window.

Confirming System Restore Settings in Windows XP

1. Open the Control Panel's System icon.

2. Click the System Restore tab.

3. **Ensure that there's no check mark by the option labeled Turn Off System Restore.**

   Yes, the check box must be empty. This is backward. Well, at least to me it's backward.

4. **Click OK to confirm your settings and close the dialog box. Close the Control Panel window as well.**

When to use System Restore

Any time you plan on changing anything on your computer, modifying Windows, adding an update, installing new hardware, or changing a system setting, you should run the System Restore program. Specifically, you should set a *restore point.* That way, if anything weird happens, you can generally recover.

The next two sections describe how to set a restore point, depending on your version of Windows.

 ✔ The Control Panel is where you go to modify various settings in Windows. Upon opening the Control Panel, you should think, "Should I be creating a restore point now?"

 ✔ Create a restore point before installing new hardware.

 ✔ Create a restore point before removing hardware.

 ✔ Create a restore point before adding or updating a new hardware driver.

 ✔ Create a restore point before installing any programs you download from the Internet.

 ✔ Be sure to create a restore point before you decide to toil with network configurations. That will really save your butt.

 ✔ If you neglect to set a restore point, don't fret! The computer automatically sets them every few days. You should be fine.

Setting a restore point in Windows Vista

1. **From the Start button's menu, choose All Programs⇨Accessories⇨ System Tools⇨System Restore.**

   In Windows Vista, you're greeted with a User Account Control (UAC) warning.

2. **Click the Continue button to dismiss the UAC dialog box.**

3. **Near the bottom of the window, click the link that says Open System Protection.**

    The System Properties dialog box appears, with the System Protection tab front and forward.

4. **Click the Create button.**

5. **Type a reason for the restore point, or enter a description about why it's necessary.**

    For example, type **Installing new mouse** or **Updating network adapter driver**.

6. **Click the Create button.**

    After a spell (or incantation — whichever), you eventually see a Success dialog box.

7. **Click OK.**

8. **Close the System Properties window and then the System Restore window.**

    You're done; go ahead and make whatever change you were planning to do on your laptop.

Setting a restore point in Windows XP

1. **From the Start button's menu, choose All Programs⇨Accessories⇨ System Tools⇨System Restore.**

2. **Choose the Create a Restore Point option and click the Next button.**

3. **Enter a description.**

    Or, type a reason that you feel the restore point is necessary; for example, **Updating video drivers** or **Adding wireless networking**.

4. **Click the Create button.**

    The next screen tells you that your restore point has been created and lists the description, date, and time.

5. **Click the Close button.**

    At this point, you can go on with the software or hardware change or whatever modifications you were going to make in Windows.

Restoring your system

When the computer starts acting goofy, and because you know that it might have been caused by a recent change, you can make the attempt at fixing things by using System Restore. You can select a restore point from the past, the most recent one, or the one you just set before you went messing with the computer and recover the system to a workable state.

To recover your system and (hopefully) fix the problem, obey the steps in the sections that follow.

The System Restore action should fix the problem, especially if it was caused by a recent system change. If not, you can try starting the laptop in Safe mode, which is covered later in this chapter.

✔ Running System Restore undoes any changes you made between now and the date and time of the restore point. Some of the changes might not have caused the problem, so don't be surprised, for example, if your screen saver changes or other parts of Windows change — parts unrelated to the original problem.

✔ System Restore doesn't delete any new files you created. It affects only the operating system and installed software.

✔ System Restore lets you reset the system back only a few days or so. Attempts to use a restore point earlier than a week before generally don't meet well with success.

Restoring a Windows Vista laptop

1. From the Start button menu, choose All Programs⇨Accessories⇨ System Tools⇨System Restore.

Be sure to click the Continue button if you're faced with a User Account Control dialog box.

2. Choose the option Choose A Different Restore Point.

I recommend this option because the Recommended Restore choice doesn't always reflect the most recent restore point you set. (It might show only the restore points created by Windows.)

3. Click the Next button.

4. Choose a restore point from the list that's displayed.

Note that some days might have more than one restore point. This is why I recommend being descriptive when you set the restore point, so that you know which one to use.

5. Click the Next button.

6. Click the Finish button.

Scary-warning time! That's okay; System Restore cannot be interrupted while it's restoring your system. That means if you're running other programs now, you should close them by clicking the No button, closing those programs, and then restarting this procedure over with Step 1. Otherwise:

7. Click the Yes button.

Hum some cheery tunes while your laptop's system is being restored. (Future releases of Windows will play elevator music here.)

8. **Be surprised!**

Yes! Windows shuts down. Don't be surprised. It's your signal that the restore operation was complete and you can, once again, log in to Windows and get work done — hopefully, without the problem you were previously facing.

Restoring a Windows XP laptop

1. **From the Start button's menu, choose All Programs⇨Accessories⇨ System Tools⇨System Restore.**

2. **Choose the Restore My Computer to an Earlier Time option.**

3. **Click the Next button.**

4. **Choose a restore point from the calendar that's displayed.**

Note that some days might have more than one restore point.

5. **Click the Next button.**

6. **Close any running programs.**

This is done as a precaution; you don't want to lose any data.

7. **Click the Next button.**

Windows logs you off and restarts the computer. This is necessary for some changes to have full effect. Just sit back and wait, or get another cup of your favorite caffeinated beverage.

8. **Click OK on the final screen.**

The final screen is displayed after the restore point is complete.

Major Troubleshooting with Safe Mode

When you need to do serious troubleshooting, Windows offers a special mode of operation called *Safe mode*. I question the name. Doesn't it imply that normally Windows is *not* in Safe mode? What is it then? Unsafe mode? But I digress. . . .

Safe mode helps determine one major thing: whether the problem is with Windows or other software. In Safe mode, only the most basic programs required to run Windows are loaded on startup. The rest of the stuff — those troublesome drivers — aren't loaded. Then, if the problem is gone in Safe mode, the problem is *not* to be blamed on Windows.

Entering Safe mode

Safe mode happens in a number of ways. Most annoyingly, your laptop starts in Safe mode when something is awry and Windows cannot start normally. See the section "Testing in Safe mode" to find out what to do, as well as the section "My laptop always starts in Safe mode!"

With some versions of Windows, you can conjure up Safe mode by pressing the F8 key when the laptop first starts. If you're quick enough, pressing the F8 key causes Windows to display a text-based startup menu. One of the options presented is Safe mode. Choose that option to continue starting the computer in Safe mode. But not every version of Windows offers this feature.

The most assured way to start your laptop in Safe mode is by using the most excellent troubleshooting tool System Configuration Utility, a.k.a. MS Config. This utility helps you troubleshoot startup problems by selectively disabling various startup services and programs.

To configure the computer to start up in Safe mode, use the System Configuration Utility:

1. **Choose the Run command from the Start button menu.**

   Or, press the Win+R keyboard shortcut; or, in Windows Vista, choose All Programs➪Accessories➪Run.

2. **Type** MSCONFIG **into the text box, and then click OK.**

   In Windows Vista, click the Allow button when you're confronted with the User Access Control dialog box.

3a. **In Windows Vista, click the Boot tab, and then put a check mark by the item labeled Safe Boot.**

3b. **In Windows XP, select the Diagnostic Startup radio button.**

4. **Click OK.**

   Wait a few seconds. The computer is "thinking."

5. **Click the Restart button.**

   Your laptop restarts in Safe mode.

Let the troubleshooting begin!

   ✔ Refer to the next section for what to do in Safe mode.

   ✔ To get out of Safe mode, repeat the preceding steps, but this time in Step 4 choose the option named Normal Startup — Load All Device Drivers and Services.

✔ For more information on the System Configuration Utility, refer to my book *Troubleshooting Your PC For Dummies* (Wiley Publishing).

✔ Another startup menu might appear on your laptop, one that gives you the option of starting the Windows Recovery Console. Using that utility is also covered in my *Troubleshooting Your PC For Dummies* book, starting with the second edition.

Testing in Safe mode

In Safe mode, Windows doesn't load common device drivers or extensions to the computer system. Therefore, the screen has a very low resolution, and some hardware features you're used to working with aren't available: Forget about networking. Forget about the Internet.

Your job in Safe mode is trying to repeat the error. Do whatever it is that's causing your trouble. If the problem exists in Safe mode, it's most likely a Windows problem. If not, and when everything seems okay, the problem is with something else on your computer — some software program or piece of hardware.

To exit Safe mode and start the computer normally, repeat the steps from the previous section. In Step 3 for Windows Vista, remove the check mark. For Step 3 in Windows XP, choose Normal Startup.

✔ Do not try to use your computer in Safe mode. Don't get work done; don't run your word processor. Don't play a game. Safe mode is for fixing the problem, not for doing anything else.

✔ When the problem is with Windows itself, which is evident in Safe mode, you should visit the Windows tech support Web site to find a solution. Restart the computer in normal mode and visit the Microsoft Knowledge Base:

```
http://support.microsoft.com/
```

Type in a few keywords to search the Knowledge Base for your problem. A solution should quickly be at hand.

"My laptop always starts in Safe mode!"

When your laptop starts in Safe mode, it means that something is wrong. Some piece of hardware or software has told Windows that it just can't function, and so the system starts in Safe mode — first, to alert you to the problem; and second, to give you the opportunity to fix things.

In most cases, the problem's description appears on the screen, and you can address the issue by reading the text that's displayed.

Sometimes, you have to check with the Device Manager to look for misbehaving hardware. Malfunctioning hardware appears on the Device Manager list, highlighted by a yellow circle with an exclamation point in the middle. Double-clicking that item displays the error message and possibly a suggestion for fixing things.

Common Problems and Solutions

It would be nearly impossible for me to mention every dang doodle problem your laptop can experience. So, rather than list every dang doodle one of them, or even 1,000 or even 100, I've narrowed the list to 5. Each of them is covered in this section.

"The keyboard is wacky!"

This problem happens more often than you would imagine, based on the e-mail I receive. The solution is generally simple: You accidentally pressed the Num Lock key on your keyboard, and half the alphabet keys on your keyboard are acting like numbers.

The solution is to press the Num Lock key and restore your keyboard to full alphabetic operation.

Making the mouse pointer more visible

The Mouse icon in the Control Panel is a hotbed of rodent-like activity. Especially if you're having trouble seeing the mouse pointer on your laptop's screen, visit the Pointers or Pointer Options tab in the Mouse Properties dialog box. The following suggestions can help you make the mouse pointer more visible:

✔ On the Pointers tab, you can choose larger mouse pointers than the set normally used by Windows. In the Scheme drop-down list, choose Windows Standard (extra large) for some supersize mouse pointers.

✔ On the Pointer Options tab, use two of the options in the Visibility area to help you find a mouse pointer on the screen. Specifically, try Pointer Trails or the Ctrl-key click option.

> ✔ Pointer Trails adds a comet-tail effect to the mouse in Windows, helping you locate the mouse pointer as you move it around.
>
> ✔ When the mouse plays Where's Waldo, you can find it with the Ctrl-key click option by pressing either Ctrl key on your keyboard. A series of concentric rings surrounds and highlights the mouse pointer's location.

The laptop won't wake up

A snoozing laptop can mean that the battery is dead. Consider plugging in the laptop and trying again.

When the laptop has trouble waking from Stand By mode — and you have to turn it off and then turn it on again to get control — you have a problem with the power-management system in your laptop. See the next section.

Power-management woes

When your laptop suddenly loses its ability to go into Stand By or Hibernate mode, it means that there might be a problem with the power-management hardware or software.

First, check with your computer manufacturer's Web page to see whether you can find any additional information or software updates.

Second, ensure that both modes are activated: Check the Power Options icon in the Control Panel.

Finally, confirm that other hardware or software isn't interfering with the power-management software. If so, remove the interfering software or hardware, or check for updates that don't mess with your laptop's power-management system.

The battery won't charge

Batteries die. Even the modern smart batteries are good for only so long. When your battery goes, replace it with a new one. When the battery goes unexpectedly, consider replacing it under warranty if it proves defective.

Rules and laws govern the disposal of batteries. Be sure to follow the proper procedure for your community to safely dispose of or recycle batteries.

"1 Need Help, and 1 Can't Find the Answer Here"

This chapter contains my best advice for troubleshooting your laptop. Honestly, these are the things I do when stuff goes wrong. Beyond that, you can get support and help from your dealer or laptop manufacturer, either over the phone or from its Web site. Again, that's what I do.

- ✔ If you followed my advice, you purchased an extended warranty for your laptop. Good. Use it in times of woe.

- ✔ Part of buying a laptop is searching for after-sale service and support. I say so in Chapter 2. You paid for that service and support, so use it! The dealer or manufacturer should be the first person you phone at the sign of trouble.

- ✔ Support for Windows is a tricky issue. Theoretically, if your laptop manufacturer provides Windows, it's bound to provide support for it.

Chapter 19

Upgrading Your Laptop

*O*ne reason that the PC is the most popular computer design ever is that the system is upgradeable. Everything in a desktop PC is modular. It's possible to replace any of several components by removing a defective something and replacing it with a better or more powerful something else. In most cases, the only skills needed are a screwdriver and a healthy respect for electricity. Laptop computers, however, aren't as upgrade friendly.

Most laptops are solid units. Sure, you might be able to swap out the CD/DVD player or hard drive. You might be able to add more memory. But beyond that, the laptop's case is a crowded, complex place with little room for civic improvements.

Despite its limitations, your laptop can be upgraded. Sometimes, it's even necessary. Beyond hardware, it has software upgrades to consider. This chapter covers both types of upgrades — software as well as hardware.

How 'Bout Some New Software?

Generally speaking, I don't recommend upgrading software. In the olden days, upgrades were necessary to add new features and expand on the abilities of older programs. But today's software is so advanced that even a program purchased back in the late 1990s would still serve you well today.

Upgrading your software

I recommend upgrading your software only when the newer version of the program offers features you need or fixes problems you have. Otherwise, my motto is "If it ain't broke, don't fix it!"

I'm serious: You can avoid a lot of trouble by not upgrading. I've seen too many stable computers become unstable after simple upgrades. I've seen printers suddenly not work. Worse yet, I've seen the chain reaction of having to upgrade more than one application just to keep things compatible. That can be expensive.

Still, upgrading can often be effortless. The newer version of the application can boost your productivity. The key is to be prepared for anything.

✔ Before upgrading, set a system restore point. It helps you recover things in case the upgrade doesn't work properly. Refer to Chapter 18.

✔ Upgrading is as easy as sticking the new program's CD into your laptop's CD drive. Everything after that should run automatically, with your input required only for a few simple questions.

✔ The hard part about upgrading is living with any unintended consequences. An *upgrade* is a change to your laptop. Sometimes, changes aren't good. Refer to Chapter 18.

✔ You don't need to uninstall the previous version of a program when you're installing an update. The only exception is when you're specifically advised to uninstall any older versions.

✔ Refer to Chapter 6 for information on removing software from your computer.

Updating Windows

Microsoft routinely updates Windows — weekly, in fact. As bugs are fixed or security issues are addressed, updates are made available. They can be automatically installed as your laptop accesses the Internet, or they can be manually installed by visiting the Windows Update service on the Internet or obtaining the occasional update CD directly from Microsoft.

When your computer is configured for automatic updates, Windows goes to the Microsoft update site and downloads the updates in the background every time you're connected to the Internet. As new updates are available, they're provided to you. Then you're informed of the updates and given the option to install them, depending on which settings you choose when you configure automatic updates (see the next two sections).

- ✔ I recommend keeping the Automatic Update feature turned on and automatic.
- ✔ Ensure that you choose a time for the automatic updates when your laptop is on and not sleeping, hibernating, or turned off.
- ✔ Your laptop should be connected to the Internet during the update time.
- ✔ It's even better when the laptop is on AC power, and not batteries, when the updates happen.
- ✔ Occasionally Microsoft releases an entire package of updates as a *Service Package* or Service Pack. Again, I recommend this is a required update.

Configuring your laptop for automatic updates in Windows Vista

1. **Open the Control Panel's Windows Update icon.**
2. **On the left side of the window, click Change Settings.**
3. **To activate automatic updates, select the first option at the top, Install Updates Automatically (Recommended).**

   You can peruse the other options, if you like, though I highly recommend the first one.
4. **Choose a proper time for the updates to take place.**
5. **Click OK.**

   Optionally, close the Control Panel window as well.

Upgrades versus updates

Computer jargon can be confusing enough without having to deal with vague terms that also exist in English. Prime examples are the words *upgrade* and *update.* They might seem like the same thing, but in the computer world, they're not.

Upgrade means to install a newer version of some program you already own. For example, you upgrade from version 2.1 of a program to version 2.2. Specifically, that's referred to as a *minor* upgrade. From version 4.0 to version 5.0 is a *major* upgrade.

Update means to improve an existing program, but not change its version or release number. For example, Microsoft routinely releases security updates for Windows. These updates, or *patches,* are applied to your version of Windows to improve things, address security issues, or fix bugs. Applying the update does not upgrade the software.

In some universe somewhere, this all makes sense.

Configuring your laptop for automatic updates in Windows XP

1. **Open the Control Panel's System icon.**

2. **Click the Automatic Updates tab.**

3. **Select the option at the top of the dialog box, Automatic (Recommended).**

4. **Set an available time for the updates.**

5. **Click OK.**

   You can close the Control Panel window.

Upgrading to a new version of Windows

I highly recommend against upgrading your laptop's operating system. Specifically, I recommend against upgrading Windows. Once upon a time, upgrading the operating system was great. But today, the improvements and changes they make to Windows are just too great to risk the stability of your computer — specifically, a laptop.

Rather than upgrade Windows, the next best thing is simply to wait until you can afford to buy a new laptop with the latest version of Windows prein-stalled. That way, you're assured that all the hardware is compatible with the new version and that it's robust enough to handle the new version of Windows. When you're upgrading an older computer, you just can't be assured of those things, so it's a risk. I don't recommend risking the invest-ment you have with your laptop.

- One thing you might not get with the update are *drivers,* or specific soft-ware that controls various parts of your laptop. These parts include the mouse pad, the wireless and Ethernet network adapters, the display, the power-management hardware — essentially, all the things that make your laptop easy to use.

- Sure, if you want to upgrade Windows, go ahead. I can't stop you. But I highly recommend against upgrading Windows.

Giving Your Laptop New Hardware

If you're fortunate enough to have an upgradeable laptop, by golly, you should take advantage of it someday!

Internal expansion options are somewhat limited with laptops. Even so, on many laptops, it's possible to replace or upgrade the hard drive and memory (RAM). Most other things on the laptop cannot be upgraded; the micro-processor, video circuitry, networking adapter, modem, and other hardware

are often all integrated into the laptop's main circuitry board, or *mother-board.* It's cheaper to buy an entirely new laptop than to try to upgrade anything on the motherboard.

If your laptop is equipped with a handy method for adding more memory, do so! Memory chips are available far and wide, though my favorite place to shop for RAM is the online memory store at www.crucial.com. The site has a configuration program that helps you select the exact memory you need. It's very handy, plus the memory chips come with good instructions on how to install them in your computer.

Some laptops allow for the hard drive to be replaced or upgraded. The easiest way to do this is when there's a drive bay option. For example, you can use a floppy drive, CD-R, DVD, or hard drive in the drive bay. So, if your computer came with a CD drive and you want to replace it with a second hard drive, the operation is not only possible, but also relatively easy to accomplish. The bad news is that the extra drives are available only from the manufacturer and are often quite pricey.

Beyond those few basic items, your laptop is essentially a closed box, and no further upgrades are offered. Don't despair! Refer to Chapter 7 for various ways to expand your laptop's universe. With the USB standard, there's really no limit to your laptop's hardware extents.

- ✔ Rather than upgrade your laptop with an internal hard drive, consider getting an external USB 2.0 drive instead. Ditto for an extra CD, DVD, or recordable media drive.

- ✔ New hardware is recognized almost instantly by Windows. A pop-up bubble from the notification area alerts you to any new hardware that Windows finds.

- ✔ When new hardware isn't automatically found, open the Control Panel and then the Add Hardware icon. Run the Add Hardware Wizard to help set up and configure your new hardware.

- ✔ Some USB peripherals might not be recognized. For example, a new USB mouse or keyboard might not cause any alerts to appear or notices to show up. That's fine. Check the device to ensure that it's working. If so, then you're doing well.

- ✔ You must add external modems manually. Refer to Chapter 11.

- ✔ Joysticks must be configured manually. Use the Game Controllers icon in the Control Panel.

- ✔ Refer to the documentation that came with your hardware for how exactly to configure it. Note that sometimes the software that comes with your device (usually on a CD) might need to be installed first, before you install the hardware. Other times, it's vice versa.

Part VI
The Part of Tens

The 5th Wave

By Rich Tennant

"In preparation for takeoff, we ask that you turn off all electronic devices, laptop computers and mainframes..."

In this part . . .

My friend Jim really needs only three fingers. That's because he uses only three items to illustrate a point. Sometimes he uses A, B, C to punctuate the items, and sometimes he numbers them. But there's always three.

When I rattle off items, I prefer to use ten, probably because I have ten figures and definitely because I think that listing ten things is more difficult than listing only three. Twelve things? Leave that for the gods!

The chapters in this section list some helpful items, tips, or suggestions to assist you and your laptop as you waltz down the merry path of harmony. Each chapter has ten items; therefore, this is The Part of Tens.

Chapter 20

Ten Battery Tips and Tricks

*J*ust about every bit of hardware on a laptop computer is somehow related to, or has a counterpart on, the nonportable desktop computer — everything, that is, except for the battery. More than a carrying handle, it's the battery that makes the laptop portable.

This chapter contains 10 tips and tricks to help you use your laptop and its battery in the most productive manner possible. Note that these aren't the standard battery tips. I'm assuming, for example, that you know better than to put your laptop's battery into your mouth. Furthermore, I assume that you won't suddenly desire to put your laptop's battery on a campfire "to see what happens." Finally, I assume that you'll never go anywhere near your laptop's battery with a can opener or soldering iron — unless it's your dying wish to see your grieving relatives try to explain your stupidity to a television news crew.

Don't Drop the Battery, Get It Wet, Short It, Play Keep-Away with It, Open It, Burn It, or Throw It Away

Enough said.

Every Few Months, Drain the Battery All the Way

To keep your laptop's battery nice and healthy, remember to drain it completely at least once every few months.

Most laptops use modern, intelligent lithium-ion batteries. Unlike the "memory effect" batteries of the past (NiCad and NiMH), you can recharge your lithium-ion batteries at any time, and they still maintain full capacity. Even so, let the battery completely drain about once every two or three months. Then recharge the battery nice and slow; probably, overnight is best. That keeps your battery healthy and happy.

Turn Down the Monitor's Brightness

To save a bit on battery life on the road, adjust the brightness on your monitor down just a hair — or perhaps as low as you can stand. That definitely saves the juice.

✔ Buttons near the laptop's LCD monitor control the brightness.

✔ Sometimes, the brightness is controlled by using special Fn key combinations.

✔ Your laptop's power manager might automatically dim the screen when the laptop is on battery power.

✔ Screen dimming can be done in Windows Vista, in the Control Panel's Mobility Center.

✔ Also check the Power Options dialog box (from the Control Panel), to see whether your laptop has any advanced or specific settings for disabling or saving power used by the display.

Scary lithium-ion battery trivia

Lithium-ion batteries are what many of us humans aspire to be: smart and popular. But there's a scary side to the lithium-ion battery. Consider this frightening lithium-ion battery information designed to literally shock you away from any thought of messing with your laptop's battery:

✔ One function of the lithium-ion battery's smarts is to prevent overcharging. Overcharging? Hmmm. . . .

✔ When a lithium-ion battery is overcharged, it gets hot. Then it explodes.

✔ The lithium metal in the battery burns inside water.

✔ The acid inside the battery is not only highly caustic, it's also flammable.

✔ I'm sure that the acid is poisonous as well, but — golly — that last sentence had me at "caustic."

✔ There's an increased risk of explosion when the battery gets too hot.

✔ You cannot recycle a used lithium-ion battery, so don't ever think of buying or using a "recycled" battery.

Power Down the Hard Drives

Power is consumed the most in your laptop the most by motors — specifically, those motors that keep the hard drive continually spinning. Sometimes, this is necessary. When you're using a program that continually accesses the hard drive, such as a database, it's more efficient to keep the drive continually spinning. But when you're working on something that doesn't require constant disk access, it's a good idea to save some juice by sleeping an idle hard drive.

Refer to Chapter 8 for more information on hard drive timeouts.

Add More RAM to Prevent Virtual Memory Disk Swapping

One way that the hard drive conspires with the operating system to drain the battery quickly is when the virtual memory manager pulls a disk swap. The way to prevent that is to add more memory (RAM) to your laptop.

Virtual memory has nothing to do with virtue. Instead, it's a chunk of hard drive space that Windows uses to help supplement real memory, or RAM. Mass chunks of information are swapped between RAM and your laptop's hard drive, which is why you never see any Out of Memory errors in Windows. But all that swapping puts a drain on the battery.

Windows does a great job of managing virtual memory. Although you can fine-tune the virtual memory manager, I don't recommend it. Instead, test the virtual memory manager this way:

1. **Run three or four of your most-often-used programs.**

   Start up each program, and get its window up and ready on the screen, just as though you were about to work on something. In fact, you can even load a document or whatever, to ensure that the program is occupied.

2. **Watch the hard drive light; wait for it to stop blinking.**

   Wait until the hard drive light on the laptop (refer to Chapter 5) stops blinking. That means hard drive access has stopped and the computer is simply waiting.

3. **Press Alt+Esc.**

   The Alt+Esc key combination switches from one program (or window) to another.

4. **Watch the hard drive light.**

5. **Repeat Steps 3 and 4 until you've cycled through all programs and windows at least once.**

   What you're looking for is hard drive access. If the hard drive light blinks as you switch between programs, it can be a sign that virtual memory is being used, by swapping from RAM to disk. Yes, your system is working harder than it should, and it affects battery life.

The idea isn't really to adjust virtual memory as much as it is to add more RAM to your laptop and prevent virtual memory from ever taking over in the first place.

- A good amount of RAM to have with Windows Vista is 1GB, although 2GB is even better.

- For Windows XP, I recommend at least 512MB of RAM, and more is better.

- To see how much memory is installed in your laptop, open the Control Panel's System icon. The amount of memory that's installed appears along with other information about your computer.

- Refer to Chapter 19 for more information on adding RAM to your laptop.

Run as Few Programs as Possible, and Close Unused Programs

Because of the multitasking nature of Windows (which is good), excess power is used to keep several programs running at a time (which is bad). To optimize performance, I recommend running as few programs at a time on your laptop when you're using the battery.

For example, you might be reading e-mail in your e-mail program, browsing the Web, editing a document in your word processor, and keeping a game of Spider Solitaire going in another window. All that activity is really unnecessary, and shutting down the programs you're not using helps save battery life.

Guard the Battery's Terminals

Like a big-city airport or a bus station or Frankenstein's neck, your laptop's battery has terminals. People don't traverse a battery's terminals; but, like Frankenstein's neck, electricity does. The terminals are usually flat pieces of metal, either out in the open or recessed into a slot.

- ✔ Keep your battery in the laptop.

- ✔ Outside the laptop, keep the battery away from metal.

- ✔ Keep the terminals clean; use a Q-tip and some rubbing alcohol. You need to do this whenever you succumb to the temptation to touch the terminals, even though you shouldn't be doing that.

- ✔ Do not attach anything to the battery.

- ✔ Do not attempt to short the battery or try to rapidly drain it.

- ✔ The terminals appear in a different location on the battery, depending on who made the battery and how it attaches to the laptop.

- ✔ To "short" a battery, you attach a wire directly connecting the battery's positive and negative terminals. Although this technique has the effect of draining the battery, the drain is created by generating heat, and heating up any battery is a Bad Thing.

Avoid Extreme Temperatures

Batteries enjoy the same type of temperatures you do. They don't like to be very cold, and they don't like hot temperatures, either. Like Baby Bear, the battery enjoys temperatures that are *just right*.

Store the Battery If You Don't Plan on Using It

You should try to avoid letting your battery sit. If you keep the laptop deskbound (and nothing could be sadder), occasionally unplug the thing and let the battery cycle, just to keep the battery healthy. That's the best thing to do.

When you would rather run your laptop without the battery inside, or when preparing a spare battery for storage, run the battery's charge down to about 40 percent or so, and then put the battery in a nonmetallic container. Stick the container in a nice, cool, clean, dry place.

- ✔ Like people, batteries need exercise! Cycle your battery every two months or so whether you're using the laptop remotely or not.

- ✔ The recommended storage temperature for lithium-ion batteries is 59 degrees Fahrenheit or 15 degrees Celsius.

- ✔ Also refer to the next section.

- ✔ A lithium-ion battery has an expiration date! After two or three years, the battery dies. This is true whether you use the battery or store it.

Understand That Batteries Drain Over Time!

No battery keeps its charge forever. Eventually, over time, the battery's charge fades. For some reason, this surprises people. "That battery was fully charged when I put it into storage six years ago!" Don't be one of the surprised; know that batteries drain over time.

Yet, just because a battery has drained doesn't mean that it's dead. If you stored the battery properly, all it needs is a full charge to get it back up and running again. So, if you stored a battery (see the previous section), anticipate that you'll need to recharge it when you go to use it again. This works just like getting the battery on the first day you bought your laptop; follow those same instructions for getting the stored battery back up and running again.

Chapter 21

Ten Handy Laptop Accessories

*O*ne thing that has kept the computer industry alive for years and years is that a computer purchase never stops with the computer itself. First comes software. Then follows more hardware and even more hardware. Peripherals! Gizmos! Gadgets! And then there are accessories, like mouse pads and tchotchkes to sit atop the monitor. The computer is endlessly expandable.

Feast your eyes, dear reader, and stretch your pocketbook on the following 10 fun or must-have items to expand your laptop universe. (Go to Chapter 7 to find out more about other peripheral devices you can use with your laptop.)

Laptop Bag or Travel Case

Buy yourself and your laptop a handsome laptop bag. Chapter 15 offers some great suggestions and recommendations.

Spare Battery

Nothing cries "Freedom!" to the laptop road warrior more than an extra battery. Having a bonus battery doubles the time you can compute without being tethered to an AC wall socket. Some laptops even let you hot-swap from one battery to another while the laptop is still running, which means that the total length of time you can use your battery greatly exceeds your capacity to do work.

Ensure that the spare battery is approved for your laptop, coming either directly from the manufacturer or from a source that is reliable and guarantees compatibility. Using the wrong battery in your laptop can meet with disastrous results.

Docking Station or Port Replicator

The way to expand your laptop's options is to add special nonportable options, such as a docking station or port replicator.

Port replicator: A port replicator snaps on to a special expansion slot or connector on your laptop. It adds the most common desktop connectors to your laptop, plus maybe more copies of ports that the laptop has too few of. The port replicator can plug into the wall and supply the laptop with power, or it can just be a "cling-on" that snaps on to the laptop's rump for added expansion.

Docking station: A docking station is a more sophisticated (and expensive) version of the port replicator. As with the port replicator, it allows you to add peripherals and expand the power of your laptop, although it's more of a base station or permanent location than a port replicator is. Some docking stations are even shaped like desktop PCs, but with open maws into which you slide the laptops. Some even allow you to add expansion cards, which makes the laptops even more like stationery, desktop PCs.

- ✔ When you're ready to go back on the road, pop out the laptop and you're gone!

- ✔ A port replicator also gives your laptop more ports and more expandability options than the laptop might come with on its own.

- ✔ The docking station and port replicator are specific to your laptop. You need to obtain them from your laptop's manufacturer or computer dealer.

Cooling Pad

The ideal accessory for any modern laptop is the laptop cooling pad. This is a device, similar to the one shown in Figure 22-1, on which your laptop sits. The device contains one or more fans and is either powered by the laptop's USB port or standard AA batteries. Your laptop sits on the device, and the fans help draw away the heat that the battery and microprocessor generate. The result is a cooler-running laptop, which keeps the laptop happy.

- Note that the cooling pad runs from the power supplied by the USB port or from its own batteries. That means it's portable.

- Sadly, you cannot use a cooling pad with a port replicator or docking station that gets in its way.

- If you're getting a USB-powered cooling pad, try to get a model that has a pass-through USB port so that you don't lose a USB port when you add a cooling pad.

- Some cooling pads also double as USB hubs.

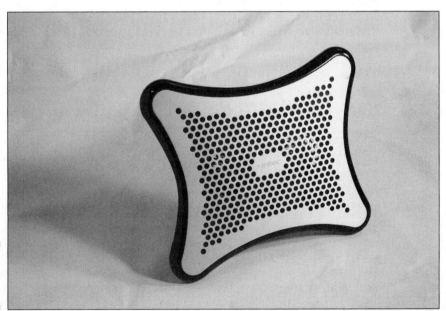

Figure 21-1:
A cool
cooling pad.

Mini-Vac

Handy for cleaning your laptop, especially the keyboard, is the mini-vac. These are found in most office-supply stores, and many are portable (battery powered). You'll be surprised (and disgusted) by the gunk that the mini-vac can suck from your laptop.

USB Lamp

Your laptop's LCD screen is illuminated and even shows up in the dark. Sadly, however, most laptop keyboards don't light up. To help you see the keyboard as well as other important things around your laptop, you can light things up with a USB-powered lamp.

The lamp plugs into a standard USB port on your laptop. It has either a stiff, bendable cord or a clamp so that you can position it. Flip the switch and let there be light!

Note that some laptops might already have built-in keyboard lights. Some IBM models, for example, feature a lamp mounted atop the LCD screen. A special function key turns the lamp on or off.

Full-Size Keyboard

Although you might not want to tote one around with you, there's a certain pleasure to be had when you're using a laptop with a comfy, full-size keyboard. Especially if you rely on the numeric keypad, either for numbers or cursor control, it's a joy to use a full-size keyboard with a laptop.

There's nothing special you need to do for a full-size keyboard, but note that most laptops don't sport PC keyboard ports. Instead, use the USB port, or if you have a port replicator or docking station, you can connect the full-size keyboard to it.

In addition to (or perhaps, instead of) a standard full-size keyboard, you can select any of a number of fun and different keyboards for your laptop. You can find keyboards with special Internet buttons, ergonomically designed to make typing easier on the human bod, as well as wireless keyboards. Because your laptop didn't come with a full-size keyboard, it's a buyer's paradise as far as choosing one for your laptop. Or, if all you need is that numeric keypad, you can get special USB numeric keypads for your laptop.

External Mouse

The only problem I have with using an external mouse on my laptop is that I neglect it. I'm so trained to use the touch pad that I forget about the full-size, comfy, and easy-to-use mouse right next to my laptop.

As with a keyboard, you aren't limited to your choice of an external mouse for your laptop. You can get a basic mouse, one of those space-age optical glowing mice, a mouse with lots of buttons, that weird mouse that you can hover in the air and use like a TV remote, a wireless mouse, a trackball mouse, one of those tiny laptop mice, and the list goes on and on.

Although you can disable the touch pad on your laptop, I recommend keeping it active when you use an external mouse. Often, when I'm browsing the Web or just reading a document, I typically revert to the touch pad rather than use the external mouse. (I'm hard to train.)

Your laptop most likely lacks a mouse port. Get a USB mouse.

ID Card or Return Service Sticker

If your laptop wore underwear, you'd most likely want to write the laptop's name on the underwear. Fortunately, laptops don't require underwear, so the next best thing is to create an ID card for your laptop.

It's common for business people to simply tape their business cards somewhere on the inside of their laptops, such as just to one side of the touch pad.

The idea here is not only to claim ownership of the laptop, but also to pray that if it's ever lost or stolen, the laptop will be recognizable as your own. A good citizen will phone you up and offer to return the laptop that he or she found with your name emblazoned on an ID card.

A better solution is to use a return service and take advantage of its tamper-resistant asset tags. Refer to Chapter 16 for more information.

Theft-Prevention System

The perfect gift for the laptop you love: some type of cable to keep your laptop from walking off, one of those annoyingly loud my-laptop-has-been-moved alarms, or that special software that tries to "phone home" should the laptop be purloined. Ease your fears! Also refer to Chapter 16 for more information on laptop security — specifically, these types of devices.

Chapter 22

Ten Things to Throw in Your Laptop Case

. . . .

In This Chapter

▶ The laptop's power cord

▶ A spare battery

▶ An external mouse

▶ Something to clean the laptop

▶ Security devices

▶ Removable media

▶ A set of headphones (or two)

▶ Handy tools

▶ Cables, cables, and more cables

. . . .

Some people just don't know how to pack. The amateur recognizes the need to cook out in the wild, but toting around your every cast-iron pot, pan, and skillet is unnecessary. After all, lightweight and resourceful camping cooking gear exists.

I suppose that it all comes down to experience. The toil and trials of toting around cast-iron cookware every weekend begs for a solution. Likewise, you want to pack your laptop carrying case with what you need and no more — especially no cast-iron peripherals. Plus, there might be some handy things to pack that you're utterly unaware of. To help in your education, this chapter presents 10 handy, useful, and necessary things you should consider including in your laptop carrying case.

Power Cord and Brick

This item is one that even I forget. Sometimes, I think "Oh, I'm only going to be gone for an hour, and the battery lasts for three hours, so I don't need the power cord." Then an appointment is canceled, and I have more time, but regret not having the power cord with me.

Always take your power cord and its adapter, or "brick," in your laptop case. You just never know when a wall socket will appear. Take advantage of it!

Spare Battery

If you're blessed with a spare battery for your laptop, bring it!

 ✔ Don't forget to charge the spare battery before you leave.

 ✔ Also refer to Chapter 8 for more information on your laptop's battery.

Mouse or Trackball

Anyone who's used to a real mouse probably won't forget to throw it in the laptop's case, but you never know. I highly recommend using a real mouse with your laptop, especially if your laptop sits somewhere on a table or desk with room for the mouse.

 ✔ The real mouse adds little weight to your laptop case.

 ✔ Get a USB mouse, or use the USB connector if you have a desktop mouse. (You don't need the green-colored desktop PC mouse adapter.) Most modern laptops sport USB ports, but few come standard with mouse ports any more.

 ✔ If your laptop is Bluetooth enabled, you can use a wireless Bluetooth mouse.

 ✔ A *trackball* is a special type of mouse, often called the "upside down" mouse. You manipulate a ball with your fingertips, and the ball spins in a stationary base. This item is often easier to use when desk space is limited. In fact, trackball users claim that such a mouse is easier to control than the typical bar-of-soap model mouse.

Screen Wipes and Cleaner

Go to the office-supply store and get some screen wipes and a small, portable bottle of cleaner. Toss 'em in your laptop bag and keep them there. If you can find the screen wipes in a smaller, portable size, buy them. Make them a permanent part of your laptop bag.

Laptop Lock

Don't forget your laptop's antitheft device. Whether it's a cable you can connect to something solid or one of those loud, loud audio alarms, you probably want to pack it in your laptop bag.

Refer to Chapter 16 for more information on laptop security.

Removable Media

Saving your stuff to the laptop's hard drive often isn't enough. It helps to have an assortment of alternatives to get that information out of the computer, especially when your laptop isn't connected to a network for easy file transfer. Two such options are CD-Rs and USB flash drives.

- ✔ I often toss one of those 10-pack, blank CD-R bundles into my laptop bag, in case I need to burn a CD-R on the road.

- ✔ CD-Rs can also be used for backing up important data.

- ✔ Ensure that your laptop has a CD-R drive before you buy the blank CD-R discs. Not every laptop comes with such a drive.

- ✔ You can also bring and use CD-RWs, though I personally just use CD-Rs. The CD-Rs are cheaper, and I rarely find myself erasing or rewriting the CD-RWs anyway.

- ✔ This same reasoning holds true for DVD-R and the other DVD writable-disc formats. Just ensure that you get the proper blank discs for the type of DVD drive in your laptop.

- ✔ USB flash drives are handy, key ring-size gizmos that plug directly into one of the laptop's USB ports. Windows instantly recognizes the new drive and lets you copy stuff to it, up to 2GB or more! The drive can then be removed and its information accessed by any other computer with a compatible USB port.

> ✔ There's a difference between a USB flash drive and the media card used by a digital camera. The media cards require some form of card reader interface, whereas flash drives do not. You can still use a media card as another form of removable storage — as long as you also pack the card reader in your laptop's carrying case.

Headphones

The computer is a musical machine! Why bring along an iPod when all you really need are your music CDs, the laptop, and . . . headphones.

I prefer using headphones with my laptop because its little internal speakers are just too feeble. Yeah, I know, they try. But with headphones, you can also turn the volume way, way up and enjoy your music without annoying anyone nearby.

When I go traveling, I take two sets of headphones with me. Then I use a headphone splitter/adapter so that both sets of phones can plug into the laptop. That way, two of us can enjoy viewing a DVD movie on the laptop during a long airplane ride.

Some Necessary Utensils

Consider packing a small "handyman" kit with your laptop. Or, include in your laptop case at least a small regular and Phillips head screwdrivers, a pair of pliers, and a small wire cutter. I also recommend a small utility knife; however, such a thing is likely to be confiscated by airport security.

Cables, Cables, Cables

Cables are good. When you can, bring spare Ethernet, phone, USB, IEEE 1394 (also called FireWire), S-video, power, and any other type of spare cables you can muster. You might never use them, but then again, you never know.

> ✔ You never know where the Internet lurks! Taking along a goodly length of Ethernet cable with your laptop is always a good idea. It allows you to instantly connect to any available Ethernet network without having to wait for or (worse) rent a cable.

> ✔ A goodly length is about 6 feet long.

✔ Cables don't have to be all tangly, either. If you don't like wrapping up your cables, look for those cables that come with their own retractable spools at any office-supply store.

✔ Another cable to have, if it's available for your laptop, is an automobile cigarette lighter DC adapter. (Some newer cars don't even call it a "cigarette lighter" anymore. No, it's the DC adapter!)

Not the End of the List

You can pack your laptop bag full of so much stuff that the bag will eventually weigh more than you do. There's only so much you can take: portable printers, USB hubs, PC Cards, external disk drives, and the list goes on.

The items mentioned in this chapter are good to *always* have in your laptop bag. Add the other stuff as you need it. Or, when you're traveling, consider putting those things in your checked luggage so that you're not toting the extra weight.

Index

Notes

Notes

Notes

Notes

Notes

Notes

Notes

Notes

Notes

BUSINESS, CAREERS & PERSONAL FINANCE

0-7645-5307-0

0-7645-5331-3 *†

Also available:
- Accounting For Dummies †
  0-7645-5314-3
- Business Plans Kit For Dummies †
  0-7645-5365-8
- Cover Letters For Dummies
  0-7645-5224-4
- Frugal Living For Dummies
  0-7645-5403-4
- Leadership For Dummies
  0-7645-5176-0
- Managing For Dummies
  0-7645-1771-6

- Marketing For Dummies
  0-7645-5600-2
- Personal Finance For Dummies *
  0-7645-2590-5
- Project Management For Dummies
  0-7645-5283-X
- Resumes For Dummies †
  0-7645-5471-9
- Selling For Dummies
  0-7645-5363-1
- Small Business Kit For Dummies *†
  0-7645-5093-4

HOME & BUSINESS COMPUTER BASICS

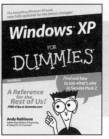

0-7645-4074-2

0-7645-3758-X

Also available:
- ACT! 6 For Dummies
  0-7645-2645-6
- iLife '04 All-in-One Desk Reference For Dummies
  0-7645-7347-0
- iPAQ For Dummies
  0-7645-6769-1
- Mac OS X Panther Timesaving Techniques For Dummies
  0-7645-5812-9
- Macs For Dummies
  0-7645-5656-8

- Microsoft Money 2004 For Dummies
  0-7645-4195-1
- Office 2003 All-in-One Desk Reference For Dummies
  0-7645-3883-7
- Outlook 2003 For Dummies
  0-7645-3759-8
- PCs For Dummies
  0-7645-4074-2
- TiVo For Dummies
  0-7645-6923-6
- Upgrading and Fixing PCs For Dummies
  0-7645-1665-5
- Windows XP Timesaving Techniques For Dummies
  0-7645-3748-2

FOOD, HOME, GARDEN, HOBBIES, MUSIC & PETS

0-7645-5295-3

0-7645-5232-5

Also available:
- Bass Guitar For Dummies
  0-7645-2487-9
- Diabetes Cookbook For Dummies
  0-7645-5230-9
- Gardening For Dummies *
  0-7645-5130-2
- Guitar For Dummies
  0-7645-5106-X
- Holiday Decorating For Dummies
  0-7645-2570-0
- Home Improvement All-in-One For Dummies
  0-7645-5680-0

- Knitting For Dummies
  0-7645-5395-X
- Piano For Dummies
  0-7645-5105-1
- Puppies For Dummies
  0-7645-5255-4
- Scrapbooking For Dummies
  0-7645-7208-3
- Senior Dogs For Dummies
  0-7645-5818-8
- Singing For Dummies
  0-7645-2475-5
- 30-Minute Meals For Dummies
  0-7645-2589-1

INTERNET & DIGITAL MEDIA

0-7645-1664-7

0-7645-6924-4

Also available:
- 2005 Online Shopping Directory For Dummies
  0-7645-7495-7
- CD & DVD Recording For Dummies
  0-7645-5956-7
- eBay For Dummies
  0-7645-5654-1
- Fighting Spam For Dummies
  0-7645-5965-6
- Genealogy Online For Dummies
  0-7645-5964-8
- Google For Dummies
  0-7645-4420-9

- Home Recording For Musicians For Dummies
  0-7645-1634-5
- The Internet For Dummies
  0-7645-4173-0
- iPod & iTunes For Dummies
  0-7645-7772-7
- Preventing Identity Theft For Dummies
  0-7645-7336-5
- Pro Tools All-in-One Desk Reference For Dummies
  0-7645-5714-9
- Roxio Easy Media Creator For Dummies
  0-7645-7131-1

* Separate Canadian edition also available
† Separate U.K. edition also available

SPORTS, FITNESS, PARENTING, RELIGION & SPIRITUALITY

0-7645-5146-9

0-7645-5418-2

Also available:

- Adoption For Dummies
  0-7645-5488-3
- Basketball For Dummies
  0-7645-5248-1
- The Bible For Dummies
  0-7645-5296-1
- Buddhism For Dummies
  0-7645-5359-3
- Catholicism For Dummies
  0-7645-5391-7
- Hockey For Dummies
  0-7645-5228-7

- Judaism For Dummies
  0-7645-5299-6
- Martial Arts For Dummies
  0-7645-5358-5
- Pilates For Dummies
  0-7645-5397-6
- Religion For Dummies
  0-7645-5264-3
- Teaching Kids to Read For Dummies
  0-7645-4043-2
- Weight Training For Dummies
  0-7645-5168-X
- Yoga For Dummies
  0-7645-5117-5

TRAVEL

0-7645-5438-7

0-7645-5453-0

Also available:

- Alaska For Dummies
  0-7645-1761-9
- Arizona For Dummies
  0-7645-6938-4
- Cancún and the Yucatán For Dummies
  0-7645-2437-2
- Cruise Vacations For Dummies
  0-7645-6941-4
- Europe For Dummies
  0-7645-5456-5
- Ireland For Dummies
  0-7645-5455-7

- Las Vegas For Dummies
  0-7645-5448-4
- London For Dummies
  0-7645-4277-X
- New York City For Dummies
  0-7645-6945-7
- Paris For Dummies
  0-7645-5494-8
- RV Vacations For Dummies
  0-7645-5443-3
- Walt Disney World & Orlando For Dummies
  0-7645-6943-0

GRAPHICS, DESIGN & WEB DEVELOPMENT

0-7645-4345-8

0-7645-5589-8

Also available:

- Adobe Acrobat 6 PDF For Dummies
  0-7645-3760-1
- Building a Web Site For Dummies
  0-7645-7144-3
- Dreamweaver MX 2004 For Dummies
  0-7645-4342-3
- FrontPage 2003 For Dummies
  0-7645-3882-9
- HTML 4 For Dummies
  0-7645-1995-6
- Illustrator CS For Dummies
  0-7645-4084-X

- Macromedia Flash MX 2004 For Dummies
  0-7645-4358-X
- Photoshop 7 All-in-One Desk Reference For Dummies
  0-7645-1667-1
- Photoshop CS Timesaving Techniques For Dummies
  0-7645-6782-9
- PHP 5 For Dummies
  0-7645-4166-8
- PowerPoint 2003 For Dummies
  0-7645-3908-6
- QuarkXPress 6 For Dummies
  0-7645-2593-X

NETWORKING, SECURITY, PROGRAMMING & DATABASES

0-7645-6852-3

0-7645-5784-X

Also available:

- A+ Certification For Dummies
  0-7645-4187-0
- Access 2003 All-in-One Desk Reference For Dummies
  0-7645-3988-4
- Beginning Programming For Dummies
  0-7645-4997-9
- C For Dummies
  0-7645-7068-4
- Firewalls For Dummies
  0-7645-4048-3
- Home Networking For Dummies
  0-7645-42796

- Network Security For Dummies
  0-7645-1679-5
- Networking For Dummies
  0-7645-1677-9
- TCP/IP For Dummies
  0-7645-1760-0
- VBA For Dummies
  0-7645-3989-2
- Wireless All In-One Desk Reference For Dummies
  0-7645-7496-5
- Wireless Home Networking For Dummies
  0-7645-3910-8

HEALTH & SELF-HELP

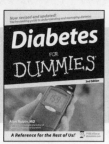

0-7645-6820-5 *†

0-7645-2566-2

Also available:
- Alzheimer's For Dummies
  0-7645-3899-3
- Asthma For Dummies
  0-7645-4233-8
- Controlling Cholesterol For Dummies
  0-7645-5440-9
- Depression For Dummies
  0-7645-3900-0
- Dieting For Dummies
  0-7645-4149-8
- Fertility For Dummies
  0-7645-2549-2

- Fibromyalgia For Dummies
  0-7645-5441-7
- Improving Your Memory For Dummies
  0-7645-5435-2
- Pregnancy For Dummies †
  0-7645-4483-7
- Quitting Smoking For Dummies
  0-7645-2629-4
- Relationships For Dummies
  0-7645-5384-4
- Thyroid For Dummies
  0-7645-5385-2

EDUCATION, HISTORY, REFERENCE & TEST PREPARATION

0-7645-5194-9

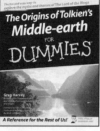

0-7645-4186-2

Also available:
- Algebra For Dummies
  0-7645-5325-9
- British History For Dummies
  0-7645-7021-8
- Calculus For Dummies
  0-7645-2498-4
- English Grammar For Dummies
  0-7645-5322-4
- Forensics For Dummies
  0-7645-5580-4
- The GMAT For Dummies
  0-7645-5251-1
- Inglés Para Dummies
  0-7645-5427-1

- Italian For Dummies
  0-7645-5196-5
- Latin For Dummies
  0-7645-5431-X
- Lewis & Clark For Dummies
  0-7645-2545-X
- Research Papers For Dummies
  0-7645-5426-3
- The SAT I For Dummies
  0-7645-7193-1
- Science Fair Projects For Dummies
  0-7645-5460-3
- U.S. History For Dummies
  0-7645-5249-X

Get smart @ dummies.com®

- Find a full list of Dummies titles
- Look into loads of FREE on-site articles
- Sign up for FREE eTips e-mailed to you weekly
- See what other products carry the Dummies name
- Shop directly from the Dummies bookstore
- Enter to win new prizes every month!

* Separate Canadian edition also available
† Separate U.K. edition also available

Available wherever books are sold. For more information or to order direct: U.S. customers visit www.dummies.com or call 1-877-762-2974.
U.K. customers visit www.wileyeurope.com or call 0800 243407. Canadian customers visit www.wiley.ca or call 1-800-567-4797.